a creation of Halcyon Enterprises

Alexander Walker

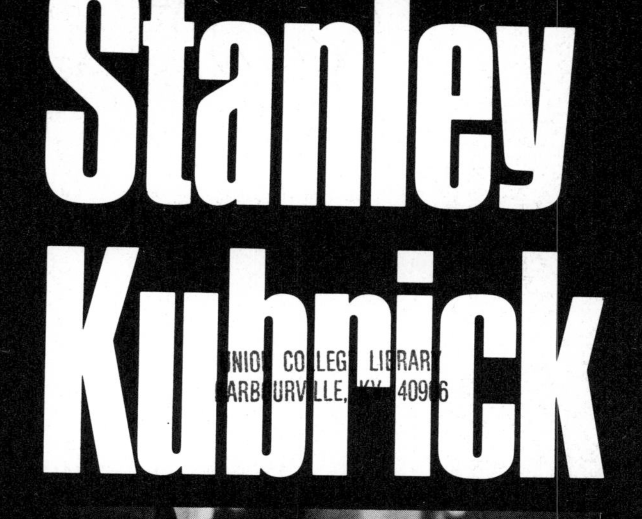

Stanley Kubrick directs

expanded edition

HBJ

HARCOURT BRACE JOVANOVICH, INC.

New York

ISBN 0-15-684892-9

Library of Congress Catalog Card Number: 77-153692

Printed in the United States of America

BCDEFGHIJ

Acknowledgments

The quotation from A Clockwork Orange, *by Anthony Burgess, is reprinted with the permission of William Heinemann Ltd. and of W. W. Norton & Company, Inc., copyright © 1962 by Anthony Burgess.*

The co-operation of United Artists Corporation is gratefully acknowledged. All photographs from Paths of Glory, Killer's Kiss, *and* The Killing *are reproduced by permission of United Artists Corporation.*

The author and publishers are grateful to Columbia Pictures for all photographs from Dr. Strangelove, or How I Learned to Stop Worrying and Love the Bomb, *copyright © 1964 by Columbia Pictures; and for photographs on page 6, page 10, title page photo of Kubrick, page 12 top right and middle row, copyright © 1964 by Columbia Pictures.*

The photographs on page 9, page 12, top left and bottom row, appear through the courtesy of Metro-Goldwyn-Mayer.

For all photographs from A Clockwork Orange, *we thank Hawk Films Limited—Warner Brothers.*

We thank Alexander Singer for the photographs on page 11.

All photographs from 2001: A Space Odyssey *are © 1968 by Metro-Goldwyn-Mayer.*

Credits for photographs on the cover are as follows. Front: *Metro-Goldwyn-Mayer. Back:* Paths of Glory, *United Artists Corporation;* 2001: A Space Odyssey, *Metro-Goldwyn-Mayer;* A Clockwork Orange, *Warner Brothers.*

CONTENTS

KUBRICK: MAN AND OUTLOOK

From Fear and Desire to A Clockwork Orange

Only a few film directors possess a conceptual talent—that is, a talent to crystallize every film they make into a cinematic concept. It is a skill that goes far beyond the mere photographing of a script, however cinematic the script may be in itself. It transcends the need to find a good subject, an absorbing story, or an extraordinary premise to build on. Essentially, it is the talent to construct a form that will exhibit the maker's vision in an unexpected way, often a way that seems to have been the only possible one when the film is finally finished. It is this conceptual talent that most strongly distinguishes Stanley Kubrick.

But to say as much is only to restate the question this book seeks to answer: What is it that makes Kubrick the kind of director he is? It even makes the task more difficult. Because almost every film Kubrick has directed has entailed constructing a new concept, he is a filmmaker who resists the customary critical approach that tries to distinguish strongly linked themes in a director's work. It is wise even to avoid the head-on approach of question and answer with Stanley Kubrick. It is not one he readily submits to or thrives on; for he knows the value of leaving the questioner, or viewer, unsatisfied, with an intensified curiosity about the complex forces shaping any action or individual.

Kubrick himself is a whole area of complex forces. Each film is a way of exploring the number of exciting possibilities it holds for him at the time he decides to make it. Each film enables him to extend his own investigation of himself by exhausting the area of research it opens up to his artistic and scientific imagination. This alone is one good reason why he is incapable of repeating a subject: it would mean repeating *himself.* And he has simply not the time or the patience for that. Thus he is freed from the deadening demands that the film industry invariably makes on its most successful directors, or at least he does not give in to the demands when they are made.

Few directors have a temperament as strongly constituted as Kubrick's to survive and create inside the industry without letting its enormous pressures rob him of his independence or impair his judgment. "Inside" is the key word here. If Kubrick keeps himself to himself—and he has increasingly done just that, until he is one of the most elusive of filmmakers—it is not because he has any need to fear the kind of "punishment" that the movie industry still metes out even in these days, when directors have more creative freedom than ever before, to those who flout commercial imperatives in their pursuit of self-expression. Kubrick knows the laws that govern success or failure in this kind of world. He works within them. As Hollis Alpert once put it, "He does not believe in biting the hand that might strangle him." Yet the fact remains that he has succeeded in reconciling his own uncompromising requirements with those of the industry. On the strength of some half-dozen films, he has won a reputation for originality of subject and treatment that is rare among international film directors.

As well as his independence he has kept his unpredictability. Each of his films, with only one exception, which he now disowns as not being "his" film, is stamped by its maker's evolving confidence in his own skill and by his curiosity in seeing how far he can extend it. He has always forced his reach to exceed his grasp. Other directors can

justifiably boast of never underestimating their public. Kubrick's has been a more characteristically private resolve: he has never underestimated himself.

Such a man takes—and gives—immense pains in carrying out a resolve like this. To be part of his team is to surrender a part of one's life in a very real sense. Self-discipline in this kind of director demands a degree of despotism—basically benevolent, yet ruthless in never allowing anyone or anything to jeopardize the work of constructing a movie in his own image of it. His immense energy recharges itself on work. Beyond a certain amount of well-being and physical comfort, the customary social pressures or diversions outside work simply do not impinge on his creative priorities. In recent years he has grown a ruff of black beard that adds a visible dimension of inscrutability to a disposition whose self-sufficiency seems at times almost monastic.

His curiosity about the world is unflagging; the capacity of a friend or associate to satisfy it is often less so. His conversation is endlessly interrogative. This is sometimes abrupt and disconcerting when rapid-fire questions push one up against the wall of one's own inability to come out with satisfying answers. In part, Kubrick's insistence on tapping one's thoughts, on eliciting responses, is connected with an interest in communication that has intensified over the years until it now occupies a major part of

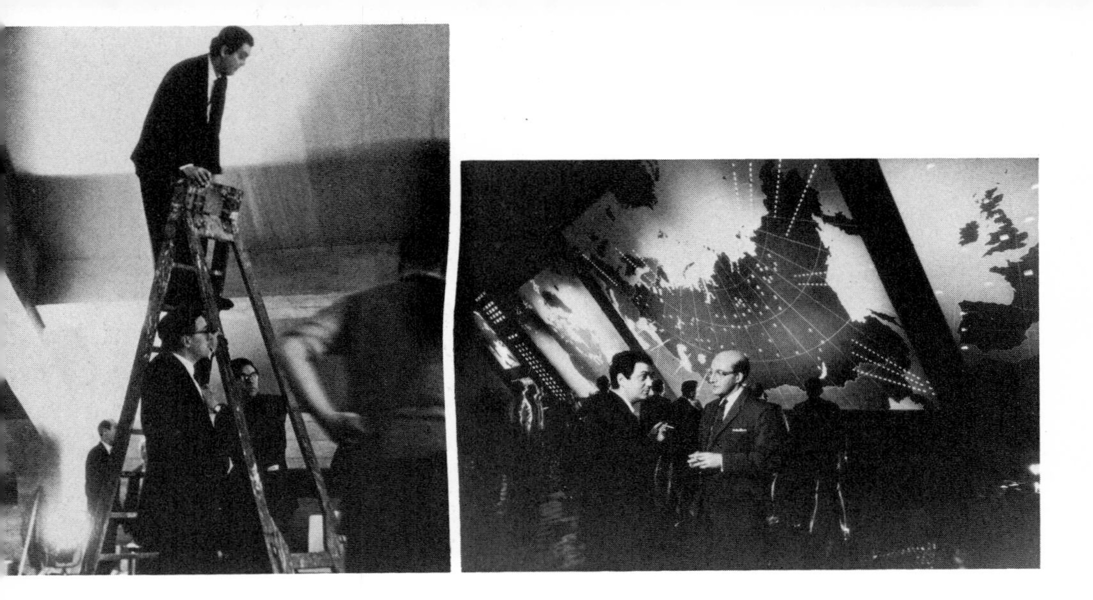

1963: On the set of Dr. Strangelove

his life and, as we shall see, forms the central concern in several of his films. Communicating with Kubrick is a kind of "debriefing"—the military term is quite appropriate —for his need to inform himself fully before he makes decisions is obsessive. It follows that his range of interests is vast. An evening's conversation with him has covered such areas as optical perception in relation to man's survival; the phenomenon of phosphenes (or "lights behind the eyes") and its connection with the "star ride" sequence in *2001: A Space Odyssey;* German thoroughness in building flash screens onto their coastal gun emplacements in Normandy so that the cannon fire would not be pinpointed by the enemy; compromised safety margins in commercial flying (Kubrick, a resolute nonflyer, had been monitoring control-tower conversation at a nearby international airport); Dr. Goebbels' role as a pioneer film publicist; the Right's inability to produce dialecticians to match the Left's; Legion of Decency pressures during the making of *Lolita;* SAM-3 missiles in the Arab-Israeli conflict; Irish politics and the possibility of similarities in the voice prints of demagogues; and, of course, Kubrick's favorite game, chess.

Chess was the first of two lifelong obsessions he ac-

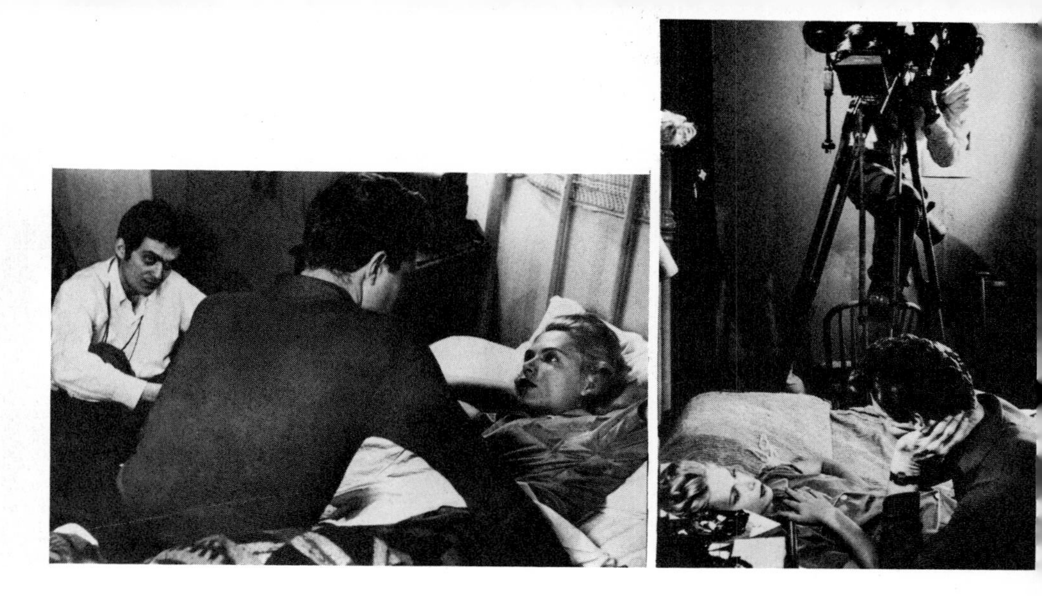

1955: On the set of Killer's Kiss

quired from his father, a physician practicing in The Bronx, New York, where Kubrick was born in 1928. The second was photography. In Kubrick's case, there appears to be a very strong creative link between chess and the camera —one is a mental discipline, the other an imaginative craft.

Chess in particular offers a clue to the elements that constitute Kubrick and helps to explain why he has made certain films and not others—and why he has made them in certain ways and not in others. For the thought that goes into moviemaking, both in the physical preparation of a production and in the conceptual structuring of the film, is closely related in the case of this director to the attitudes that chess playing develops.

"If chess has any relationship to filmmaking," says Kubrick, "it would be in the way it helps you develop patience and discipline in choosing between alternatives at a time when an impulsive decision seems very attractive. Otherwise it is necessary to have perfect intuition—and this is something very dangerous for an artist to rely on." It is hard to find the right criteria for making the dozens of decisions daily facing a director when they appear to have only small pluses or minuses attached to them. But the pondering of the choices, as in chess, enable him, per-

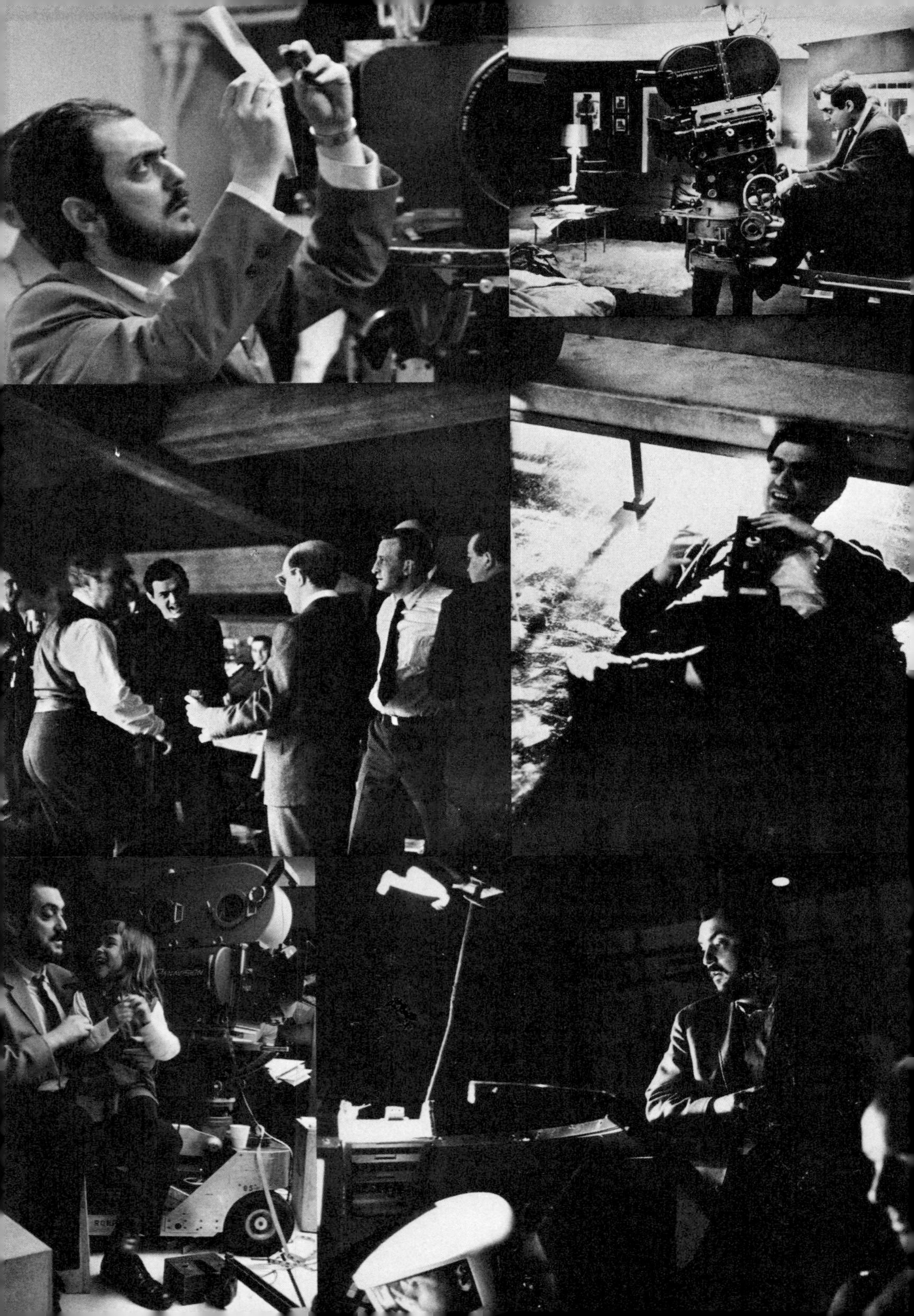

haps, to make more good ones than if he had impulsively reached for the first one that looked interesting.

Chess also sharpens one's awareness of the time factor. In tournament chess, a level Kubrick attained but stopped at, unwilling to make the total commitment required by serious championship play, the players are matched against a clock as well as against each other. There is a clear analogy between this rigorous framework and a film's budget and schedule, which relate to the time it will take to shoot. "You have a problem of allocating your resources of time and money in making a film, and you are constantly having to do a kind of artistic cost-effectiveness of all the scenes in the film against the budget and time remaining," says Kubrick. "This is not wholly unlike some of the thinking that goes into a chess game." The chessboard finds its way into scenes in several Kubrick films; and the narratives of *The Killing* and *Dr. Strangelove* are structured around the race against time and the consequences of "moves" made by the characters or by objects virtually independent of the characters. But whether there is this kind of internal evidence or not in a Kubrick film, its whole feeling suggests it has been shaped by a particular kind of mind, intuitively aware of choice, consequences, and the pattern of play—and chess has been a part of this conditioning discipline.

Formal education certainly provided very little of it. Kubrick at school was not even a "late beginner." Interestingly, physics was the most satisfactory among his subjects, in which he earned undistinguished grades, at Taft High School. Perhaps the failure of most of his teachers to hold his attention, much less ignite his imagination, helps account for the compulsive desire to connect with an audience that runs so consistently through his filmmaking. (Boredom taught him at an early age the distinction between artistic creation and public communication. Though this distinction is a primary concern of all filmmakers of stature, it is temptingly easy for a self-absorbed artist to lose sight of it.) The only instructor at Taft that he found stimulating was the English teacher Aaron Traister, who at least attempted to make Shakespeare's plays interesting; it was he who figured in a piece of photojournalism that Kubrick, spurred on by his father's gift of a camera, sold to *Look* Magazine while he was still at Taft.

After high-school graduation he quickly landed a job with *Look.* The magazine became for all practical purposes his university. "Four and a half years of working for *Look* Magazine, traveling all over America, seeing how things worked and the way people behaved, gave me some useful insights plus important experience in photography." At the age of seventeen, in short, he had "backed into" the kind of opportunity that builds optimism and assists the belief that one can accomplish anything—a feeling that certainly doesn't hurt at this age. It also allowed Kubrick to save a few thousand dollars, enough to make a short movie called *Day of the Fight* (1950), an example of photojournalism, on the middleweight boxer Walter Cartier. Filmed with a small, 100-foot daylight-loading Eyemo camera, it cost $3,900; RKO bought it for just a few hundred dollars more and played it at the Paramount Theatre in New York.

Fired by this first success, Kubrick quit *Look.* He was then twenty-one. His youthfulness was an important factor, for had he got his job on the magazine in his late twenties or early thirties, a much more usual age, he might not have found it so easy to leave such a good post; but his lack of family responsibilities at this age allowed him to pursue the far riskier livelihood of a filmmaker.

Kubrick's curiosity about the world, aroused by his experience with the magazine, now prompted him to get the education he had missed at Taft by monitoring courses at Columbia University. Among his teachers were Lionel Trilling, Mark Van Doren, and the classicist Moses Hadas. From this time on he became an omnivorous reader; in a sense, dropping out of school made him into a lifelong student.

The reading that influenced him as a child certainly wasn't done in the classroom, but at home, where his father's office shelves and bookcases held translations of European fairy stories, folk tales by the brothers Grimm, tales from Greek and Roman mythology, and other similar works. Because he read them at a formative age, they had, Kubrick acknowledges, a considerable effect on his filmmaking. They showed the inadequacy of naturalism as the mainspring of a plot. "Naturalism finally does not elicit the more mysterious echoes contained in myths and fables; these resonances are far better suited to film than any other art form. People in the twentieth century are increasingly occupied with magic, mystical experience, transcendental urges, hallucinogenic drugs, the belief in extraterrestrial intelligence, et cetera, so that, in this sense, fantasy, the supernatural, the magical documentary, call it what you will, is closer to the sense of the times than naturalism." His films show recurring evidence—sometimes in the selection of the main event; sometimes in the guise of a character, the concept of a set, the atmosphere of a scene—of this early, persistent interest in the symbolic analysis of society through its enduring myths and fables.

What place did films have in Kubrick's youth? During and after his stint on *Look* he used to haunt the Museum of Modern Art's film shows, going "as often as they changed the program." But his early curiosity was mainly about technique, not content. Editing in particular had exciting mysteries for a still-photographer bent on making movies. "The most influential book I read at that time was Pudovkin's *Film Technique.* It is a very simple, unpretentious book that illuminates rather than embroiders. It certainly makes it clear that the film cutting is the one and only aspect of films that is unique and unrelated to any other art form. I found this book much more important than the complex writings of Eisenstein. I think it's worth-while for anyone interested in filmmaking to study the contrast between the films of Eisenstein and those of Chaplin, which is another way of referring to the difference between style and content. The greatness of Eisenstein's films represents the triumph of cinematic style over heavy-handed, often simple-minded content. Chaplin's films are masterpieces of content, taste, and sensibility over what is virtually a noncinematic kind of technique. If I had to choose between the two, I would take Chaplin: fortunately the two approaches are not mutually exclusive."

Nevertheless, one early memory of a film that impressed

him because of a marvelous combination of music and action was the sequence of the Battle on the Ice in Eisenstein's *Alexander Nevsky*—a display he has often alluded to in later interviews. But when his own film career was under way and he had cut his artistic teeth on technique, he speedily recognized the limitations of pure composition. Eisenstein's reputation as the master of montage probably influenced Kubrick later to give more and more attention to content. Although Kubrick does not acknowledge that the films of Fritz Lang that he saw—he liked in particular the Dr. Mabuse series and *"M"*—had any direct influence on him, Lang's concern with myth, legend, and the Teutonic unconscious seems clearly analogous to Kubrick's evolving interests.

Kubrick's paternal grandmother had come from Rumania and his paternal grandfather from the old Austro-Hungarian Empire. Whether these family origins played any part in determining the direction his tastes took is a matter Kubrick prefers not to speculate on. But he readily concedes that, of all the directors whose work he saw at this time, "I did very, very much like Max Ophuls' work. I loved his extravagant camera moves which seemed to go on and on forever in labyrinthine sets. The staging of these great camera moves appeared more like a beautifully choreographed ballet than anything else: a spindly waiter hurrying along with a tray of drinks over his head, leading the camera to a couple dancing, who, in turn, whirled the camera to a hussar climbing the stairs, and on and on the camera would go, all to beautiful music. I don't think that Ophuls ever received the critical appreciation he deserved for films like *Le Plaisir, The Earrings of Madame de —,* and *La Ronde.* When I went to Munich in 1957 to make *Paths of Glory* at the Geiselgesteig Studios, I found the last sad remnants of a great filmmaker—the dilapidated, cracked, and peeling sets that Ophuls had used on what would prove to be his last film, *Lola Montes.*"

However, Kubrick is not aware that he derived an overwhelming experience from any particular film he viewed before striking out on his own movie career—except, he adds dryly, from the *bad* films. "I was aware I didn't know anything about making films, but I believed I couldn't make them any worse than the majority of films I was seeing. Bad films gave me the courage to try making a movie."

But what he absorbed in movie theaters wasn't immediately apparent in his own films. After making a second short for RKO, *Flying Padre* (1951)—which was about a Roman Catholic missionary who got around his 400-mile parish in the Southwest by plane—Kubrick raised about $10,000 from his father and an uncle to direct his first feature, *Fear and Desire* (1953). He describes it today as "undramatic and embarrassingly pretentious." One suspects that he does not find it disagreeable to know that the only traceable print of it is in private hands and unavailable for public screening at the moment. It was the story of four soldiers lost behind enemy lines in an unnamed war and trying to find out who they were as well as where they were. A poet friend of Kubrick's, Howard Sackler, who has since become famous as the author of *The Great White Hope,* wrote the screenplay. "The ideas we wanted to put across were good," says Kubrick, "but we didn't have the experience to embody them dramatically. It was little more than a thirty-five-millimeter version of what a class of film students would do in sixteen millimeter." Nevertheless its distributor, the late Joseph Burstyn, got it into art houses, where it collected an appreciative notice or two. It also provided Kubrick with formative experiences. One was the overriding necessity of a realistic and engrossing story. The other was the value of creative freedom. For even films financed by one's relatives can commit a director to burdensome contract stipulations.

But the greatest benefit of all was simply the experience of shooting a feature film. "The entire crew of *Fear and Desire* consisted of myself as director, lighting cameraman, operator, administrator, make-up man, wardrobe, hairdresser, prop man, unit chauffeur, et cetera. The rest of the crew consisted of a friend of mine, Steve Hahn, who was an executive at Union Carbide and who took his holidays with us and knew something about electricity; another friend, Bob Dierks, who was the studio assistant at *Look* Magazine, helped me set up the equipment and put it away, and did a thousand other jobs; my first wife, Toba, who tried to cope with all the paperwork and minor administration; and three Mexican laborers who carried the cases around. Particularly in those days, before the advent of film schools, Nagras and lightweight portable equipment, it was very important to have this experience and to see with what little facilities and personnel one could actually make a film. Today, I think that if someone stood around watching even a smallish film unit, he would get the impression of vast technical and logistical magnitude. He would probably be intimidated by this and assume that something close to this was necessary in order to achieve more or less professional results. This experience and the one that followed with *Killer's Kiss,* which was on a slightly more cushy basis, freed me from any concern again about the technical or logistical aspects of filmmaking."

Fear and Desire ran into post-production problems of a technical nature that cost an additional $20,000. It never showed a profit on the investment; but its maker thought it expedient to get another film out quickly while it was still in the program at the Guild Theatre, in New York. Again with Sackler, he strung together some action sequences—they had to be reasonably cheap to shoot—and then filled in a story entitled *Kiss Me, Kill Me,* about a girl who is kidnaped by the sadistic owner of a dance hall and rescued from his clutches by a gallant young boxer. "While *Fear and Desire* had been a serious effort, ineptly done, *Killer's Kiss,* as it was later known, proved, I think, to be a frivolous effort done with conceivably more expertise though still down in the student level of filmmaking."

Killer's Kiss (1955) inevitably involved Kubrick in far more than editing—again in just about every technical job there is in filmmaking. Except for a few scenes with the boxer and the girl in their tenement rooms, which were shot in a tiny studio, it was all done on New York locations. It took twelve to fourteen weeks—"a generous time. But everything we did cost so little that there was no pressure on us—an advantage I was never to encounter again." The equipment was excellent—Mitchell and Eclair cameras, which were hired on a deferred-payment basis, as were laboratory, dubbing, and editing facilities. "All the dialogue was post-synched, which accounts for a slight zombielike quality to some of the acting. Money began to run out in the editing stage, and being unable to afford even an editing assistant, I had to spend four months just laying in the sound effects, footstep by footstep." Along with the main player, Frank Silvera, as the dance-hall boss, the cast worked for a pittance; Kubrick was surprised at how much actors would forgo just for the chance to act. It cost about $40,000, raised by Kubrick from friends and a relative, Morris Bousel, a Bronx pharmacist; but the final cost was $75,000, after deferred payments were made and union rates met.

To the limited number of critics who saw the film on release, *Killer's Kiss,* with its sense of violence and urban desperation, offered evidence of a highly original new talent, capable of refreshing the crime-film genre. However, Kubrick, still conscious today of the film's limited intentions, or perhaps regretting a story fitted together for effect rather than content, stubbornly refuses to acknowledge the values in it that others find. "It was John Grierson who said of Von Sternberg that 'when a director dies, he becomes a photographer.' *Killer's Kiss* might prove that when a director is born, the photographer doesn't necessarily die. The only distinction I would claim for it is that, to the best of my belief, no one at the time had ever made a feature film in such amateur circumstances and then obtained world-wide distribution for it."

One of the most important consequences of having made this film was Kubrick's meeting with James B. Harris. Harris, also twenty-six, was, like Kubrick, passionate about films. (The mutual friend who brought them together was Alexander Singer, who had acted as stills-photographer on *Killer's Kiss* and has since become a director himself.) Harris and Kubrick subsequently set up a producer-director partnership that lasted for three films. Through his family's interests in TV and film distribution Harris was able to provide the finances Kubrick needed to buy a property and make a really professional film.

Their first film in partnership, *The Killing* (1958), is also the first on which Kubrick is proud to have his name. Critics have praised it chiefly for the brilliance of its construction, the precise working out of the race-track robbery in it and the way in which events that overlap in time are integrated into the suspense by audacious and ingenious flashback techniques. In view of this acclaim, Kubrick's comment is wryly amusing: "Jim Harris and I were the only ones at the time who weren't worried about fragmenting time, overlapping and repeating action that had already been seen, showing things again from another character's point of view. In fact, this was just the structure in Lionel White's thriller, *Clean Break,* that had appealed to us and made us want to do the film. It was the handling of time that may have made this more than just a good crime film."

Now, the importance of the story is a fundamental aspect of Kubrick's working methods. He is a filmmaker who puts his trust in the old atavistic appeal of a story, in its ability to focus his own talent, retain the attention of his audience, and at the same time underpin his exploration of the areas of special interest within that story. In this respect he is a traditionalist, compared with avant-garde filmmakers who have freed themselves from the tyranny of the story by abolishing it. Kubrick acknowledges this is a strong temptation; but he is fond of quoting the passage in E. M. Forster's *Aspects of the Novel* in which this novelist and critic writes: "Neanderthal man listened to stories, if one may judge by the shape of his skull. The primitive audience was an audience of shock-heads, gaping around the camp-fire, fatigued with contending against the mammoth or the woolly rhinoceros, and only kept awake by suspense. The novelist droned on, and as soon as the audience guessed what happened next, they either fell asleep or killed him."*

For Kubrick, finding a story he wants to film is probably the most important yet least successfully dealt with part of his work. The question "How did you find the story?" is to him like asking, "How do you fall in love?" "I have always found it to be an accidental process, and never one which can be attacked head-on." He will ponder the op-

**Aspects of the Novel* (New York: A Harvest Book, Harcourt Brace Jovanovich, Inc., 1956), p. 26.

portunities a potential story contains for months before even beginning to do anything about it. "You must be receptive, certainly—but you have to reflect on them very realistically. Many apparently attractive stories mislead you by a narrative trick incapable of translating into a film." If pushed, he concedes that a story is a film's most artificial aspect, too, since a well-organized narrative is seldom met with in life. But naturalism, as we know, is not the frontier of Kubrick's interests; he continually crosses it. The story is one device for doing so. It satisfies the primal curiosity, a point often lost sight of in films; if the magical ingredients are present, the story also extends the imagination into the director's own sphere of concern. The excitement that the discovery of the right story releases in Kubrick is intensely creative, as it draws on and adds to and becomes converted into whatever other thoughts and interests obsess him at that particular time. He sets immense store on it. "Just as actors have nightmares that they'll never get another part, I have a recurring fear that I'll never find another story I like well enough to film."

E. M. Forster defined the story as "a narrative of events arranged in their time sequence." This hints at the special appeal *The Killing* probably made to Kubrick underneath its "good story." It posed the intellectually stimulating problem of dislocating the time sequence as the separate events overlapped in the race-track robbery; and it offered him the emotional gratification of keeping the narrative pressing ahead in simple fulfillment of the audience's curiosity about "what happened next." This combination of intellectual precision and narrative satisfaction is one of Kubrick's strongest identity marks, as the analysis of his films will show.

The Killing was made for $320,000, a budget larger than the one before but still minute by today's Hollywood standards. Surprisingly, perhaps, it was shot entirely on film sets, except for scenes at the race track and airport. The largest set used was the race-track betting area; this was made up of just a few wood-and-plaster flats, yet the film's air of total realism transfigures it. Now that his film had conventional Hollywood status, union regulations prevented Kubrick from doing the photography himself, and this led to a certain tension when his cameraman, a Hollywood veteran, objected to panning or tracking shots involving a twenty-five-millimeter lens, fearing that distortion would result. (The twenty-five-millimeter lens was the widest-angle lens available in 1956. Now, everyone tracks and pans with eighteen-millimeter, fourteen-and-one-half-millimeter, even nine-and-eight-tenths-millimeter lenses.) The confidence that his own thorough grounding in photography gave Kubrick now paid off; the tracking shots were perfectly realized using, at his insistence, the twenty-five-millimeter lens. The greater means at his disposal meant he was able to afford better actors than in *Killer's Kiss,* though, characteristically, he found at least one member of the cast, the wrestler who diverts the police by staging a brawl, in a chess club he often frequented on Forty-second Street. *The Killing* was the first film in which the satisfaction he gets from directing extended to all the performances from his actors; there was not a weak one anywhere.

The Killing was followed by months of total indifference from Hollywood. Then Kubrick and Harris were signed to develop properties for Dore Schary, who was head of production at MGM. Kubrick prepared a script based on a Stefan Zweig story, "The Burning Secret," in collaboration with the novelist Calder Willingham; and when Schary lost his job in a company shakeout, and his protégés also left, it was with Willingham that Kubrick developed the scenario of his next film.

He reached back to a Humphrey Cobb novel whose story had fascinated him as a child. It was called *Paths of Glory,* and was based on a true incident in World War One. *Paths of Glory* had the obligatory obsessional element to grip Kubrick's imagination in its deep sense of injustice at the fate of three soldiers executed as scapegoats because their commandant had set his men an impossible military objective. Jim Thompson, the thriller writer who had coauthored the screenplay of *The Killing,* joined Kubrick on the new film and contributed, with Willingham, much of the fine dialogue.

But Kubrick controlled the over-all construction.

The script was turned down by every one of the major Hollywood studios until Kirk Douglas agreed to play the main role. His fee claimed $350,000 out of the budget of $900,000, but without a star of his magnitude there would have been small chance of getting the film financed. It was made in Germany, partly for economy, partly because the story's anti-French bias made French locations inadvisable.* It is the first of Kubrick's major films, a totally confident advance from the action drama into the cinema of ideas and human values. Its performances were strong, subtle, and detailed; its visual impression of warfare at that period is still unequaled on the screen—no less an authority than Winston Churchill commended its authenticity.

Kubrick, however, tends to play down the technical virtuosity of the film as well as the difficulties of working in a foreign country with a crew who did not speak much English. (At that time far fewer American films were produced abroad than has become the case in recent years.) He says: "I had no qualms about the technical side of filmmaking; after all, I had done most of the jobs myself. The Germans were superb technicians, totally work-oriented." The German extras, however, were almost too fearless for Kubrick's liking. He had to keep reminding the hundred or so German police cast as French infantrymen that they were supposed to be raw troops under terrifying and unaccustomed fire. Only then did they get the knack of acting scared and stop performing foolhardy examples of physical courage that could have been dangerous; the shell holes they tumbled intrepidly in and out of were mined with explosives able to inflict severe burns. "For this sequence," he says, "we had six cameras, one behind the other on a long dolly track which ran parallel to the attack. The battlefield was divided into five 'dying zones' and each extra was given a number ranging from one to five and told to 'die' in that zone, if possible near an explosion. I operated an Arriflex

*The film is still banned in France, and the ban imposed by the Swiss authorities at the time of its release, out of respect for their neighbor's feelings, was not lifted until early in 1970. The film was also originally banned in U.S. military establishments in America and abroad.

camera with a zoom lens and concentrated on Kirk Douglas."

Another justly celebrated scene, General Mireau's first inspection of the "trench world" that forms so horrifying a contrast to the elegant château that houses the commanders, was done in a single long take. Both sides in the war, Kubrick explains, floored their trenches with duckboards because of mud; this historical detail made it a simple matter to lay the dolly straight on top.

As well as complete technical mastery, *Paths of Glory* (1957) showed Kubrick's developing authority with actors. While the cast of *The Killing* performed well without exception, they nearly all came from the sturdy, dependable ranks of Hollywood character actors. In *Paths of Glory* the stars have gained an extra dimension; the quality of Kubrick's intelligence is ingrained in their performances, in a superb alliance between their own skills and personalities and the photography, editing, and direction that the filmmaker has imposed. Critics generally agreed that Kirk Douglas surpassed himself as the humane Colonel Dax; much of this was due to the quality of the direction he received.* Kubrick totally dismisses stories that Adolphe Menjou, as the utterly corrupt General Broulard, was "difficult," resented his director repeating takes, and only grudgingly agreed to an additional reading after one *he* had considered his best. On the contrary, says Kubrick, Menjou was a consummate craftsman when it came to taking direction—and the fixed right-wing attitudes the actor held were not unhelpful in such a role.

Early in his career Kubrick had given himself a crash course in the theory of directing actors. "The equivalent to Pudovkin's book on film editing is a book oddly enough about Stanislavsky, not by him: *Stanislavsky Directs,* by Nikolai M. Gorchakov. It provides a very detailed and practical description of Stanislavsky at work on different productions. I would regard it as an essential book for any intending film director."

---

*Douglas has since shown himself oddly self-denying in *his* rating of his performance. Interviewed by Michel Ciment in *Positif* (January, 1970), he ranked *Paths of Glory* last of all the films for which he had a personal preference, after *Lonely Are the Brave, Spartacus, Champion, Lust for Life,* and *The Vikings.*

Kubrick asserts that it is the director's own imagination, the quality of *his* ideas, that plays the principal part in keying his actors to the pitch necessary for a good performance. "A director's job working with actors is much more like a novelist than the traditional image of a Svengali; it's essentially a problem of the right idea, the right adjective, the right adverb. These are the things that finally produce results. The right idea is like having the right tool for the job: you feel it as soon as you start work. Teaching actors how to act is something that should be done by somebody else." If actors perform better for Kubrick than for other directors, maybe the quality of the ideas he gives them is better. Invariably, he works with professionals—actors who can "home" onto an idea he feeds them, or hit the same mood intuitively, and who can generate subtle forms of feeling every moment the camera is turning. Certain actors, Kubrick has found, can do "a psychological rope trick," using their own taste, imagination, and judgment to come reasonably close to a characterization on their own. But even their awareness can be made much sharper by a director who is creating the right ideas for them and recognizes in which takes, or in which part of one take, they are at pitch. He will not allow people to "walk through" a rehearsal at 7:30 a.m. He wants the real thing produced for his inspection—"otherwise," he says, "why are we rehearsing?"

In his most recent films he has eagerly used technology to aid his actors, usually by expanding the time available to him for directing them. A Polaroid camera shoots a scene for the lighting qualities, and after Kubrick has scanned the instant print and issued any necessary instructions for adjusting the lighting effect he wants, the time saved is at the service of his players. Time has become more and more precious to him. He now uses Videotape for screen tests by a casting director, so that he can scan the results quickly and, if need be, painlessly at home.

Face-to-face encounters can be painful for Kubrick, especially with strangers, and it follows that the relationship he develops with his principal players is not just a process of directing them in front of the camera, but of growing to know them over what is often a lengthy preshooting period. One feels he is prying them open for inspection. A part can often be made to follow a character trait. He certainly explores all the choices it offers, inventing, elaborating, selecting, rejecting. Intelligence or intuition is what he always hopes to find in his players: the often complex work of transferring ideas on the set, occasionally replaced by a kind of imaginative shorthand between director and actor, is thus made easier. The relationship eventually becomes so close that a code is elaborated in which Kubrick will say, when he wants, for instance, a certain degree of smiling reaction, "I think that calls for a three and a half."

Some of those who have worked with him recently talk of Kubrick's preoccupation with finding "the moment" in every scene—the revelatory detail, be it a gesture, a look, the way a word is said, even an inanimate object, that electrifies the effect of the playing. Comedy thrives on such moments; and more than anything else, one feels, Kubrick's success in finding them explains why he has become such a brilliant director in that most difficult genre. If he works his actors hard, it is usually in the mutual search for "the moment." But it is *co-operative,* this relationship; not dictatorial. "With Kubrick," says Malcolm McDowell, "you are encouraged to go out on a limb, often breaking away from the script (which has to be good in the first place, so that he has the confidence to roam free of it), but you always know that he is there somewhere with you, sustaining and assisting you."

In spite of tremendous critical acclaim for *Paths of Glory,* Kubrick found his career stalemated by nonevents. It was now 1959. He had gone to Hollywood in 1958 and developed two scripts, an adaptation for Kirk Douglas and an original for Gregory Peck. Neither one was ever used. A contract to direct Marlon Brando in *One-Eyed Jacks* came to nothing but six months of frustrating, time-consuming discussions. Kubrick was finding out how Hollywood eroded a filmmaker's creative stamina by running him up dead-ends. Then came an emergency call from Kirk Douglas. *Spartacus* had run into trouble after its director, the late Anthony Mann, had fallen out with Douglas after only a few days of shooting. Douglas asked

Kubrick to take over.

If any event decisively confirmed Kubrick's determination totally to control his own films—from inception to last shot, and then on through the promotional publicity to the *première* and even afterward—it was the experience of directing *Spartacus* (1960). He did not control this film; he was simply an employee who could be fired at the will of its star, whose own production company was making it. Nonetheless things started off well. The early sequences of the gladiators training and dueling were rewarding to do, says Kubrick, perhaps because they were action sequences, not dependent on a screenplay whose dialogue and characterization the director regarded as poor for his purposes. He had criticized both and had believed his criticisms were accepted. After a few months' filming, however, it became clear to Kubrick that his suggestions for improving the script were not going to be adopted. Reasons for this differ, and Kubrick is still reticent about scraping away protective scar tissue. But one well-placed observer close to Kirk Douglas believes that the star at first accepted his director's revisions in the script until Howard Fast, author of the original novel, viewed footage from the film and told Douglas what a miracle it was he had found a talent like Kubrick. Though well-meant, it was tactless to give a star the impression that his film's success was largely dependent on its brilliant director.

Kubrick stuck out the difficult months that followed, unable to have any say in the script, but fearing that if he quit, someone else might make it worse, and vaguely hoping that at some stage, perhaps in the editing, it might be made better. He regards it as his most difficult and fruitless period. A couple of years later he permitted himself a rather sarcastic reference to his powerlessness when Peter Sellers, in the character of Quilty in *Lolita,* lisps, "I am Spartacus; set me free." The experience had an annealing effect on Kubrick. He henceforth never relinquished the power of decision making to anyone—"a simple matter if it's in your contract, a great deal of trouble if it's not." Many filmmakers pursue the goal of artistic independence, but few with the tenacity Kubrick has shown since *Spartacus.* And now, of course, commercial success has confirmed his independence.

It was while *Spartacus* was being painfully pushed forward that Kubrick and James Harris announced they had bought the screen rights of *Lolita*—for a reported $150,000 —and had engaged Vladimir Nabokov to write the screenplay. In view of thoughts he expressed at the time on adapting literary works, it was an odd choice for Kubrick. His preference had tended toward work that was little known, short in scope but well furnished with psychological insights, so that the action could be justified—an important need for him. Now he committed himself to filming a book of world-wide literary acclaim, with a theme that defied the censors and, most said, even the filmmakers.

One element he certainly found appealing in the book was the obsessional quality of Humbert Humbert's love for the nymphet. The conventional love theme had so far had absolutely no appeal for Kubrick; he is basically a skeptic, not a romantic. But while exploring the bizarre he has always liked to profit from the restraining discipline of the realistic and the conventional. Consequently, a forbidden devotion like that of Nabokov's hero, pursued under the surface of apparently orthodox society, put out ironic vibrations for him. "The literary ground rules for a love story are such that it must end in either death or separation of the lovers and it must never be possible for the lovers to be permanently united. It is also essential that the relationship must shock society or their families. The lovers must be ostracized. It is very difficult to construct a modern story which would believably adhere to these rules. In this respect I think it is correct to say that *Lolita* may be one of the few modern love stories."

He also believed it possible to devise a cinematic style corresponding to the book's erotic wit. He felt strongly that what could be described could be filmed. Nowadays he concedes that much less could be filmed in the mid-1960s and that *Lolita* would be a different film if it were made today. The book's witty, allusive style encompassed material it was then imprudent to put on the screen or even imply. Moreover, some aspects of the film's promotion, such as restricting it in America to audiences over the age of eighteen, was interpreted less as appeasement to morality groups like the Legion of Decency than as an additional allure for those who expected to see sex-play between a grown man and a virtual infant.

False expectations did harm the film's reception to some extent, but in addition Kubrick had also to deal with the very real restrictions then imposed on the film industry. The Legion of Decency (since then much reformed in its ways and now known as the National Catholic Office for Motion Pictures) was naturally concerned with the theme; its concern extended even to details like the scene in which a burial urn containing the ashes of Lolita's father happened to be placed next to a religious triptych. Kubrick was told that to juxtapose an illustration of Catholic piety with evidence of a cremation was totally unacceptable; and in the final print a photographic process had to be employed to blur the religious image. One can imagine from this example what a blast would have occurred had the film contained more overt sexuality. Kubrick now says:

"Naturally I regret that the film could not be more erotic. The eroticism of the story serves a very important purpose in the book, which was lacking in the film: it obscured any hint that Humbert Humbert loved Lolita. One was entirely satisfied to believe that he was erotically obsessed with her, and one believed his repeated comments that it would be necessary to get rid of her when she was no longer a nymphet. It was very important to delay an awareness of his love until the end of the story. I'm afraid that this was all too obvious in the film. But in my view this is the only justifiable criticism." (Again one notes his constant concern with justifying his effects.)

Some critics expressed the view that Sue Lyon looked too old for Lolita, but Kubrick rebuts this by pointing to the maturity of many an American nymphet of Lolita's age. Moreover, he points out as further justification of his casting, Sue Lyon bears a rather close resemblance to the nymphet named Annabel in the novel who seduced Humbert Humbert early in his life and whose spell, according to Nabokov, he managed to break by "incarnating her in another"—that is, in Lolita.* "I went to a party with Nabokov after the *première,*" says Kubrick, "and he was very jolly and very flattering about the film in every respect. At no time during or after the production did he ever express any doubts about Sue Lyon looking too old."

The screenplay credit on *Lolita* is taken by Nabokov only, but Kubrick added many touches of his own sardonic invention. The entire table-tennis encounter between Quilty and Humbert Humbert in the opening sequence is his conception; so is the ironic scene showing Humbert Humbert soaking complacently in the bathtub while receiving his neighbors' condolences on his wife's death. Kubrick also encouraged Peter Sellers, as Quilty, to improvise the surrealistic scenes he figured in, under several disguises.

All this is in line with Kubrick's views on scripting, which have not changed much over the years. He always tries to get as complete a script as possible before shooting, allowing himself the privilege of changing it as things evolve. The moment the actors begin to play the scene is often the only time when the story's fullest possibilities become apparent; and he likes to be flexible enough to take advantage of this. "One has to work out very clearly what the objectives of a scene are from the point of view of narrative and character, but once this is done, I find it much more profitable to avoid locking up any ideas about staging or camera or even dialogue, prior to rehearsals. I try to leave enough time between the writing of the script and the working out of the ideas of the scene, and the actual shooting of the scene, so that I can arrive in some way as an observer looking at something that has a degree of freshness to me. It's important to be able to respond to some extent in the way the audience will eventually respond."

Kubrick believes firmly in working out what his actors should do in terms of the scene, not the shot. He will sometimes alter what they do, in order to improve a shot—"but not too often, for things that are arranged for the

---

*"I see Annabel in general terms as 'honey-coloured skin,' 'thin arms,' 'brown bobbed hair,' 'long lashes,' 'big bright mouth.' "—*Lolita,* by Vladimir Nabokov.

camera generally result in cliché compositions." In other words, the visual aspect of an acting scene has to take second place to the performances. Since Kubrick has learned to work fast on the visual side, and the new techniques already mentioned have helped him, it presents no daunting problems for him; he is one of the very few film directors competent to instruct their lighting photographers in the precise effect they want: for a time he held a union card in New York as a lighting cameraman. But always in his work, achievement has to do with content, not effect. "The important thing is not to put the cart before the horse and to set things up for the camera before you've made something happen worth filming."

After *Lolita*'s release the partnership with James Harris was amicably ended, for Harris wanted to direct his own films. Kubrick had gone to England to make *Lolita* on account of the funds that the financing company had available in Britain. And Kubrick has continued to make his films there. Still, he has never considered himself an expatriate American. With his aptitudes and craft rooted in communications media, he finds it easy and attractive to keep in contact with the international film scene, and, indeed, with the larger world, from wherever he happens to be. (More often than not, a discussion with him is punctuated by the buzzing of his wrist-watch alarm announcing that someone, somewhere, is waiting for a call, or is ready to put in a call to him.)

But the change of work base has had deeper effects on Kubrick. He lives in the English countryside where time, energy, inspiration, confidence cannot be eroded by too much contact with the world, especially the movie world; this has provided him with a highly favorable psychological climate in which to function. His present environment respects his privacy. Though he is remote from the Hollywood power struggles, the available mass media facilitate his spectator enjoyment of following these struggles, move by move, without being submerged by them. And finally, it allows him to initiate action, rather than be on the receiving end of it. All these factors are important for a director determined to keep total control of his movies.

Between shooting films, Kubrick works from his home,

a large house with a rambling family look to it, set in semirural Hertfordshire, about a half hour's drive from London. Built in a style of airy yet settled solidity, it indicates the English affinity for a Chekhovian life style. A film studio is nearby. His third wife is the painter Christiane Harlan, who has exhibited in London galleries and at the Royal Academy.* In the days when she was an actress in her native Germany, she played the frightened girl who is pushed out onto the stage to sing to the troops at the end of *Paths of Glory.* The Kubricks have three children.

His permanent business aides are few; one of them is his brother-in-law. This sense of a business center running imperceptibly into a family household has probably given Kubrick's creative life the kind of stability that is not easy to find in New York City or Beverly Hills today (see page 12, Kubrick and his daughter). The flow of visitors who come by invitation is matched by the flow of films, old and new, sent for him to see in his home cinema—he rarely goes to see them in London—and both visitors and films maintain the flow of that essential nourishment for Kubrick, information. Thus his ever-curious intelligence sharpens his protective life style, while his relatively fixed abode supplies him with time for reflection, for "pondering the choices," which the hectic activity of wheeling and dealing in panicky circumstances denies many other filmmakers.

Perhaps it is accidental that the neighborhood he inhabits was the site of an English monastery many centuries ago; but it is certainly an appropriate location. The life of reflection, information, and stimulation that at any moment can be turned into action may have influenced Kubrick in fixing on some of his more recent film subjects. They have come to him by more indirect means than the usual scanning of publishers' galleys for likely properties. They have crystallized out of his more general concerns, rather than out of any specific need to find a story to do. In particular, they have come from the wide diversity of material he reads, all bearing on some area of interest. When his attention is focused on a particular topic, he

*Kubrick's earlier marriages were to Toba Metz, at the age of eighteen, and later to Ruth Sobotka, a dancer with Balanchine's City Center ballet company, who made a brief appearance in *Killer's Kiss.*

devours all the relevant material he and his aides can lay their hands on. Other things, too, keep feeding his interest: a news item in a paper, a piece of information a friend sends him, a chance conversation with a visitor, a radio report. The phenomenon of finding all kinds of additional information flowing in coincidentally from all sides, like magnetized particles, once some main area of interest has absorbed one's attention, is not an uncommon experience among creative people in the arts or sciences; but Kubrick seems particularly susceptible to it, perhaps because he arranges his life to facilitate it, and there is no doubt that it is a powerful factor in giving conceptual shape to the final film.

The strong interest he already had in the nuclear impasse was intensified in the early 1960s when he began subscribing to military magazines and other official or semiofficial publications dealing with the subject. "I started out being completely unfamiliar with any of the professional literature in the field of nuclear deterrence. I was at first very impressed with how subtle some of the work was—at least so it seemed starting out with just a kind of primitive concern for survival and a total lack of any ideas of my *own.* Gradually I became aware of the almost wholly paradoxical nature of deterrence or, as it has been described, the Delicate Balance of Terror. If you are weak, you may invite a first strike. If you are becoming too strong, you may provoke a pre-emptive strike. If you try to maintain the delicate balance, it's almost impossible to do so because secrecy prevents you from knowing what the other side is doing, and vice versa, ad infinitum. . . ." This is the paradox that, once Kubrick perceived it from his involvement in the subject, inspired *Dr. Strangelove, or How I Learned to Stop Worrying and Love the Bomb* (1964).

More out of interest in survival, rather than art, he turned to the Institute for Strategic Studies with the request for guidelines on more serious reading. In the course of his inquiries he asked the head of the Institute, Alastair Buchan, if he knew of any worth-while fiction on the subject. Buchan, Kubrick recalls, mentioned the book on which he subsequently based his film. This was *Red Alert,* a straight suspense thriller by an English author, Peter George, who had been a Royal Air Force navigator. *Red Alert* contained two critical ingredients—a powerful story, which characteristically was what first caught Kubrick's interest, and a brilliant premise. In other words, its plot construction was logically justifiable, and this, to a mind like Kubrick's, rendered it doubly attractive. Even the premise had a Kubrick flavor—the impossibility of constructing a perfect plan, because, inevitably, every foolproof system has its built-in contradiction. Peter George had reasoned that although it is desirable to have a controlled nuclear-deterrent system that cannot be activated by middle-echelon officers, nevertheless a country's leaders cannot be the sole persons with the power to order a nuclear attack; they are far too conspicuous and hence too vulnerable. So the questions at issue were: How many other people were there with the power to issue the "Go" code? Where were they in the chain of command? And were there ways to launch weapons other than as instruments of national policy?

The film bore out the logical consequences of the premise. It took a situation that had been carefully designed to be fail-safe and turned it inside out, so that the man who sent the system wrong did so in a way that prevented others from setting it right again. But Kubrick did not get very far in constructing a serious suspense story for the screen. "As I tried to build the detail for a scene I found myself tossing away what seemed to me to be very truthful insights because I was afraid the audience would laugh. After a few weeks of this, I realized that these incongruous bits of reality were closer to the truth than anything else I was able to imagine. And it was at this point I decided to treat the story as a nightmare comedy. Following this approach, I found it never interfered with presenting well-reasoned arguments. In culling the incongruous, it seemed to me to be less stylized and more realistic than any so-called serious, realistic treatment, which in fact is more stylized than life itself by its careful exclusion of the banal, the absurd, and the incongruous. In the context of imminent world destruction, hypocrisy, misunderstanding, lechery, paranoia, ambition, euphemism, patriotism, heroism, and even reasonableness can evoke a grisly laugh."*

Through Kubrick's temperament runs a strong fascination with the nightmare side of existence. He has a willingness to face the catastrophe he suspects to be imminent with an inquiring mind and release the pessimism he feels in savage laughter. Exactly what has shaped this outlook is probably impossible to pinpoint precisely. One is tempted to seek its origin in the racial resilience of the Jews, whose historically helpless plight has given rise to some of the world's blackest humor. Kubrick, however, does not incline to this view; and certainly immersion in the film industry offers an artist enough occasions for acquiring a satiric cast of mind without his having to suffer additional persecution on account of his faith!

The world, as Horace Walpole said, is "a comedy to those that think, a tragedy to those that feel." And Kubrick appears to be a product of the creative tension between the two states of mind. On occasion, he has spoken of Peter Sellers in terms that may very well apply to himself. "Peter has the most responsive attitude of all the actors I've worked with to the things I think are funny. He is always at his best in dealing with grotesque and horrifying ideas. I've never felt he was as funny in conventional comedy roles; his greatest gift is for the grisly, horrifying areas of humor that other actors wouldn't think playable at all."

Comedy, for Kubrick, makes it possible to deal with issues that would be unbearable in any other form. But such an attitude makes his position exceedingly complex regarding some of the issues his films raise. Though he has made two major films that leave no doubt about his basic attitude to war, he cannot be classified simply as a pacifist. His fascination with the subject also stems from the grotesque, often comic, ways that war throws human nature into relief. He sees war as an irrational situation that swiftly forces attitudes out into the open, attitudes that in less critical times might take longer to de-

*A paradox borne out again and again by some of the extraordinary moments of nightmarish "comedy" that William Manchester reported in his analysis of the aftermath of the Kennedy assassination in *The Death of a President.*

velop and have to be presented on the screen in more contrived forms. Being the most extreme example of a pathological situation, war holds enormous dramatic attractiveness for Kubrick. The psychotic behavior need not be treated crudely; on the contrary, his films have proved what a wide range of ironic subtleties it is possible to explore. Preferably, though, the grotesque occurrence has a surrounding framework of realistic technical data or conventional social values; these set off the abnormalities of the situation and heighten the behavior of the characters. To keep one foot in nightmare and the other in reality, a director requires a very sure sense of balance. This Kubrick has to an exceptional degree. His skepticism about the upward progress of mankind, which sharpened the barbed pessimism of *Dr. Strangelove,* is linked with his own high regard for reason, logic, and precision—all qualities in dire jeopardy where the malfunctioning human animal is concerned.

The humanist in Kubrick hopes that man will survive his own irrationality; the intellectual in him doubts it. Both attitudes contributed to his choice of space exploration and man's first contact with extraterrestrial forms of life as the subject of his next film, *2001: A Space Odyssey* (1968). But no sooner has the "subject" been thus labeled than one has to qualify it. This is the "subject" as the casual eye might register the events in the film. In fact, Kubrick's chief concern in *2001* was with the concept of intelligence and its transformations. This enormously complex film does not date simply from the time Kubrick and his cowriter, Arthur C. Clarke, began to elaborate the narrative side. *2001* is the product of interests that were engaging Kubrick's attention in the years before a word of the screenplay was put on paper. The concept of communications was one of these.

On the most basic level, communications underpin the whole process of making a film. The organization of his film in the preshooting stage—never mind the task of communicating what he wants it to say to future audiences during shooting—is a process that stretches every faculty Kubrick possesses. This is often where his team of collaborators feels the going is toughest. Some have formed the impression that shooting the film is actually a relief to Kubrick, for he strives for perfection in every memo, message, order, inquiry, suggestion, and revision he initiates. A man who makes communication a central feature of his working life will very easily extend it into the intellectual concept of his film.

Moreover, one of the additional working tools Kubrick has used in recent years has been the computer. It saves him time and enables him to predict the consequences of apparently equally attractive moves. Doing everything—from adding a column of figures to charting a film's critical path analysis—the computer can give Kubrick a rational means of dealing with the constrictions of budget and schedule—and more, too. The prospect of programing a computer would afford him the satisfaction of organizing an intelligence fit for his needs—an intelligence without, he hopes, many common human shortcomings. Now a computer that plays a certain role in planning a film can very easily, by one imaginative leap, be cast for a major role *in* a film; especially if the film speculates on the relationship between man's intelligence and the way he has used his tools to embody and extend it. The stages by which HAL 9000 was promoted from a minor functionary in an early draft script of *2001* to being an active protagonist in the finished film are things Kubrick prefers not to discuss. But of the underlying interest which HAL extends to sections of the film, Kubrick says, "One of the fascinating questions that arise in envisioning computers more intelligent then men is at what point machine intelligence deserves the same consideration as biological intelligence. Once a computer learns by experience as well as by its original programing, and once it has access to much more information than any number of human geniuses might possess, the first thing that happens is that you don't really understand it anymore, and you don't know what it's doing or thinking about. You could be tempted to ask yourself in what way is machine intelligence any less sacrosanct than biological intelligence, and it might be difficult to arrive at an answer flattering to biological intelligence."

With these interests so much a part of his daily activity, Kubrick's imagination only needed a productive jolt to set it on course for the "subject" of *2001*. "I had always been surprised at how little interest anyone seemed to show in the quite respectable and widely held view by scientists that the universe was undoubtedly filled with intelligent life. As someone once quipped, 'Sometimes I think we're alone, and sometimes I think we're not. In either case, I find the idea quite astonishing.' The reasons for believing we are not alone are quite compelling. First of all, from spectrographic analysis of the stars we know the universe is made of the same chemical elements. Recent experiments have gone a long way to confirming the theory that life was created by random chemical reactions which took place over billions of years in the primordial soup. Now there are about 150 billion stars in our galaxy, each star and sun something like our own. And there are about 150 billion galaxies in the visible universe. The formation of planets around a star is now thought to be a common occurrence. So you are left with a staggering number of possibilities for the formation of planets in stable orbits which are not too hot and not too cold and from which it can be presumed that life will eventually arise after a few billion years.

"Eventually biological life forms will develop and one of these will be as ill-adapted to its environment as it is believed our ancestors were. To these creatures intelligence will become an evolutionary survival trait, and a process not entirely unlike our own should follow. Having physical mediocrity as the *sine qua non* for intelligence becoming a survival trait, these creatures will probably channel their intelligence along the lines of the tool-weapon culture and they will start on the relatively short road to modern science. Since the age of the stars in the universe varies by millions of years, it is also reasonable to imagine intelligence far older than their own and possessing capabilities which to us would seem magical, even godlike."

Once this idea was started, the creative process of *Dr. Strangelove* repeated itself. Kubrick let the amassing of scientific data lead him on to a search for meaningful fiction. Arthur C. Clarke's writing supplied it, especially his short story "The Sentinel," which sketched the notion of a cosmic "burglar alarm" placed on the moon by extraterrestrial beings to forewarn them of man's approach.

Kubrick, as we have seen, already shared Clarke's belief in the power of myths and legends to set up echoes in human awareness. From the very start, even when the project was titled *Journey Beyond the Stars,* the pair were concerned to find a term for the film that would replace the overused and imprecise "science fiction." They came up with the word "odyssey"—"a space odyssey," said Clarke at a press conference, "comparable in some ways to the Homeric *Odyssey."* Given all this, it is not surprising that Kubrick cast his film about intelligence in the form of a myth—"a mythological documentary" is the term he was to apply to it—and gradually, unconsciously perhaps, and then with increasing awareness of their potential, drew on his other concerns and interests as he and Clarke developed the screenplay.

But what ultimately made the film unique was Kubrick's gradual perception of the perfect cinematic concept for the film as a nonverbal visual experience, one that would resist neat categorizing by dialogue or narration and, instead, penetrate an audience's consciousness at a deeper and more stimulating level. Most of Kubrick's earlier films had leaned upon the use of some kind of commentary or first-person narration, which he had used, he says, when it seemed necessary to compress and convey information of a kind that is not easy, or realistic, to put into dialogue. Narration helped him put this across without having to slog through the conventions of a stage play.

Now, narration, and quite extensive narration, too, did exist in one early script for *2001,* dated mid-1965, some six months before shooting began. Most of it was in the Dawn of Man prologue. Yet the first words spoken in the finished film do not come until well after this sequence and, in all, there are only about forty minutes of dialogue. The early difficulty that narration presented was that to make the events remotely comprehensible to people with little scientific knowledge would require too much spoken commentary. Then as he made the film it came to Kubrick that words were actually working against the visual experience he wanted to convey. Kubrick had engaged Douglas Rain, a Canadian actor, to speak some narration for the film. But he kept postponing this as the conviction hardened that a nonverbal approach was the only appropriate one. Eventually Rain's contract was about to expire when Kubrick asked him, instead of supplying narration, to re-record a part that had already been spoken by another actor, with not entirely satisfactory results. The part was that of the computer, HAL 9000. It proved one of the best choices Kubrick has ever made.

Not counting the time spent on preparing the screenplay, *2001* still took about two and one half years to make: six months of preshooting activity, four and a half months of filming with the cast, a year and a half working on the 205 separate special-effects shots. It absorbed the efforts of a vast team of technicians. And, characteristically, Kubrick took great pains to justify the elements in the film; consultations were held with nearly seventy industrial and aerospace corporations, universities, observatories, weather bureaus, laboratories, and other institutions, to insure that the forecast of life in space in A.D. 2001 was based on information that already existed or could be predicted. The budget, originally six million dollars, escalated to ten and a half million. The reason for this was that the repertoire of special-effects techniques was inadequate to produce the shots needed, and equipment had to be designed and built, techniques experimented with, and all of this in an expensive film studio, rather than a factory or a laboratory. Obviously budgetary increases resulted. But the film's profitability continues to grow. So does its extraordinary power to win adherents among the young—not by any means all from the "hippie" subculture so fond of the film's reputed (and overstressed) hallucinogenic properties. Many of the critics who at first failed to appreciate the film were later converted when, as Joseph Gelmis put it, "understanding became a function of the emotions, rather than one's reasoning powers."

Considering the scale of *2001* and his success in fulfilling his ambitions in making the picture, it was hardly a surprise when Kubrick announced in 1969 that the subject of his next film was going to be Napoleon. This film has not yet been made. The main preparation for it had been completed and a general staff of historians and researchers had supplied every relevant detail of what was envisaged as a huge canvas encompassing all the major events in the Emperor's life, when the project was suddenly canceled for financial reasons. Hollywood's financial crisis of the late 1960s had shattered the confidence of some film companies as to their ability to commit themselves to a large-scale film, especially at a time when the small, youth-oriented picture was in vogue.

Fortunately, the disappointment over having to put off Napoleon until more propitious times did not last long. Almost on the rebound, Kubrick found the subject of his next film. The old self-responsive process led him to Anthony Burgess's novel *A Clockwork Orange.* First published in 1962, *A Clockwork Orange* deals with the future, an area that Kubrick has made very much his own on the screen. The novel has been called the most cogent and terrifying vision of things to come since George Orwell's *Nineteen Eighty-Four.* Like that book, it cloaks its prophecy about society's evolution in a good story—a persistent attraction to Kubrick. It takes the form of a nightmarish thriller narrated with vivid directness by Alex, the teen-age antihero, whose generation of young hoodlums fraternizes in its own private language, called "Nadsat," and takes over society after dark, terrorizing town and country. Beneath the violence, though, the aim is satirical and even didactic. Burgess extrapolates a feature of contemporary life into the near future, certainly a couple of decades short of 2001, and exaggerates it in a savage, Swiftian way so as to reflect a distorted yet recognizable image of ourselves. Despite the stridently "Pop" tone of the first-person narrative, the theme is a Christian one. It is redemption. The premise implied by the odd title is that it is far better for an individual to possess free will, even if it is exclusively the will to sin, than for him to be made over into a clockwork paradigm of virtue.

Seized by the state police after a particularly grisly bout

of thuggery, Alex undergoes the "Ludovico Treatment," a savage system of aversion shock-therapy that reconditions his responses and turns him into a model but mindless citizen—in short, a "clockwork orange"; a mechanized being who only appears to be organic.

The interlocking ironies of humans who act like machines and a machine that is almost human have been already deeply implanted in *Dr. Strangelove* and *2001: A Space Odyssey.* And the overlapping "areas of interest" do not end there. Alex's fate continues Kubrick's concern with the ambiguous nature of science, whose capacity to enhance life is contrasted with the misuse men make of it to circumscribe freedom and even extinguish existence. The theme has the intellectual excitement Kubrick finds stimulating; in giving shape to Alex's world, the imaginative possibilities—a sex-obsessed yet loveless society filled with the tensions created by the amoral young, their hostile but listless elders, and the repressive zeal of the authorities—are just the kind he can rework meaningfully in his own way. One of the problems confronting him is how to take an evildoer like Alex, who knows no remorse and experiences no love, for whom girls are simply objects to rape with "the old in-out in-out," and turn him into someone who inspires pity, in the same way HAL did once the avenging astronaut had dehumanized what ought not to have been considered human in the first place.

Kubrick and Burgess share the same involvement in what is perhaps the most ingenious feature of this novel: its creation of a teen-ager language, Nadsat, whose abusive terminology runs like a vocal manifesto of violence through Alex's unrepentant chronicle, giving it a quality of absolute and unashamed candor. Here, for example, is Alex's commentary on his arrest by the police: "All the time we were sirening off to the rozz-shop, me being wedged between two millicents and being given the old thump and malenky tolchock by these smecking bullies. Then I found I could open up my glaz-lids a malenky bit and viddy like through all tears a kind of streamy city going by, all the lights like having run into one another. . . . I knew I was going to get nothing like fair play from these stinky grahzny bratchnies, Bog blast them." Becoming easily intelligible through context and repetition, this language has the same purpose as the hypersophisticated whorls and loops of Humbert Humbert's erotic syntax in *Lolita:* it establishes a precise tonal connection between the hero and the audience. It continues the preoccupation with language that was noted earlier in the euphemisms of nuclear strategists, the professional off-handedness of the moon scientists, the paranoid officialese or bigoted malapropisms of the military mind in *Dr. Strangelove;* in short, Nadsat brings Kubrick back to "the magic of words," the ways of using vocabulary and locutions to show attitudes of mind and project states of heightened, sometimes irrational experience. Nadsat fulfills the same purpose. Its vocabulary is not without logic, but is derived from such roots as Russian, gypsy argot, Cockney rhyming slang, portmanteau words, baby talk connoting a reversion to womblike pleasure, and onomatopoeic expressions that sound like the violence they describe. This "justification" for a language that at first seems baffling must have been an attractive feature to Kubrick.

The shooting schedule lasted through the winter of 1970–71. Kubrick used a compact and extremely mobile crew, for virtually all of the film was shot on location in and around London or at an old factory converted into a production headquarters and *ad hoc* studio. He made use of a conventional film studio for only a day or two, in order to shoot some special effects. Technically, this spareness seems to signal a return to the stripped-down conditions of *Killer's Kiss*—with, of course, a much larger budget—and in the cutting Kubrick is engaged in finding out about the film he has shot and, by extension, about himself. The curiosity that serves him in place of a need for community is the most driving part of his nature today. What he discovers and formulates into an experience becomes the film *A Clockwork Orange.*

As ever, Kubrick would prefer to leave the film as the only real comment he can make on his work. The answers he gave to a series of questions in the spring of 1971 may not bear directly on *A Clockwork Orange,* the work then in progress. But they do indicate accurately how his self-scrutiny is linked in his mind with the process of creation. They reveal with almost painful honesty his refusal to argue from a preconceived theme or theory; they also show his fascination with the technical evolution of his craft as well as his consistent subordination of techniques to the need to communicate with people, hold their attention, and gratify their curiosity without abandoning his own vision. They confirm important aspects of his outlook and method; they convey information that may assist fledgling filmmakers, and do so with an evident honesty of self-response. They deserve quotation as evidence of the continuous process of exploration, hesitation, and conviction that makes Kubrick a major artist.

Walker: What attracted you to the subject? What do you hope to achieve with the film?

Kubrick: These are the questions I always find impossible to answer. I believe that the questions are asked with the hope of getting a specific answer like "This is the story of a man's search for his own identity," or any number of similar replies ranging from middle- to high-brow, with or without social conscience. I don't want to sound pretentious or cranky, but I think questions like that can only produce a reply which is either gimmicky or irrelevant. It comes down to about as much as saying, "*Hamlet* is about a man who couldn't make up his mind." Somehow, the question also presumes that one approaches a film with something resembling a policy statement, or a one-sentence theme, and that the film proceeds upwards like some inverted pyramid. Maybe some people work this way, but I don't, and even though you obviously have some central preoccupation with the subject, somehow when you're telling a story (and I know this sounds trite, but it's true anyway) the characters and the story develop a life of their own, and, as you go along, your central preoccupation merely serves as a kind of yardstick to measure the relevancy of what the imagination produces.

I also think that it spoils a great deal of the pleasure of the film for anyone who happens to have been unfortunate enough to have read what the filmmaker "has in mind." As a member of the audience, I particularly enjoy those subtle discoveries where I wonder whether the filmmaker himself was even aware that they were in the film, or whether they happened by accident. I'm sure that there's something in the human personality which resents things that are clear, and, conversely, something which is attracted to puzzles, enigmas, and allegories.

Walker: How deeply are you involved in the administration when you make a film like *A Clockwork Orange*—or indeed any of your films?

Kubrick: I am deeply involved in the administration, because it is in this area that many creative and artistic battles are lost. You've got to have what you want, where you want it, and at the right time, and you have got to use your resources (money and people) in the most effective way possible because they are limited, and when they are seriously stretched it always shows on the screen. Because I have to be, I am very interested in organizational problems, and the conclusion that I have come to is that the making of a film is one of the most difficult organizational and administrative problems to exist outside of a military operation. Running a business is unfortunately never a useful analogy, because the key to the successful operation of all businesses is the establishment of routine and the breaking down of jobs into simple, definable, understandable functions which can be performed by normally adequate people.

Whereas in films almost everything is a "one-of" problem, it is almost impossible to establish a routine, and the work done is so diversified that if it were to be broken down as in a manufacturing process, you would need ten times as many people, which you could not afford.

Filmmaking violates the old adage that what is wanted is a system designed by geniuses which can be run by idiots. It has always been the other way round with films. However, I keep trying and keep coming up with new systems, new means of displaying information, remembering, reminding, following up. I risk my popularity with some of my department heads by continually pressing home the point that merely giving an order to somebody is only a fraction of their job, that their principal responsibility is to see that the order is carried out accurately, on time, and within the budget.

Walker: Can you give me an example of some of the systems you used in *A Clockwork Orange,* on the production side—to find locations, say, in a country to which you are a relative stranger?

Kubrick: Apart from all the normal procedures you'd expect your art department or production office to come up with, such as going out and looking, it seemed a logical idea on *A Clockwork Orange,* since it was necessary to find modern architectural locations, to go through the appropriate magazines and literature. I purchased ten years of back issues of three different architectural magazines and spent two solid weeks with my art director, John Barry, turning and tearing out pages. The material was put into a special display file, manufactured by a company in Germany, called Definitiv. The system encompassed various signals, colored, alphabetical, and numerical, which were displayed when the file was hanging in a rack. These signals allowed the material to be cross-referenced in almost an infinite number of ways.

Walker: I am sure you know how much time and trouble some filmmakers put into the credit titles of their films. With your emphasis on the visual, how do you feel about this?

Kubrick: I never worry about the main titles. I have seen some very clever ones which I have admired, but I think that clever main titles are just a waste of money and a disservice to the film. I have a very simple-minded point of view, in that the first shot of the film should be the most interesting thing that the audience has seen since it sat down. In addition to winning the audience back from the credits to the "anticlimax" of the film itself, clever titles mean animation, trick effects, opticals, and usually a very expensive designer; and this means they cost a fair amount of money. I would rather put the money into the film itself.

Walker: It seems to me you approach the task of editing your films with as much involvement as, if not more than, the actual shooting, is this so?

Kubrick: I love editing. I think I like it more than any other phase of filmmaking. If I wanted to be frivolous,

Man having his responses mechanically conditioned: Malcolm McDowell (with his director) begins the grueling scene in A Clockwork Orange *where Alex, the young thug, is given the Ludovico Treatment to turn him into a model citizen.*

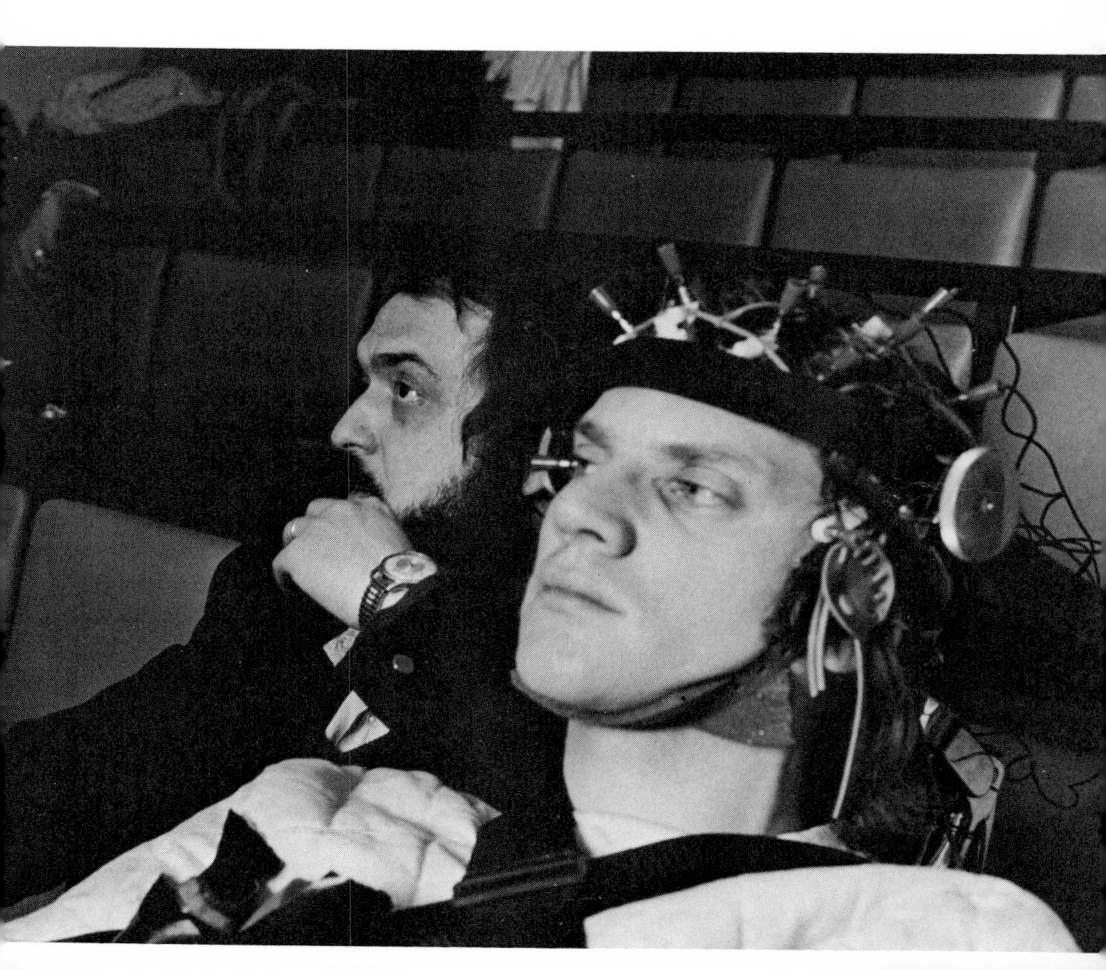

(Above) Psychedelia in A Clockwork Orange: *the Korova Milkbar, hangout for dropouts and teen-agers, where plastic nudes form banquettes and the moloko, or milk, comes mixed with vellocet, drencrom, or some other "Nadsat" drug, which, in Alex's words, "give you a nice quiet horrorshow fifteen minutes admiring Bog and All His Holy Angels and Saints in your left shoe with lights bursting all over your mozg."*

Machines for mechanical violence, Alex and his gang beat up helpless citizens of a society that is limp and listless except for the teen-agers and the totalitarian rulers.

(Left) While Alex's gang of thugs in weird all-white combat suits stand by, Kubrick lines up a shot in the Korova Milkbar. Statuary, with its air of hygienic eroticism, recalls the nude dummies that were witnesses (and sometimes weapons) in the fight at the end of Killer's Kiss.

(Left) As in his first film, so in his latest, Stanley Kubrick supervises every detail personally.

(Below left) Trapped by the Cat Woman wielding a bust of Beethoven, Alex counterattacks with a gigantic sculptured phallus. Kubrick spent most of a day filming the bizarre duel, much of it with a camera hand-held by himself (seated at left), moving round and round with the weaving, thrusting combatants in furious 360-degree circles until they almost collapsed from exhaustion.

(Below right) Kubrick, behind the cone of lights, prepares the sequence in A Clockwork Orange *where Alex and the Cat Woman (Miriam Karlin, on the right) fight to the death.*

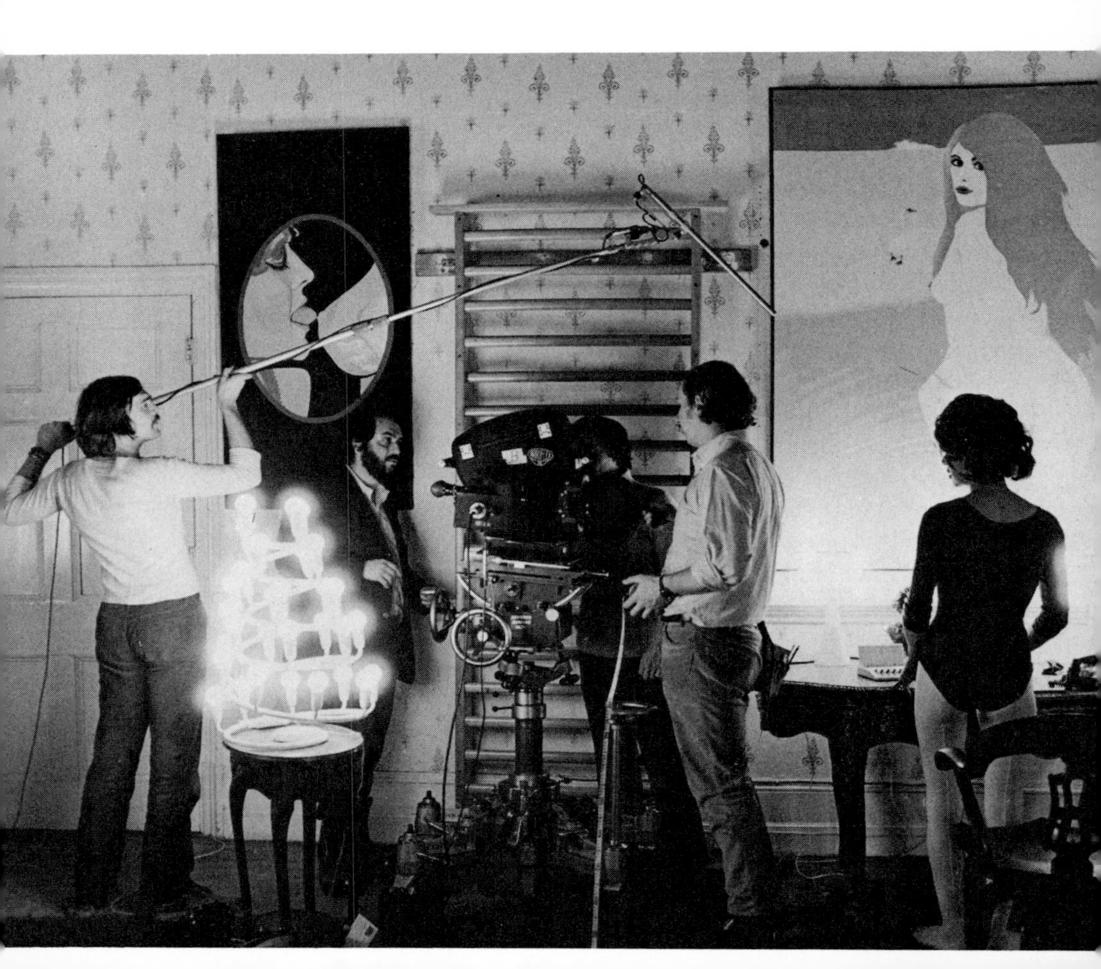

I might say that everything that precedes editing is merely a way of producing film to edit.

Editing is the only unique aspect of filmmaking which does not resemble any other art form—a point so important it cannot be overstressed. (I know I've already stressed it!) It can make or break a film.

The basic equipment I use is two Steenbeck editing tables and a Moviola. I use the two Steenbecks for selection, and by having two of them I can continuously look at the film without waiting for the last roll to be taken off and replaced by another. I don't feel too guilty about having the two Steenbecks, because their combined rental cost is only a small fraction of the daily interest charges which exist on the production loan of even a small film during the editing phase of a production. I find the Steenbeck marvelous for selection. It allows the fast forward and reverse and runs very quietly at normal speed. But for the actual cutting of the film and the handling of small bits of film, the Moviola is far superior, for all of its noisy, clattery, old-fashioned self.

When I am editing, I work seven days a week. In the beginning I work ten hours a day and then as we get closer to the deadlines I usually push that up to fourteen or sixteen hours a day.

Walker: You have shot virtually all of *A Clockwork Orange* on location. Can you tell me what special equipment you made use of?

Kubrick: There is some marvelous sound, lighting, and camera equipment available today which makes it possible to shoot anywhere on location without suffering any disadvantage in comparison with working in a studio. This means that one can benefit from realistic surroundings and cut costs significantly.

Specifically, on the photographic side, one now has lightweight fiberglass blimps which allow hand-held sound takes, ultra-fast lenses (f. 0.95) which permit shooting under extremely low light levels, and extremely wide-angle lenses (9.8 millimeter) which allow long shots in even the most confined rooms.

Sound recording has traditionally been the reason why people have thought it necessary to work within the soundproof walls of a film studio. But sound technology has advanced more strikingly than any other technical side of filmmaking. Aside from lightweight portable sound recorders which can be slung over a shoulder (formerly a sound truck with a man inside served the same purpose), there is a diverse range of microphones which allow excellent recordings to be made under the worst conditions. We had a scene in *A Clockwork Orange* that took place under the Albert Bridge. The traffic noise was so loud that you had to raise your voice just to be heard in a conversation, but with the aid of a Sennheiser Mk. 12 microphone no larger than a paper clip, stuck into an actor's lapel, it was possible to produce a sound track which had only a very pleasant hum of activity in the background.

As for lighting, I should say that eighty-five per cent of *A Clockwork Orange* was lit either by replacing normal light bulbs in existing lighting fixtures with photo floods, or by the use of very lightweight Lowell 1,000-watt quartz lights, bounced off either ceilings or special reflective umbrellas. At other times it was necessary to use brute arcs for which there is no substitute when large expanses have to be lit at night, or when a one-source light effect has to be achieved in a large interior.

KUBRICK: STYLE AND CONTENT

Without *Fear and Desire* and *Spartacus*—the one film an initial practice piece and the other an assignment picture he now virtually disowns—each of the films of Stanley Kubrick has a strong, unifying aspect. But it would be rash to say that all of them bear witness to strong, unifying themes. Kubrick clearly does not work thematically, with deliberate intent, from one picture to the next. He works by discovery. He works by accidentally happening on a subject, usually one with the lure of a good story; then, by pondering the problems and possibilities it offers for development, he conceptualizes a way of telling the story in film terms that fit it with imaginative precision.

He also works by "surprise," in the sense that Cocteau has used the word. And Cocteau borrowed it from Diaghilev, a creative autocrat, in some respects like Kubrick, who employed it in the impresario's challenge, *"Etonnez-moi."* Kubrick guards the element of surprise, of revelation, in his films, for his own sake as well as the audience's. He wants the unfolding films to surprise *him,* too, which is why he avoids saying much about them before they are made. Prior discussion might exhaust the power of suggestive thinking, just as deciding a camera set-up too early could curtail the development of a scene.

Even on a film like *Spartacus,* where he was not only a hired hand but a tied one, he was able to convey an unmistakable sense of his own fascination with the possibilities the film had, but which were never realized in Dalton Trumbo's banal and sentimentalized script. Significantly, these moments occur where the script merely indicates action—and where the action ties up the star, to the director's distinct advantage. One such scene permitted Kubrick to deal with the techniques of gladiatorial training and the scientific emphasis on reducing men to being efficient killing machines. Others occur in the battlefield perspectives at the end; resting his camera on an Olympian cloud, Kubrick surveys the rival armies of Romans and Spartacists with a detached, aesthetic appreciation that anticipates his later fascination with the order, precision, and lethal beauty of Napoleon's maneuvers in classical warfare.

Much that is integral to Kubrick's movies comes from the way his compulsive curiosity pushes radically different subjects into his own areas of interest. Perhaps *Killer's Kiss* comes low in his own estimation because it reflects so few of his present interests. But it is an oddly compelling work that tells much about the young Kubrick and explains why he stirred up immediate critical notice. The story, as he has said, was deliberately built around surefire action sequences. Yet what critics sensed as novel in this modest film were precisely those moments of rest, when nothing visibly happens on the screen, but Kubrick's camera (operated by himself) brings people or objects into meaningful relationship and seems to make everything "happen." The young boxer, at the start as captive as his own goldfish in the bowl in his dingy tenement room, sits out the last hour or two before his big fight; across the courtyard a lighted window reveals a girl getting ready for her night's stint at some treadmill job. One life can look through the New York darkness into another life, yet the two lighted squares of glass only emphasize the couple's apartness. They are unaware of each other

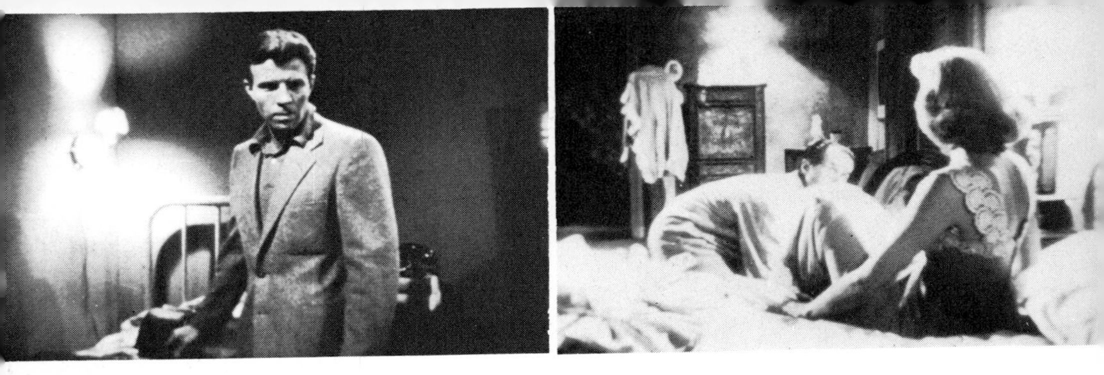

***Lighting and grouping:** Kubrick establishes character and mood by using sharply defined areas of illumination and shadow to set people in relation to their environment or to each other—(left to right) the boxer's loneliness in* Killer's Kiss; *the husband's subservience to his wife in* The Killing; The Killing*'s criminals huddled together in conspiracy (see General Ripper "lost" in his own fantasy of Communist conspiracy in* Dr. Strangelove, *page 185); Humbert Humbert's fearful isolation in a motel room.*

to the point of invisibility, each self-isolated, virtually imprisoned in lives that are soon revealed as humiliating and hopeless.

What is immediately evident is Kubrick's talent for lighting and photographing a scene so as to abstract its latent emotional value. He trusts to the power of the lens to crystallize moods and confer values on objects. *Killer's Kiss* has more shots of objects with affective associations, like the mental inventory that the hero makes of the girl's bedroom while she sleeps, than any later Kubrick film. It is an accomplishment that clearly derives from his years as a photojournalist. He was quickly and increasingly to make it serve his attitudes to events in a film, not substitute for them. Perhaps a lingering connection with the magazine photo-essay today makes him disparage his achievement in *Killer's Kiss.* He was soon to insist that style is attitude, not applied photography.

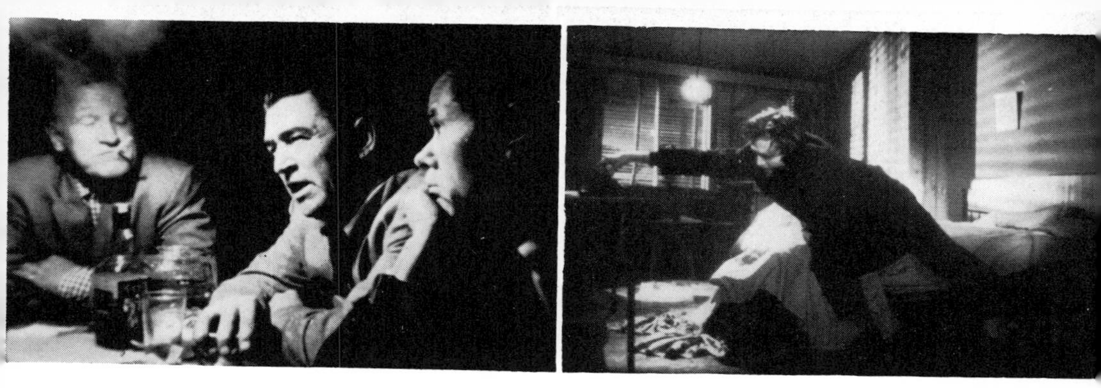

The other striking feature of the film is its tone, one of urban loneliness, almost melancholy. Its three main characters, Davy, the boxer, Gloria, the girl, and Rapallo, a brutish dance-hall owner infatuated by her, are people defeated by life. Professional failure, family tragedy, a kink of nature have them trapped. Davy's career is on the skids; Gloria's life as a dance-hall hostess is a kind of penance for her sister's suicide; Rapallo's slightly sadistic passion turns to crazed despair when Gloria walks out on him, and he is driven to kidnap her. Beaten people in the penumbra of the underworld, they foreshadow the gang of small-time crooks taking their last chance to make it big in Kubrick's next film, *The Killing.*

But *Killer's Kiss* adds a dimension of poetry to its characters' desperation by the way it interlocks their fates. While an action-thriller on the surface—fast, violent, charged with suspense and physical climax—its undertones are as disturbing and omnipresent as one of those self-fulflling curses laid on the virtuous characters in a German folk tale from the brothers Grimm. The story readily resolves itself into the archetypal fable of a maiden rescued by a valorous knight from the clutches of an ogre whose obsessive love for her she cannot return. And the impression of a fable is strengthened by an extraordinary sequence in which the girl tells Davy her life story; this is a harrowing tale of Gloria's devotion to a sister who trades her gift as a ballet dancer to marry a rich man and support her father, and who kills herself after her father's death, since she has nothing left to live for. As Gloria tells what amounts to a complete short story, Kubrick's camera shows the sister (played by

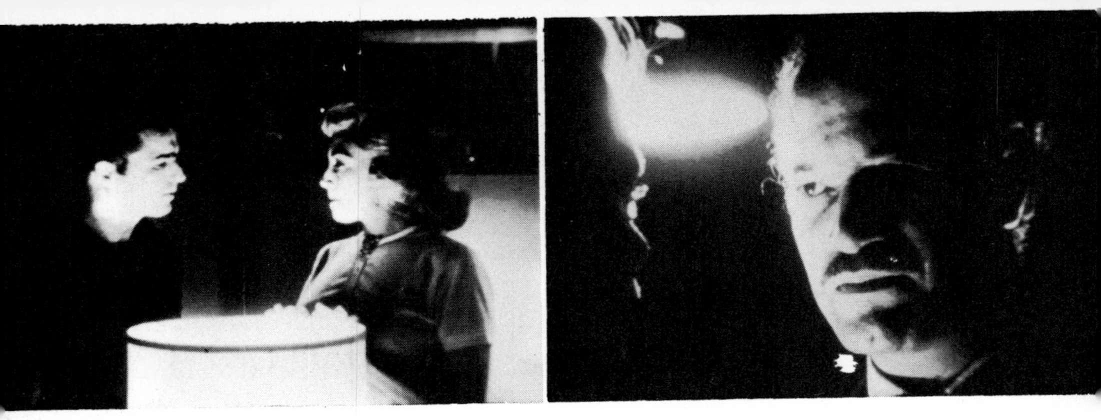

Realism in lighting: *Kubrick's early preference for light that comes from a natural source, generally an overhead lamp, is simple and brutal in effect. Pictures 1, 3, and 4 are from* The Killing; *picture 2 from* Killer's Kiss. *The meeting that takes place directly under this source of light, which increases the sense of confrontation, is a favorite Kubrick composition. (See* Paths of Glory, *page 95;* Dr. Strangelove, *page 175.)*

Kubrick's second wife, Ruth Sobotka) dancing a sad, haunting *pas seul* before an unseen audience. By the laws of logic, Gloria's flashback has no right to be in *Killer's Kiss* at all, for throughout the film it is supposed to be Davy who is telling the story in flashback. It was put in, says Kubrick, to add interest to Gloria's character and also as a tribute to his wife's talent. Yet it works poetically in the traditional way that a character in a folk tale or fairy story can embellish the tale by embarking on his own narrative within the framework of the main tale.

Kubrick has spoken of his early love of fables and fairy tales; and his belief in the energizing power of myth to work on our unconscious or touch the memory-trace of our race finds a place in several of his movies. It is implicit in the whole concept of *2001;* and to discern its early manifestation in *Killer's Kiss* is not overfanciful. It even shows up in *Lolita,* itself based on a novel by a writer powerfully attracted by the creative force of myth

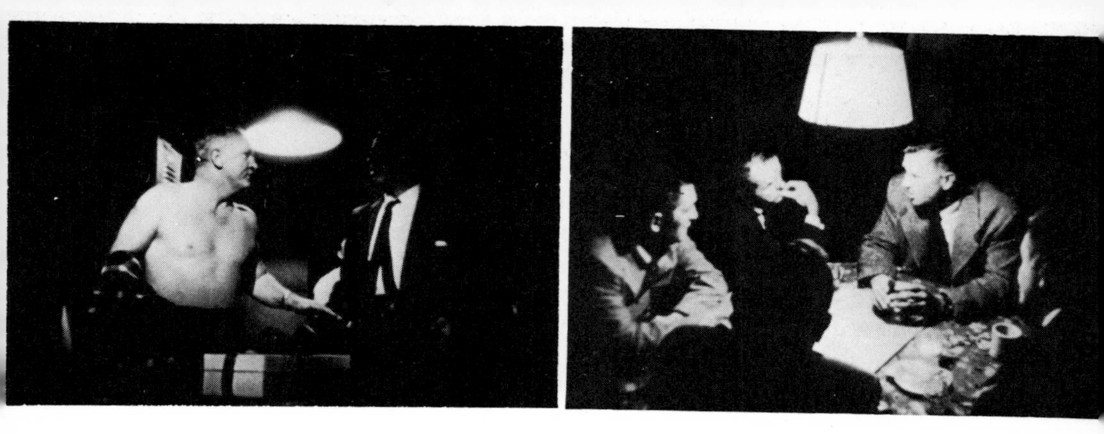

and legend. Indeed, *Lolita*'s story of a girl abducted from her true lover by a wicked ogre has a slight but eerie similarity to *Killer's Kiss.* Humbert Humbert driving to Quilty's mansion, vengeance-bound at the start, emerges out of a ground mist that might have drifted over from German legend. "I pushed the front door," Nabokov writes at this point, "and, how nice, it swung open as in a medieval fairy-tale." Kubrick follows to the letter a novelist's direction that was so congenial to his own temperament and, how nice, even improves on it by permitting a glimpse of Quilty's home, with its machicolated roof like that of an enchanter's castle.

Something else seems to connect *Killer's Kiss* with this insubstantial world of suggestion. Its actual events of boy meeting girl, girl being abducted, boy getting her back again, cover at least a few days—and Kubrick's early skill in editing turns them into a tight, dynamic story; yet all seem to happen within the ambiguous time span of a dream that may have lasted only a few minutes or a few hours. Davy, at one point, has a premonitory dream, or nightmare, which the camera records by traveling down straight, endless streets photographed in negative, the onward impetus recalling the low-flying B-52s' mission of destruction in the last reels of *Dr. Strangelove* and the cosmic ride in *2001.* Dawn, dusk, and darkness, the times when one is most aware of one's loneliness, are used by the director-photographer to light his moods as well as his locations. And the fatalistic sense of trouble that comes from involvement with total strangers is fixed almost tangibly in this world where it is either nighttime or else light is just breaking or just fading.

Kubrick's handling of action is also masterly. The sequence of Davy being chased by Rapallo's men begins with the boxer dwarfed by perpendicular blocks of riverside warehouses, like a mouse in search of a hole; the camera rises with him as he scales a fire escape, and the chase again becomes horizontal as Davy scuttles round the perimeter of a vast expanse of rooftop. Kubrick keeps his camera immobile, watching him, catlike. The subsequent fight between him and Rapallo reveals Kubrick's early flair for the grotesque. Boxer and gangster confront each other in a bizarre, cramped storeroom full of naked and partly dismembered tailor's dummies. They lunge at each other—Rapallo with an ax, Davy with a pike —but sometimes each repels the other with a fusillade of limbs and torsos. The sense of amputation that surrounds the men conveys a savage suggestion of what such

Composition in depth: *In moments of crisis in his films, Kubrick tends to compose his action in depth, framing it in narrow but natural confines. The boxer, pursued by the gang in* Killer's Kiss, *runs toward the stationary camera through the "bolt holes" of New York's back streets. (See Colonel Dax's purposive march through the trenches, advancing into a highly mobile camera, in* Paths of Glory, *pages 103-105, to lead his men over the top and into battle; and the astronaut in* 2001: A Space Odyssey, *page 233.) But the hero is usually speedily diminished again by his environment, whether a battlefield or . . .*

jousting may do to *their* bodies, while the impassive nudity of the dummies contrasts with the sweaty, panting desperation of the humans.

Halfway through *Killer's Kiss* is a sequence repaying detailed analysis. It is the murder of the boxer's manager by Rapallo's henchmen, who have mistaken him for Davy. Here is early evidence that Kubrick can build a sequence like a chess game; one move determines the next, and that one a still later move, until out of a coolly manipulated consecutive structure there is created a cumulative menace.

Davy is waiting outside the dance hall for Gloria to join him with her final paycheck; then they aim to leave New York for good. Suddenly, by a quirk of fate, two drunken conventioneers playfully filch the boxer's scarf, and he takes off after them in their clownish retreat up the street. Meanwhile his manager appears, having arranged to bring over Davy's share of the earnings from his last fight. He stations himself against one half of the plate-glass door leading to the dance hall, and waits for his friend. Gloria, after an angry, inconclusive interview with Rapallo, comes down the stairs and, not finding Davy, takes up her stance against the other half of the door. She and the manager do not know each other. Kubrick's camera looks obliquely down at their backs from the top of the inside staircase. One of Rapallo's henchmen descends the stairs to tell Gloria, in dumb show through the glass, that her boss wants another word with her; actually, it is just a trick to get her out of the way while he and a buddy rough Davy up. The camera is still at the top of the stairs as Gloria re-enters the lobby. "WATCH YOUR STEP," says a notice

. . . the skyline of warehouse roofs.

suspended over the steep staircase; a touch Kubrick swears was already a feature of the location he used. As Gloria passes the camera we see that the henchman has taken her place outside, his back to the plate glass, beside the unsuspecting manager; he has, of course, been mistaken for Davy and will soon be beaten to death out of sight up a back alley while his giant frightened shadow is seen writhing expressionistically on the alley wall.

This smooth manipulation of the action, pure movement without a word spoken in our hearing, has a preconceived pattern and a tense symmetry that characterize moments of climax in later Kubrick films. It directly anticipates the very last shot of *The Killing;* the armed FBI men advance with synchronized caution toward the robber, who stands, his will for flight paralyzed, outside the airport's plate-glass doors, which the agents proceed to open in balletic unison. Kubrick's camera has already an impulse to seek order and balance in what it frames as a visual equivalent of the mechanistic way that human behavior interlocks and settles people's fates.

The Killing attracted Kubrick both for the good story it tells and for the test of telling it. Other features, too, made it ideal for his temperament. It is the story of a race-track robbery which takes Time—abstract and capitalized—and reorders it as the plot dwells on the different parts of the robbery assigned to each of the gang. It is like playing chess against the clock; for the robbery has to be carried out within very tight limits of time, precisely within the start and finish of the seventh race, the $100,000 Lansdowne Stakes, at one mile. Actually, the limits are extended a little. The gang gains time by shooting down the favorite horse in mid-race, thus delaying the payout to bettors and giving Johnny, the ringleader, an additional few minutes to hold up the cash office. But the sense of action synchronized against measurable time (and distance: one mile) is deftly conveyed, projected into the events so accurately that one can tell to the half-minute when the race horse hits the turf with a bullet in its flank.

Yet all perfect plans are only as foolproof as the people who execute them. Humbert Humbert in *Lolita,* thinking wishfully of his wife's demise, reflects, "No man can bring about the perfect murder: chance alone can do it." In Humbert's case, chance co-operates to an ironic degree, but in most cases it frustrates the grand design. It is characteristic of Kubrick that while one part of him pays intellectual tribute to the rationally constructed master plan, another part reserves the skeptic's right to anticipate human imperfections or the laws of chance that militate against its success. Kubrick, for example, praises the novelist Peter George, who coauthored the screenplay of

Kubrick's often-repeated "corridor" compositions: the hallway of the dance hall, where a murder is lined up by one precise move after another; and the nightmare street ride taken by the sleeping boxer, both in Killer's Kiss. *(See the astronaut's psychedelic ride down the space corridor in* 2001: A Space Odyssey, *page 235; Mandrake's walk down the hall in* Dr. Strangelove, *page 205; and the next page.)*

Dr. Strangelove, for inferring the premise on which the nuclear fail-safe system must be based: which is, that there must be people other than the ones in the top echelons of command who know the "Go" code. But once this premise is noted, it suggests an inherent human weakness in the system; and it is this weakness that *Dr. Strangelove* exploits so savagely.

Moreover, accurate prediction is an essential part of the filmmaking process, particularly in the preproduction stages. It is one into which Kubrick puts fanatical effort. His recent films, as has already been noted, have used computers in the planning stages, to determine, among much else, the critical path analysis of the projected film. So it is no wonder that the "perfect plan," whether it has to do with criminal conspiracy to rob a race track, with nuclear strategy, or with film production, occupies so much of a mind already intellectually absorbed by it. Of course, the computer that goes wrong, as HAL 9000 does in *2001,* is only the most sophisticated example of an old human mistrust in perfection. *The Killing* is the first

Depth and symmetry: *the horses' stalls in* The Killing; *Humbert Humbert observing the mysterious car that always keeps an unsettling distance from him and Lolita; the the marksman's targets in* The Killing, *popping bizarrely up at the start of a sequence; the last shot in the same film, showing FBI men advancing in synchronized motion on the beaten crook as the targets come to life. (See* 2001, *page 237.)*

Kubrick film to make this interest dramatically apparent. It is constructed on a parallel pattern. While a "flawless" scheme is pushed forward step by predetermined step, at the same time chance, accident, and irrational forces lodged in its executors are bringing about its failure.

The viewer realizes the film's full cinematic originality only when the race-track robbery begins. Instead of cross-cutting between the parts of the raid that are overlapping in time, Kubrick films one part as it is carried to its climax, then puts the clock back several hours and takes another part to *its* climax. At 2:30 p.m. on the day of the race, for example, the massive wrestler hired to stage a brawl in the betting area leaves his chess club, after making arrangements for his coming spell in jail; at 4:23 p.m. precisely, with cops clinging to every limb, he is dragged away while Johnny is given the chance to slip unobserved into the now unguarded cash office. Then we flashback to 11:40 a.m. that same day, as the hired marksman leaves his farm, arrives at the track, brings down the favorite at 4:23½ p.m. exactly, only to be lying dead himself at 4:24 p.m., when the tire of his getaway car is punctured by a "lucky" horseshoe—the first of those chance accidents—and a policeman shoots him. We flashback to 2:15 p.m. that afternoon, and Johnny's story is taken to its climax as he holds up the cash office wearing a rubber clown's mask—another bizarre Kubrick touch—and throws a kit bag stuffed with bills through the window. Not till the raid is all over and the crooks are assembled, waiting for the payout, do we learn what happened to the loot after this point. "Nobody saw the bag come through the window," says one of the gang, a venal cop, and a brief,

laconic flashback shows him stowing it away in his waiting patrol car. It has the conclusive force of perfect logic.

The parts of the film before and after the raid have their particular style, too. Instead of using the dynamic cutting and the multiple cliff-hangers of the central episode, the members of the gang are introduced in vignettes that fit together like jigsaw pieces, until the larger plan of which

The time element: *simultaneous events in time in* The Killing. *Kubrick "puts back the clock" as each portion of the race-track robbery reaches climax, and begins again on the next. Repeated shot of dray horses hauling the starting gate into position provides a time check or an "edge" to each cliff-hanger episode: the brawl at the bar (top right) which keeps the cops preoccupied as the marksman (middle right) prepares to shoot down the favorite horse, thus delaying the payout and giving Johnny (bottom right), in his bizarre clown's disguise, the necessary time to hold up the pay office. Repeated shots also occur in* Paths of Glory *(see pages 120, 122, 124), where Kubrick shows the simultaneous lives being led in trench and château by giving the action of the former, cutting to binoculars through which the general is looking at this action, then coming back and enclosing the general's world with more action in the trenches, which, in turn, leads into the binocular framing again.* Dr. Strangelove's *action (pages 181-183) happens in three distinct locations, War Room, B-52, and air base, each remote in space from the other, but all linked by the temporal continuity of events until the final H-bomb blasts, triggered by the Doomsday Machine, unite them in an over-all apocalypse and, appropriately, the end of all temporal relevance.*

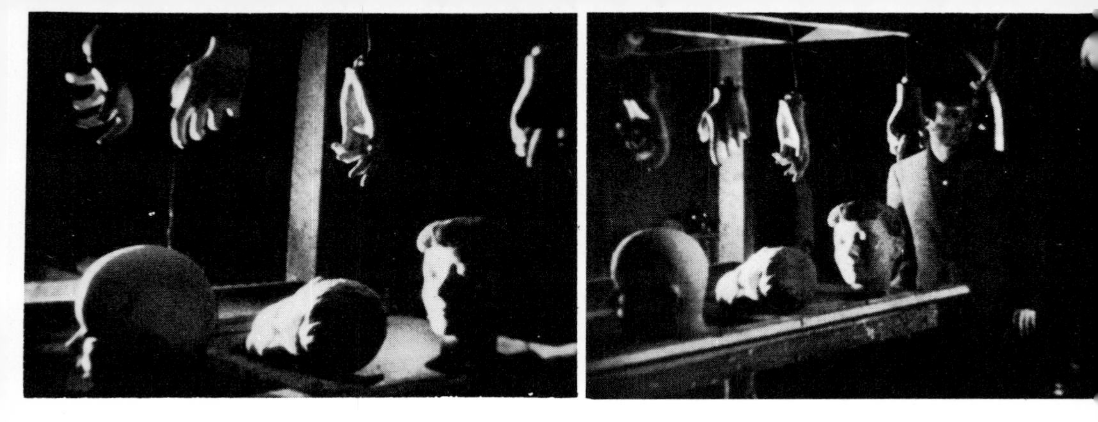

they are part begins to emerge. These scenes are written like good memoranda; they look simple, but they say much. As well as establishing motives—a sick wife, gambling debts, a man's need to gain status in the eyes of his trampish wife—they hint at weaknesses in character or relationships that will bring the whole scheme down. The trampish wife, for instance, weasels the plan out of her husband and blabs it all to her boy friend, a rival hood; he, in turn, stages his own "killing," which goes fatally wrong and leaves nearly everyone full of lead, stiffening almost visibly like wet cement sacks on the floor of the dingy living room where he has ambushed them before the share-out.

A director like John Huston, involved in the loyalties of the furtive underworld he exposed in *The Asphalt Jungle,* would probably pay respect to the courage of men of action, even when they are criminals. He might allow all of them some individual decency in death. Not Kubrick. His criminals are as human as Huston's, and even more subtly individualized, but he stays detached, cynical. Like a psychologist supervising a devilishly constructed maze, he knows it does not pay to get too fond of the rats. The sense of detachment is underlined by the use of a disembodied narrator to introduce each conspirator and tell us who he is, what he does, and also the day, the hour, sometimes even the minute, of some action or encounter involving his part of the master plan. He keeps temporal tabs on his characters and ticks off the countdown with fateful precision. In this, one hears the echo of *The March of Time* technique—so aptly named in this case—which

Kubrick's surrealism: *Parts of tailors' dummies provide a bizarre environment in* Killer's Kiss *and suggest what horrors of amputation the men fighting with pike and ax may inflict on each other.*

Bodies after the mayhem in The Killing *stiffen into the lifeless image of disposed-of dummies. Men behave like robots, and robots have the appearance of men. The mechanism that distinguishes the two stops with death, but even in life it shades human reactions into mechanistic responses. (See* Paths of Glory, *page 141;* Dr. Strangelove, *pages 180-181;* 2001, *pages 230-231.)*

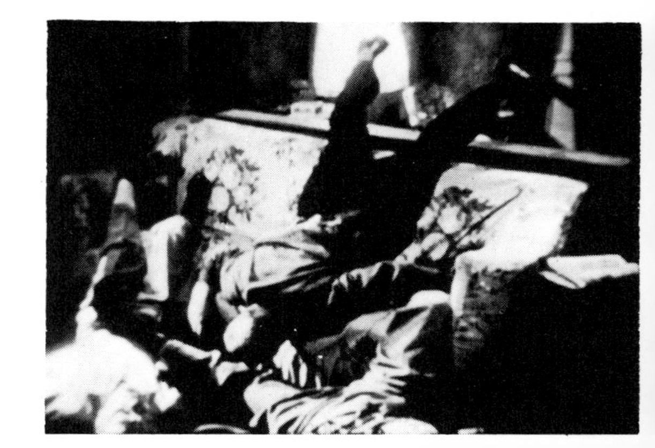

Birth of an obsession: Humbert Humbert sees Lolita for the first time . . . the monster in a drive-in cinema terrorizes Humbert, Lolita, and her mother—compressed into a few brief sequences are the object of desire and the figure of supernatural horror as Kubrick establishes the fairy-tale trio of hero, princess, and ogre beneath the erotic surface of Nabokov's novel.

Louis de Rochement extended into feature films like *The House on 92nd Street* and *Naked City.*

It may be pertinent to note that Kubrick's first short, *Day of the Fight,* was deliberately aimed at the same market as *The March of Time.* Of course, his fondness for narrative exposition cannot be explained this simply. Kubrick, it is worth remembering, belongs to a pretelevision generation whose sense of drama was still shaped to some degree by the aural impact of radio. Narration is a strong identity mark of his films. It is one way, as he says, of cutting directly through stage convention and conveying essential information without tedious use of dialogue or other expository scenes. One grants him this. Yet the narration, usually brief and resonant with foreboding even when it has a ticker-tape succinctness, as in *The Killing,* is like an aural note he strikes to which he tunes the rest of the film. It teases the expectations of an audience by the intimations of menace, mystery, or doom, as in the opening phrases of *Dr. Strangelove.*

The casting and acting in *The Killing* mark an impressive advance from *Killer's Kiss.* Not that the latter is badly acted. Kubrick really underrates it when he refers to the slightly "zombielike quality" conferred on the acting by post-synching. His own ear is too well tuned to let him do a botched job. With the exception of Frank Silvera, as Rapallo, the members of the cast of *Killer's Kiss* do not do much evident "acting," but they have the right weight and quality for the small-time people they portray. In *The Killing* the casting was more ambitious, and the partnership with James Harris provided more cash to pay some of Hollywood's sturdiest character actors. The lived-in faces of the aging crooks—the only young, virile figure is, significantly, the rival hood—need only an overhead lamp bulb and the simplest of camera set-ups to give a contour of reality to scene after scene. And the dialogue by Jim Thompson, author of thrillers about desperate, obsessed people, like *The Getaway* and *The Killer Inside Me,* provides Kubrick with openings into character that his camera can enlarge revealingly. From a man who starts off boasting that criminals are artists admired for their daring, Sterling Hayden, as Johnny, adroitly scales himself down into a deflated dummy as he sees his suitcase full of dollar bills upset at the airport by one of the film's chance accidents, involving a runaway lapdog—the least successful "accident" because it is seen coming a long way off—and the loot being blown literally out of his grasp in a blizzard of money. Best of all the players is Elisha Cook, Jr., as the little race-track clerk desperate to impress his shrewish mate, and Marie Windsor, who plays

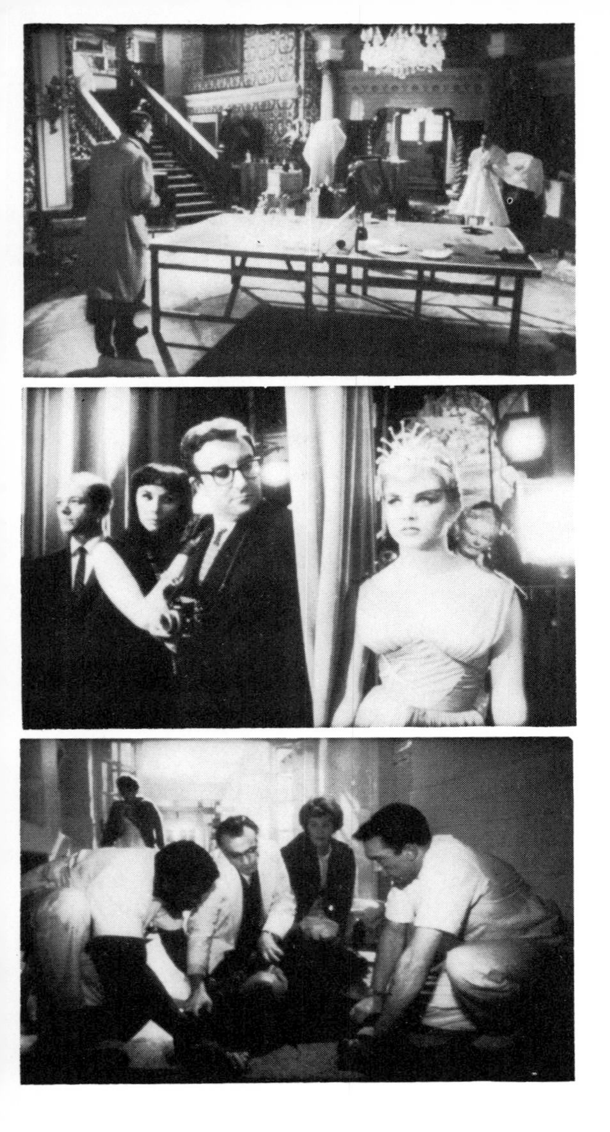

Surreal elements amidst Lolita's *realism: Humbert Humbert arrives in the Gothic shambles of the ogre's castle (top left); under the enchanter Quilty's spell, Lolita has the frozen look of a fairy-tale princess (middle left); horror materializes out of an apparently secure environment as doctors detain the hero and try to pronounce him insane (bottom left).*

More use of Kubrick's Gothic techniques and lighting in Lolita: *Quilty in the "transformation" of Dr. Zempf awaits Humbert's return to his darkened house.* *(See* Dr. Strangelove, *pages 190-191.)*

his wife. Kubrick, with *Lolita* to come, is already very much at home with this kind of pathetic infatuation. A whole marriage is laid bare as the cheap, worthless wife peels off her false eyelashes in front of her husband as unconcernedly as if they were her gloves. Their relationship could be the subject for an entire film. From Kubrick, it draws only a subjective note, when his camera, after dispassionately scanning the bodies of the men killed in the gangster's ambush, adopts the unsteady viewpoint of Cook lurching across the room homeward bound, mortally wounded, to wipe out his treacherous wife. For a moment or two, we have left the privileged enclosure of all-knowing, all-seeing observers and become part of one pathetic man's tragedy. Kubrick carries us powerfully along the impetus of Cook's homicidal advance—his stumbling return to his own apartment, his wife's desperate kidding, her panicky attempt to ignore his plight ("You look terrible," she snarls as blood seeps through his shirt), and, finally, Cook's pumping slug after slug into her while a parrot in the cage he has upset squawks out its own alarm at this mild man transfigured by murderous hate, by "the killer inside me," as Jim Thompson calls that other self which stirs in the human consciousness. To find another scene as grotesque and horrifying in Kubrick's work, one had to wait for *Lolita.*

Kubrick acknowledges with regret that when he made *Lolita* it was not possible to portray Humbert Humbert's obsession on the screen with all the physical eroticism suggested in Nabokov's novel. The problem was more social than aesthetic. Public opinion was not ready to let the screen follow perversion into the same arcane areas

open to a writer; even the novel *Lolita* had been rejected by many good publishers in New York and London as too risky, and was only brought out after much defensive use of "authoritative" critical opinion vouching for its artistic integrity. A film version started with this handicap. The only real physical intimation in the film of Humbert Humbert's sexual enslavement by the nymphet Lolita occurs in the visual metaphor that backs the credit titles. A girl's foot and leg are extended imperiously into the frame and a man's hand receives the limb in a kind of loving clasp while his other hand wedges lint between the toes and fondly enamels the nails.

Instead of sensuality, the pilot light that burns through the rest of the film is ironic comedy. If the screenplay necessarily omits the physical lusting, Kubrick and Nabokov deserve credit for sticking so closely and successfully to the comedy of a man trapped between a voracious mother and her precociously seductive daughter, struggling to free himself from the clutches of the one to attach himself concupiscently and pathetically to the other. On this level, *Lolita* is extraordinarily successful. Its dialogue respects the psychology of the novel, while Kubrick sharpens the comedy by his casting of the principals and by the intelligent direction he gives them and their response to it.

A critical controversy has raged over the film's construction. Some critics call the opening sequence a serious error. They complain that by letting Humbert Humbert kill Quilty at the start, the film sacrifices the hideous pathos that his revenge contains when it follows Quilty's seduction of Lolita, as it does in the novel. This sequence certainly involved a major decision for Kubrick—an agonizing one, too, to deprive oneself of a perfect climax by transferring it to the prologue. Yet the film as a whole gains from that opening on several grounds. One is the peculiar tone Quilty's murder immediately gives the movie. It is a mood of brilliantly organized black comedy, happening in a world that is realistic enough to contain terror, pain, and death, yet fantastic enough to surprise and amuse. The baroque rooms of Château Quilty, the gloomy air of "the morning after," the dust sheets under which the owner, then yet alive, is discovered like a premature "stiff" in his own shroud, the whole debris of orgy and decadence marvelously assist the grotesque comedy. (It also usefully removes Lolita from the "normal" world, where film censors might expect Lolitaphiles to do their hunting.) Vaguely aware of menace somewhere in his vicinity, the bleary-eyed Quilty temporizes with Humbert Humbert in a variety of ways. He kids. He play-acts, putting on a Gabby Hayes accent when required to read out, in verse, the confession Humbert Humbert has penned for him. He starts a nervy game of table tennis (a favorite Kubrick pastime with *his* house guests), in which the relationship between him and his intendant killer is broken open by the pit-pat of the ball, and then shattered completely by the sudden crash of Humbert Humbert's gun, amplified to bone-jarring volume by the emptiness of the house.

There is another good reason, besides black comedy of the most inventive, subtly played kind, for Quilty's muzzy-minded horseplay. In the novel, he and Humbert Humbert never meet face to face till the showdown. In the film, they are introduced early on. Had the retribution come at the end of the film, it would have been harder to explain Quilty's failure to recognize Humbert Humbert and guess what was coming to him. Logically, he should still have done so in the film; but one fails to notice this slight cheat when death comes before introductions. With Quilty's demise—sheltering from a hail of bullets that perforate the innocence of a Gainsborough-type painting behind which he crawls, lugging his wounded leg behind him as a final horrifying detail—the film flashes back to "Four Years Earlier," and *Lolita* proper begins. The result, as Kubrick foresaw when he decided to shoot the film this way, is to exchange the suspense of waiting for fate to overtake Quilty for the suspense of waiting, in the book, for Humbert Humbert to bed down with Lolita. This gives Quilty a much greater role in the film than in the book. He appears throughout in the multifaceted impersonations of Peter Sellers: first as his bland yet sinister self eying people as if he were casting them for parts in a private orgy; then in

Sellers' dexterous improvisation as the cop at a police convention, prying into Humbert Humbert's private life with garrulous innuendo; finally, in the most bizarre shape of Dr. Zempf, the college psychologist, unnerving Lolita's stepfather-lover with vaguely couched threats of exposure. The director and his star play the Quilty character as if he were a fugue, producing inspired passages of inventiveness, yet always integrating him with the rest of the film. Kubrick deserves more credit than he got at the time for placing a surrealistic figure so firmly in an otherwise realistic film; and it is this coexistence of reality and fantasy that powerfully anticipates the style of *Dr. Strangelove.*

The film of *Lolita* reinforces the black fairy-tale aspect of the novel out of Kubrick's own admitted fascination with "magic," especially its darker sides. Apart from the atmosphere in the prologue, already referred to, when Humbert Humbert enters Quilty's Gothic mansion as if it were an ogre's castle, one early sequence sums up the erotic relationships in classic fairy-tale terms. This is the scene at the drive-in cinema where the introductory "shock" cut of a monster in some horror film rears above the watching Lolita and Humbert Humbert, confronting them with a menace that the as-yet-unmaterialized threat of Quilty will turn into a real crisis when the evil spell he throws over Lolita enables him to carry her off in the traditional way of horror-film monsters. The trappings and lighting of horror films, weird attendants, transformations into different shapes, unexpected materializations and disappearances accompany Quilty through some of his main sequences, most strikingly in the prologue but also in the comic-macabre scene when Humbert Humbert returns home late at night to discover Quilty, as Dr. Zempf, awaiting him in a darkened room in a pose that already conjures up the sinister, chair-bound presence of Dr. Strangelove.

The director is not so successful with another risk he took—reducing the novel's eroticism—for without evidence of Humbert Humbert's carnal obsession, audiences might assume that he is simply in love with Lolita. The nymphet philosophy, spelled out succinctly early in the novel, had now to be conveyed by looks: Humbert Humbert glancing over his book at Lolita twirling a hula hoop around her desirable pubescent hips; his fixated eyes peering satyr-like through the decorative foliage at a college dance; and the reflex action at the drive-in cinema, where the horror movie brings him and his loved one (and, alas, her mother) physically together for a moment's shared fear. Where it should have been gradual and cumulative, the rhythm of eroticism has here had to be sudden and conclusive. It is too sudden. And it is not really conclusive enough. No sooner is Humbert Humbert's more than ordinary interest in Lolita established than certain aspects of the film throw doubt on its being a profane passion. The insistently lush "Lolita theme" music smacks of love, not lust. And the music "leads" some scenes. The shot of Humbert Humbert burying his face in the pillow on the nymphet's deserted bed after her mother has packed her off to summer camp loses its desperate pathos in a backwash of melodiousness.

What preserves the truth, if not the taint of the relationship, is Kubrick's handling of his cast. True to his belief that actors are allies in a film's success, he adopts a self-effacing camera style. He uses noticeably long takes, but often very simple set-ups. The camera stands there, usually with the characters in medium shot, while the actors play an often lengthy scene involving quite intricate dialogue and interplay of emotional nuances. He lets the rhythm of a performance do the "planting" of a point, an end that is more usually achieved by cutting.

Shelley Winters, as Lolita's mother, gives what is possibly her best film performace. She is a potent mixture of bossy momism, ten-cent intellectualism, women's club energy and sexual thirst. From the first genteel chime of her doorbell at Humbert Humbert's arrival, Kubrick helps project her as a beady-eyed epitome of the All-American matron-vampire; playing up to her personable prospective lodger by praising the rudimentary nature of the bathroom plumbing as if it, too, were proof of old European values, she leans in the doorway barring his departure while her well-preserved body assumes a provocative posture almost as a reflex action. James Mason, a sharp, sardonic, intelligent actor, conveys the undertones of Humbert Humbert even if he is denied the obsessive notes.

Sue Lyon has the "eerie vulgarity" and provocative whine of the novel's Lolita. That she may look "too old" in some scenes merely emphasizes the discrepancy between the mind's eye, to which the novel is directed, and the more literal camera's eye as it registers the authentic way American adolescence annihilates the pubescent gap between childhood and adulthood. Sue Lyon does not violate the nymphet theme even though she may occasionally look older than some people expect; and when violated herself at the end, pregnant, married, and beginning to assume her mother's blowsy vulgarity, she has a commonplaceness totally appropriate for Mason's flood of grief, guilt, and remorse.

Kubrick turns the necessity of not showing the pair of them in bed together into a virtue by substituting slapstick for seduction and forcing the man to sleep on a folding cot—a typical piece of antihuman mechanism—which he has ordered to be sent to their motel room as a "cover" for his intentions. Moreover the myth of Lolita's sexual innocence is exploded by her own confession in the morning, before she and her stepfather presumably have sex together. Afterward, when she has learned of her mother's death, her childish weeping is used by Kubrick to purge the relationship of sexual content and key the second half of the film to a new note of sadness, disenchantment, and frustration, as Lolita turns from desirable love object into infuriating bitch.

Two scenes are particularly characteristic of what Kubrick brought to the filming of Nabokov's novel. One is the bizarre "happening" of Lolita's mother's death, by a chance road accident, just as she has made the discovery that her second husband is a "monster." At first the scene follows Nabokov closely. Humbert Humbert is fixing a drink, while considering what story to spin his wife to allay her alarm; when the phone rings, he calls up to his wife, whom he left locking herself in her room. "There's this man saying you've been killed, Charlotte." So she has. By suppressing the event and inserting only the effect, the movie conveys the sense projected in the novel of the world moving suddenly an inch or two from under one's feet. But Kubrick tops the disconcerting effect of random tragedy—though a tragedy so completely in line with Humbert Humbert's wishes—by the irony of the next scene. The new widower, minutes after the accident, is soaking in the bathtub with his Martini floating beside him, as he accepts condolences from the neighbors with a contentment that they take to be shock. What makes this marvelously funny is the absolutely normal act of taking a bath set within the completely incongruous tragedy that has just struck. It foreshadows the way *Dr. Strangelove* builds comic effects out of the ironic incongruities of actions and circumstances and the disparity of causes and effects.

Kubrick brings his own characteristic feeling to another scene through the way he "magnetizes" particles of madness to come rushing out of a seemingly normal environment. It occurs when a group of calm, methodical night doctors at the hospital suddenly jump on Humbert Humbert when he flies into a panic on learning Lolita has fled from her bed with a mysterious stranger (Quilty). "Get a straitjacket," cries one man in white with lustful eagerness. Flat on his back, with people holding him down at every extremity and one medic spotlighting the white of his eye with a surgical light, Humbert desperately tries to prove his sanity by snatching at the most English brand of understatement. "I really ought to move on now," he murmurs. It is the same sharp use of language and locutions played against the grain of an event, in this case the man's pinioned position, that Kubrick developed into the vastly sophisticated verbal comedy of his next film.

If social pressures and film-industry prudence compelled Kubrick to jettison the erotica of *Lolita,* he gained powerful compensation by the chance it allowed him to formulate his flair for grotesque comedy. With *Dr. Strangelove* he extended his talent beyond one man's obsession into the collective folly of mankind.

PATHS OF GLORY

Paths of Glory is Kubrick's graduation piece. Before he made it, he had the reputation of an interesting newcomer who used highly original techniques to refresh the Hollywood thriller. After it was produced, he was recognized as a significant American director. It revealed a talent able to work in a tradition of individual statement—and, indeed, able to work in Europe, too, for there were far fewer expatriate directors or "runaway" productions being set up on the Continent then. And the era and milieu of the film, the 1914-1918 conflict, brought an American film-maker face to face with the challenge of a particularly European experience beyond the direct recall of all but a few of Hollywood's veteran directors. The fact that some favorably compared the film to the work of Max Ophuls is one measure of Kubrick's growth as an artist.

But even more impressive is the humanist response that beats like a pulse through a brutally cynical story, lifting it out of its particular place and time. *The Killing* had its limits inside a genre crime story; and though it stretched them imaginatively, it remained a heartless illustration of criminal ingenuity and its unforeseen consequences. *Paths of Glory* finds Kubrick dealing in the wider realm of ideas with a relevance to man and society. Without casting off any of his innate irony and skepticism, the director declares his allegiance to his fellow men.

The film has sometimes been compared to *All Quiet on the Western Front,* which Lewis Milestone made in 1930. This is a natural, yet a misleading, comparison to make. Both are American films that sink their national identity into a depiction of "foreign" combatants in World War One—in Milestone's film, the Germans; in Kubrick's, the French. Both are

General Broulard's arrival at the château

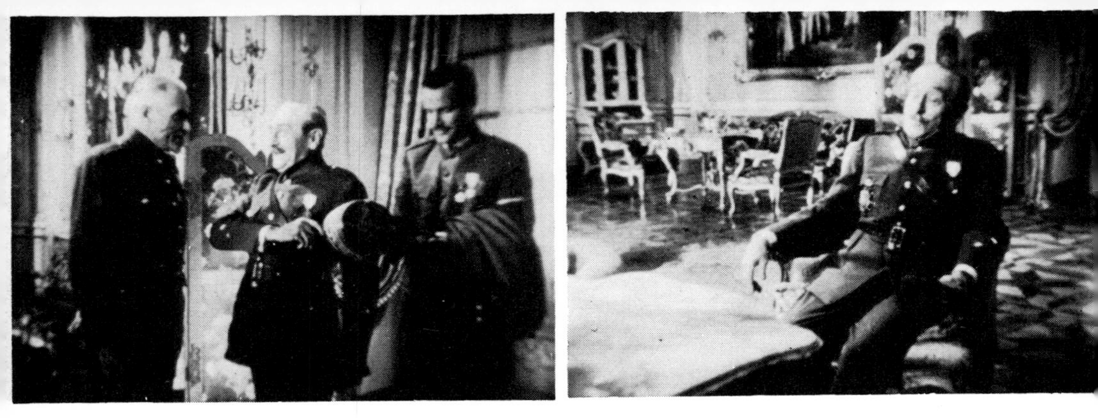

unsparing of their battlefield detail. But Milestone argued that the good man's only response to war is pacifism; his film's emphasis on sacrifice in battle is what keeps his protest reverberating still. It shows lives wasted. Kubrick's film, on the other hand, takes its stand on human injustice. It shows one group of men being exploited by another group. It explores the social stratification of war. No man's land is not really the great dividing barrier between the two sides in *Paths of Glory;* the "two sides" actually wear the same uniform, serve the same flag, and hold the same battle line, though in vastly differing degrees of comfort. The actual division, the deeper conflict, is that between the leaders and the led. It exists whether there is a war or not, but a war situation widens the division fatally. Only by implication is *Paths of Glory* a protest against war as such; it is much more pertinently an illustration of war as the continuation of class struggle. The paths of glory in the title are not the ones that lie across the battlefield; they are the avenues to self-advancement taken by the generals in command, with the utmost indifference to the fate of the men in the trenches.

The film's brief and brilliant opening exposition

prepares all the other moves that follow. A narrator sets the war-front scene in a few communiqué sentences as General Broulard, played by Adolphe Menjou, arrives at the grandoise château commandeered as field headquarters by the French. This masterly casting of Menjou confirms Kubrick's instinct for an aspect of filmmaking that often predetermines much of a film's effectiveness, before the camera starts turning. From the first second of his entry—he hands his hat to his aide without a glance toward him, confident that the man knows his place and will be standing there—Menjou radiates the air of someone used to warming both hands before the fire of human life. His acute-angled glances shot from under hooded lids play off chillingly against the carefully cultivated air of bonhomie with his crony and subordinate, General Mireau.

Equally indicative of the moral ambiance is the physical setting. The château is a place of order and elegance—all mirrored walls, shining parquet, baroque furnishings, and palatial staircases—yet somehow corrupt and eerie, like a vampire's castle in the Old High German cinema.

The use Kubrick makes of such a set was to occur

Kubrick shows Broulard leading Mireau morally astray in a winding choreographic pattern *(see page 16)* *as he suggests an attack on an impregnable enemy position. Human lives are adjusted to fit the policies of leaders.*

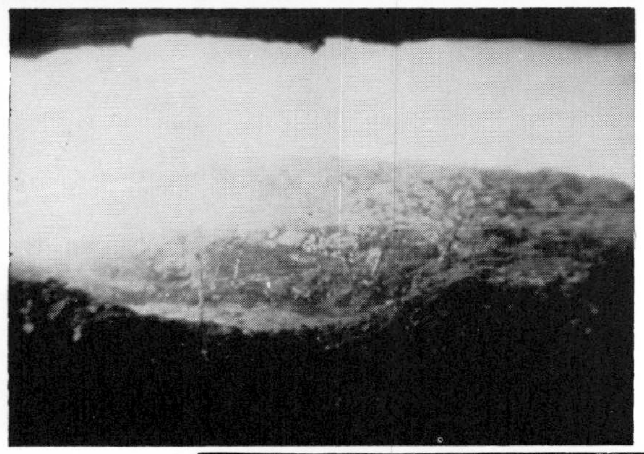

The trench world: Kubrick cuts from the elegance of the military Establishment to the reality of war.

General Mireau's machinelike incitement to the troops:

Hello, soldier! Ready to kill more Germans? Hello, soldier! Ready to kill more Germans

Hello, soldier! Ready to kill more Germans? Are you married?

again in his later films—most strikingly in *Lolita,* which opens, like *Paths of Glory,* in an eerie and decadent mansion, cavernous and deserted except for the two protagonists, Quilty and Humbert Humbert, who proceed to lead each other through the baroque furnishings in a way that recalls Mireau and Broulard. And although the keynote is black comedy in *Lolita,* whereas it is ironic tragedy in *Paths of Glory,* the impression both films convey is that of an obsession which will overwhelm and destroy those who feed on it. In the opening scenes of *Lolita* it is the resolution of an obsession—love of a forbidden kind—which Kubrick makes us witness. In *Paths of Glory* it is the sowing of an obsession—ambition of a monstrous degree. In both obsessions, needless to say, lies death.

The visitor proposes, ever so subtly, for the good of morale back home, an attack on a German emplacement that is clearly impregnable. As Broulard perambulates beside the ambitious General Mireau (played by George Macready), in ever more winding circles among the gleaming furniture, Kubrick's camera starts moving too, duplicating physically the devious moral seduction of Mireau away from all reality and reason. The deal is closed as Mireau

Soldier: "My wife . . . I'm never going to see her again. I'm going to be killed."

General Mireau: "You act like a coward.

agrees to order the offensive that will decimate his men but perhaps capture the hill and gain him promotion. It is partly the tone of cynical decadence, the baroque decor, and the camera's labyrinthine movements that have prompted the comparison between Kubrick and Ophuls.* The comparison is valid, yet largely irrelevant. Kubrick's camera follows character —the character of two corrupt militarists—rather than the stylistic example Ophuls set in the cinema.

Since Kubrick is a director whose attitude to a subject forms his style, he resists getting involved too early in the visual possibilities of a sequence. But throughout *Paths of Glory* the moral content of a sequence has its effect on his choice of camera technique. In this respect, it is a far more complex film than those of his earlier American subjects, which depend primarily on the action content of the story. The château scenes with the devious commanders in *Paths of Glory* are shot with a continually curving mobility; the trench scenes force the camera to follow, without choice, the shape of the dugout

---

*Partly, too, Kubrick's placing of Ophuls at the top of his list of directors whom he particularly admired, in a *Cahiers du Cinéma* interview, July, 1957. Also see page 16.

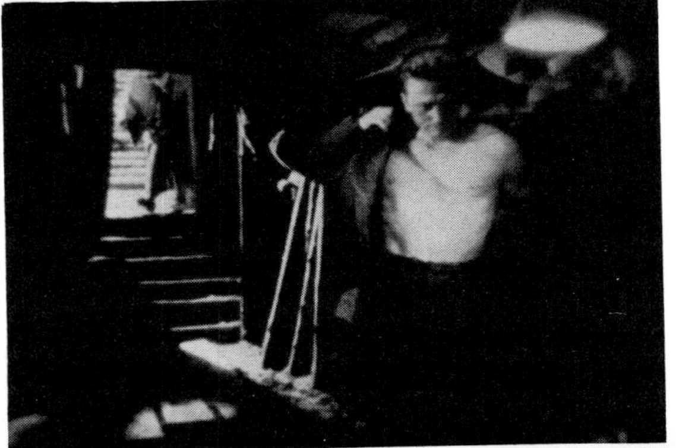

Lighting and space sharply define the physical reality of Dax and his world. Mireau views the objective from a safe distance. Mireau's view (below), through binoculars, one of the devices Kubrick uses to emphasize war as a spectator sport for the High Command

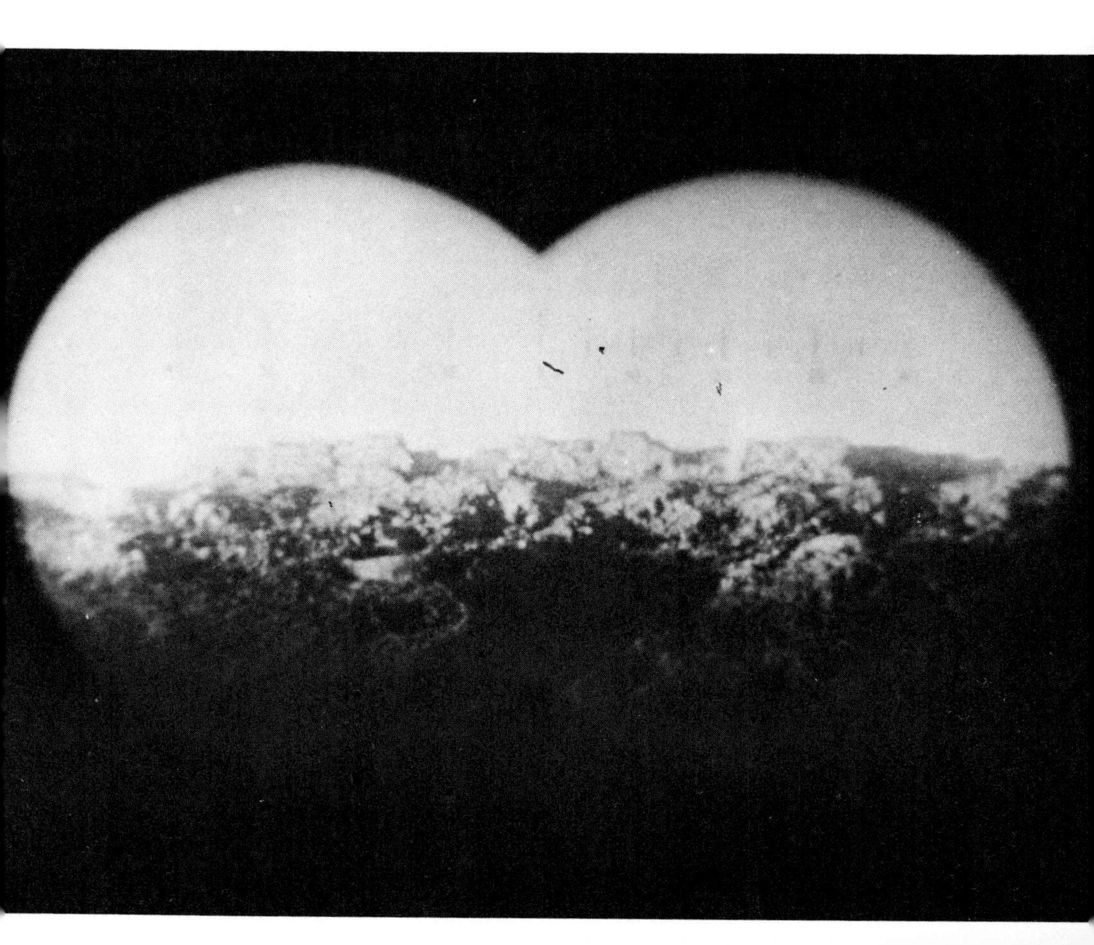

Direct confrontation in contrast to the château's labyrinthine machinations. The brutal responsibility of the plan is passed on to Dax —the man who will have to carry it out.

Dax orders a reconnaissance of no man's land . . .
but it ends with the Lieutenant killing one of his own men and hiding his responsibility for it.

maze that has conditioned men to obey; and the scenes of court-martial and execution have a geometrical rigor that reflects the predetermined verdict and the preordained fate of the accused men.

In contrast, Kubrick maintains an honest directness of camera angle to characterize the relationship between the ordinary men in the line and Colonel Dax, who is a man of moral conscience. Dax belongs to the trench world, which is the polar opposite of the château society. When General Mireau visits Dax in his dugout, he moves, ill-at-ease, through the tortuous trench system stiffly complimenting soldiers with hollow exhortations to valor; but Dax, taking the same route before the attack, moves like a man among his fellow men. His military obedience has a place in it for human values; he is the only officer who has not let a gap develop between himself and his men. Kirk Douglas' strong bone structure and physique, so often used to give his screen roles a barely suppressed threat of violence, serve here to

Corporal Paris: "You ran like a rabbit after you killed Lejeune."
Lieutenant Roget: "I don't like your tone. You're speaking to an officer, remember that."
Corporal Paris: "Oh well, I must be mistaken then. No officer would do a thing like that. A man wouldn't do it . . . only a thing *would. . . . You're in a mess, Lieutenant."*
Lieutenant Roget: "You're in a worse one. First, insubordination, second, threatening your superior . . . third, disobeying an order and inciting others to disobey."

A single source of illumination intensifies the bluntness of the encounter (see The Killing, *pages 58-59. See also page 185).*

give a dimension of moral stature as he stands up for the rights and lives of his men. But Dax is a soldier, too. When ordered by Mireau to lead the attack on the enemy emplacement, known as Ant Hill, he protests passionately—but he obeys.

The cynical calculation of the potential casualties that prefaces this offensive is almost a pilot study for *Dr. Strangelove*'s nuclear overkill. Five per cent killed going over the top, says Mireau, another five per cent as the advance starts, "let's say another twenty-five per cent in actually taking the Ant Hill—we're still left with enough men to keep it." Such mental arithmetic resembles General Turgidson's call for all-out nuclear war on Russia in *Dr. Strangelove,* on the ground that retaliation will mean "only ten to twenty million people killed, tops, depending on the breaks"; the difference is simply that the Bomb makes multiplying easier. Mireau's calculation of casualties also has its cynical concomitant in reverse, after the raid has failed; the angry, humiliated general now demands the lives of hundreds of his own men before the firing squad, so as to "encourage" the others. Gradually the numbers of scapegoats are whittled down, like a business deal being done between him and the more politically

Day breaks with Dax passing on orders, giving his men encouragement. Kubrick shows the noninvolvement of the leaders, who drink to a success for which others will spill their blood.

prudent General Broulard. The "hundreds" become "dozens" and finally "one man from each company, three in all." This *reductio ad absurdum* could not be more horrifyingly rendered.

The gathering enormity of the affair is rendered audibly in the echo effect taken on by the voices of the bargaining men. Kubrick will use a similar hollowness, presaging doom, in *Dr. Strangelove.* But something else can be detected as well, a minor but telling Kubrick characteristic. This is General Mireau's shortness of breath, which lends to his character at this point a panicky indignation, part anger at the catastrophe, part fear that his own *faux pas* will be revealed. While it is dramatically right in this context, the kind of asthmatic fear the sound embodies, the sense of entrapment and enclosure, seems to have a special appeal to Kubrick. Claustrophobia is the last thing one is prepared for in the infinity of space, but the breathing of the astronaut marooned outside his craft in *2001* is the only audible sound at that point in the film and it illustrates his sense of isolation more dramatically than would any

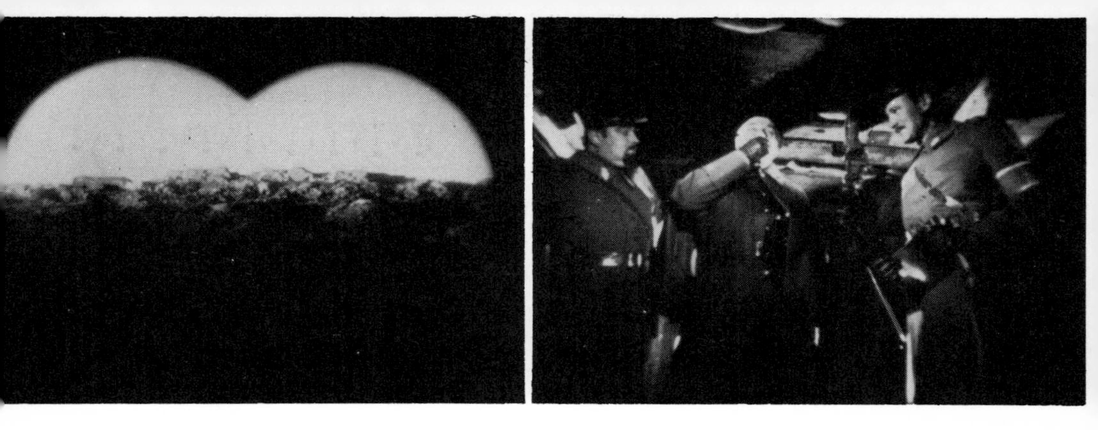

music score.* A man as protective of his private life and guarded about his personal independence as Kubrick is particularly alert to situations in which one might no longer be in full control; this awareness has made him sensitive to, and predisposes him to use, these highly appropriate sounds of unease.

The most justly famous sequence in *Paths of Glory* is the attack itself and the prelude to it. It has all the shattered details of old World War One photographs and an emotional thrust that rides on the shock waves of slaughter. Kubrick's subjective camera "stands in" for Dax as he strides through the endless wormlike trench. The waiting infantry making way for him (and the camera) look in the flat gray light like figures in stone relief already carved into the plinth of a war memorial. Soldiers loom like apparitions through the smoke, or dust, at the far end of the trench. Now and then a mobile overhead camera keeps the grim-visaged Dax under dispassionate

---

*Composer Alex North contributes a wry memoir in this respect in *The Making of Kubrick's* 2001, edited by Jerome Agel (New York: Signet Books/New American Library, 1968), p. 199.

scrutiny while the pace of his inspection builds up a purposive momentum. Then the attack! It is a marvel of composition in depth and detail. The movement is now sideways, keeping pace with the packs of crouching men scurrying like rats up and down the inhuman contours of the shell-pocked ground, shrouded in smoke one second, showered with earth, shrapnel, and debris the next. On and on and on they go, in an animated mural of death. The sound of battle has a dreadful distinctiveness, too. Like all Kubrick's movies, *Paths of Glory* uses sound to emotionally supplement perception. Over the noise and panic shrills the call-to-duty piping of Dax's whistle. A zoom lens operated by Kubrick himself continually "homes" in on Dax, catching his growing despair as the thinning ranks of the living betray both the failure of the attack and the lack of support from the French soldiers in the other trenches, who are unwilling, or unable, to advance through the German fire power. A furious Mireau orders his own artillery to fire on these "cowards," but he is met with the artillery commander's refusal except on written orders. Mireau snaps, "If the little sweethearts won't face German bullets, they'll face French ones."

Cut instantly to the château. The random slaughter of the battlefield is succeeded by selective killing through court-martial and execution. As Broulard says, "Soldiers are like children. They need discipline." The discipline he recommends is "shooting a man now and then." The isolation of ordinary soldiers from the officers who command them is emphasized throughout *Paths of Glory* in a variety of ways. It is explicit not only in the main story, but also in the well-integrated subplot, in which a cowardly lieutenant, ordered to make a reconnaissance sortie

Trench: Dax's walk to his battle position . . . gives Kubrick's ever-tracking camera, as it retreats before him or now and again assumes his subjective point of view, the chance to express the documentary feel of this confined and seemingly endless world of the common soldiers.

Dax reaches the end of the trenches and . . .

for an instant Kubrick conceals unnervingly in the dust what lies ahead, but as the leader goes over the top, the screen opens up from the constricted trenches to show the horizontal panorama of blind destruction.

Kubrick keeps zeroing in to close-ups of the horrified Dax as the camera, hand-held by Kubrick, follows the horizontal sweep of the battle. (See page 23.)

into no man's land before the attack, sends a soldier out in front of him, panics when the man does not return, and then thoughtlessly kills him himself when he lobs a grenade into the dark at the imagined foe. He later tries to conceal his criminal callousness by condemning the one eyewitness to the deed as one of the three scapegoats picked for execution. The gap between leaders and led is implicit in the film's settings as well; it has already been noted how the characters belong either to the château or to the trenches, with Dax the only man straddling the two worlds. But there is a third visual device that Kubrick uses, to the extent of making it almost a leitmotiv. This is his repeated framing of a view of no man's land, or the actual battle, inside the double lenses of a pair of field glasses. The binocular effect is employed no fewer than four times. Each time it allows the military command to look on what are (or will be) the horrifying consequences of their orders without suffering the moral responsibility of physical involvement. Apart from Dax, the commanders' role is

limited to that of spectators. (General Mireau does intervene in the action, it is true, but only to order gunfire on his own troops.) Protocol also makes them voyeurs at the execution of the scapegoats; the huge château in the background appears to observe the deaths in the morning with the same chilly aloofness. And General Broulard even improves on this detachment—for, his foxy nose scenting the risks of involvement in even this formal encounter, he makes up his mind not to attend the court-martial, thereby effectively putting the consequences of his strategy right out of sight.

Paths of Glory opens with the blare of the "Marseillaise" behind the credit titles, but despite the brazen orchestration it has an ironically hollow ring. The citizens' song has become the anthem of an Establishment that uses men for its own cynical ends, in war as in peace. And war gives the leaders an advantage in permitting them to take short cuts to power and privilege that need at least the plausible processes of government in peacetime. A well-aimed

Dax realizes the attack is failing. . . .
Where are the rest of his men?

bullet is the extreme sanction of the Establishment; war facilitates it.

The court-martial, at which Dax, a lawyer in civilian life, defends the three accused men, is a mockery of justice. Kubrick shoots it in a way that emphasizes the inhumanity inherent in the ritual. The camera tracks laterally along behind the officers of the court as the prosecutor makes out a case as if the result was a foregone conclusion—which indeed he knows it is. Then it repeats the movement in parallel fashion, though this time behind the accused, as Dax makes his plea. Symmetry is all. The guards' rifles are grounded and angled at precisely the same degree, the three accused men are so symmetrically positioned that one half of the white, gleaming, light-filled hall looks like a mirror image of the other. Such inflexible lines have something sacrificially ritualistic about them.

One of the strongest impressions *Paths of Glory* leaves on a viewer is the extreme mobility of Ku-

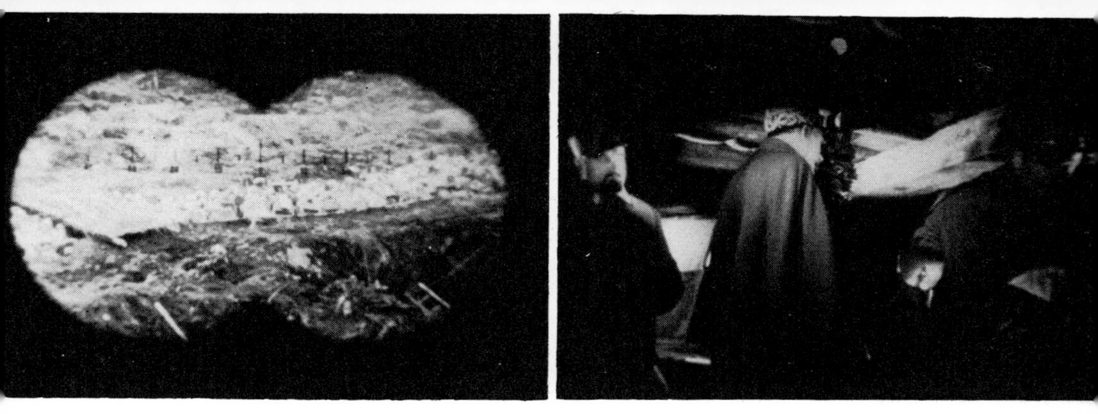

Back to Mireau's view of the attack: "Where in heaven's name are they?" he storms. "Miserable cowards, they're still in the trenches!"

brick's camera. In sequence after sequence the arrangement of the shooting angles is planned with a view to the camera's participation in the action. Kubrick is extraordinarily successful in inventing visual movements that are the equivalent of the drama created by events or latent in the atmosphere of a scene. The lateral movements already described in the court-martial sequence, the horrifying horizontal advance of the camera in line with the no-man's-land battle, along with the "zooming" incursions into the midst of the carnage, and the long backward track of Dax's trench walk are all ways of visually dramatizing what is happening. They are also ways of relating the viewer to the space on the screen by involving him in that space—moving him through it. Far more than in the earlier films, Kubrick is at pains to ensure that the mechanical factor does not stand as a barrier between the spectator and the film. And in *2001: A Space Odyssey* he was to use such movements extensively with the same aim in mind.

In the court-martial sequence Kubrick employs a visual device that crops up in other films—*The Killing, Dr. Strangelove*—for various reasons. This is the repetition of an image or a series of images. His repeated use of the "binocular" image has already been referred to. In the court-martial section of the film he starts off the testimony of *each* of the three prisoners with the *same* visual composition, a high-angle shot of the stiffly aligned soldiers placed geometrically on the chessboard floor of the huge salon. He then comes in to show us the prisoner facing the camera (the judges), the soldiers behind him, so that the man appears to be clamped between the jaws of a vise. The camera then cuts between close-ups of the prisoner, the judges, and General Mireau. The separate human individuals are all caught in the same machinelike action.

The whole execution scene continues the build-up of formal procedure, only now it is pierced through and through by the piteous spectacle of the condemned men, one insensible and tied to a stretcher, one crying and being comforted by the whining pieties of a priest, and one resigned and somber. Their plight is contrasted with the rigidity accompanying the execution of the sentence—the stiff ranks of sol-

diers, the upright execution posts, the monotone beat of the drums, the two statuesque generals, Broulard and Mireau, the cart waiting with the caskets. The silence after the shots is suddenly filled with bird song, a kind of gentle "Amen," brutally truncated by a cut to the château and Mireau's relishing remark, "The men died wonderfully!" as he butters his breakfast *croissant.* Condemned men, of course, get fed. Generals go to watch executions on an empty stomach: it sharpens their appreciation.

The firing-squad scene is all the more stark at first viewing because Kubrick has previously, and very subtly, aroused false expectations that Broulard will intervene at the last minute to halt the affair. The night before, Dax has gone to the château to make a last plea for mercy. Characteristically, the camera finds the generals and their guests in the middle of a waltz and sidles deferentially in a smooth arc round the perimeter of the parquet until an aide informs Broulard of the colonel's arrival—and then, unhurriedly, it sidles back again, playing up the feeling that men die at dawn, but generals dance at night. In the hush of the library, the self-possession of the urbane Broulard, who has treated Dax's plea almost as a *faux pas* in military protocol, is severely shaken, just

"Order the seventy-fives to fire on our positions."
Soldier: "I can't do that, sir, without a written order."

A dead body prevents Dax from returning to the attack. From the battlefield Kubrick cuts directly to the château and a furious Mireau.

as he is about to bow himself back to his guests. As Broulard places his hand on the doorknob, Dax reveals that Mireau was ready to order artillery fire on his own men. The door snaps closed, betraying the snap of surprise in the general's mind. Menjou (Broulard) blinks—one of the most potent of his battery of fastidious effects. He sees the risk of scandal to the high command. By using a slow fade-out after the message has got through to Broulard, Kubrick implies that military vengeance will now be tempered by expedient mercy. Throughout the rest of the film he has frequently used direct cuts from sequence to sequence. This device, not so commonplace in 1957 as it has since become, stretches the story line out tight and confers an inexorable logic on events. But Kubrick avoids it at this point, and allows the scene to fade on a close-up of Dax's face and a shot of Broulard impassively taking his leave of Dax, a stratagem that adds doubt to the suspense about the execution, which follows. Of course, the finality of the act, without the anticipated reprieve, is another well-planned device. We realize over the generals' breakfast that what Broulard decided was not to save

Confrontation after the failed attack. Mireau demands scapegoats and is opposed by Dax.

In cramped, dark quarters, Dax puts hope into the accused. Kubrick cuts to the inhuman immensity of the château, in which the environment created by humans also controls humans.

Stiff and statuesque compositions emphasize the feeling of legal hypocrisy as the examination proceeds. Humans are shown as pieces in their own games.

Judge: "The indictment is lengthy and there's no point in reading it. The charge is cowardice during the attack on Ant Hill."
Major Saint-Auban: "Did you advance? How far?"
Private Ferol: "To about the middle of no man's land, sir."
Major Saint-Auban: "Then what did you do?"
Private Ferol: "Well . . . I saw that me and Meyer . . ."
Major Saint-Auban: "The court has no concern with your visual experiences!"

Major Saint-Auban: "Did you urge your comrades forward?"
Private Arnaud: "Most of them died as they left the trenches."
Colonal Dax to Arnaud: "Aside from your sad failure to utter battle cries, was your behavior different from the others? Is it true that you have been designated a coward by lot?"
Judge: "It's accepted practice in the French Army to pick examples by lot."

Colonel Dax: "Corporal Paris . . . why didn't you leave the trenches?"
Corporal Paris: "Major Vignon was shot, and he fell on me and knocked me cold."

Judge to Paris: "Have you any witnesses?"

the three scapegoats, but to add a fourth to them—Mireau, whom he now throws to a court of inquiry, although with the fair certainty that he will "honorably" blow his brains out before things get that far. The outrage to human decency is compounded to the utmost limits when Broulard offers Dax the expendable general's job, with a congratulatory murmur at having intrigued so well for it. With this cynical old man's utter inability to tell the difference between an act of humanity and a bid for promotion, *Paths of Glory* delivers its final moral shock.

Kubrick's problem now is how to end the film with some sense of catharsis. He solved it in an allusive, indirect way that intensified its deeply humanist resonance. By a deliberate change of key, he puts an unfocused but powerful emotional experience in the place of the austere cynicism of the rest of the film. As Dax returns to his quarters after his interview with Broulard, he stops momentarily in the doorway of a tavern, where a captured German girl is being made to sing to the troops. With obvious

Major Saint-Auban: "And I submit that that attack was a stain upon the flag of France, dishonoring every man, woman, and child in the French nation."

distaste he sees the muddled animal sentiments on the faces of men whose comrades have been shot like pigs a few hours earlier. If Broulard was wrong when he quipped, "There's nothing so *stimulating* to a soldier than seeing someone else die," then these men whistling lecherously at the frightened girl also give the lie to Dax's faith in humanity. The girl is coerced into nervously starting a song. Gradually she asserts herself through the wolf calls, and though the words are in German, their undertones of memories of homeland and loved ones soften the battle-hardened soldiers and set them humming the melody. Dax's mind ceases to judge them. The sound reaches his heart as a guarantee of their basic humanity. He carries it within him, sustaining him, as news comes that the army has been ordered to the front. Man is capable of the noblest as well as the basest of emotions. "We know," wrote Hollis Alpert, who found this moment profoundly moving, "that Colonel Dax and his soldiers have made their odyssey and returned home safely."

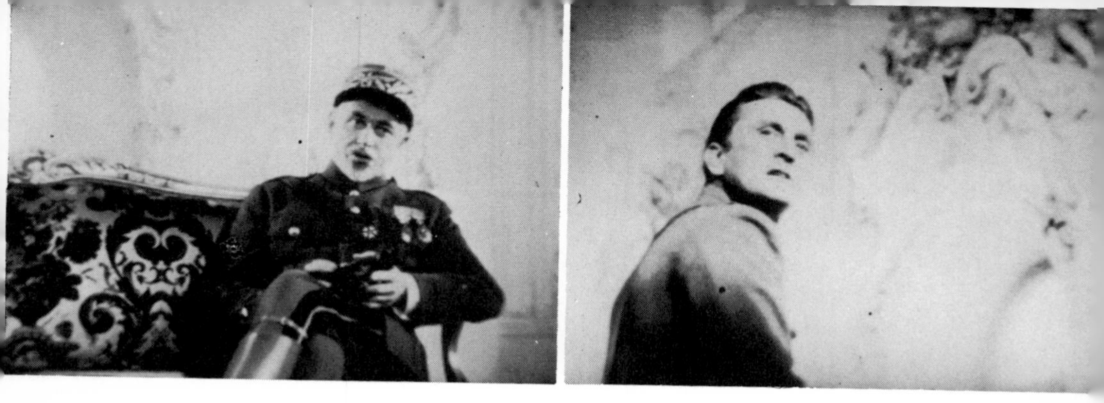

Dax's movement is filmed in severe geometrical lines as he is caught between the accused and the accusers. Colonel Dax: "Gentlemen of the court, to find these men guilty will be a crime to haunt each of you to the day you die! I can't believe the noblest impulse in man, his compassion for another, can be completely dead here. Therefore I humbly beg you . . . show mercy to these men."

Judge: "The court will deliberate."

Space, light, and shadows: Kubrick focuses on the confined agony of men awaiting execution.

Paths of Glory is a film held so truly on course and with such a confident balance between characters, casting, and moral and physical ambiance that its ideas on inhumanity and injustice permeate dramatically, not didactically, the nature of the events. It has not one weak sequence. If the scenes describing the three condemned men's captivity are cruder than the rest, this is because the emotions conveyed are cruder than those underlying the sophisticated double-talk of the generals—and also because the American accents of the cast are more obtrusive in their attempt to portray French peasants or the middle class. All the same, Kubrick and his coscenarists, Calder Willingham and Jim Thompson, do come up with a crudely effective irony, as when one of the victims laments that a common cockroach will be nearer his wife than he will because "we'll be dead, it'll be alive." And his comrade squashes the cockroach with the quip, "Now you got the edge on it."

Paths of Glory is the first Kubrick film in which the characters' relationship to their surroundings is more than physical. The architecture embodies them and

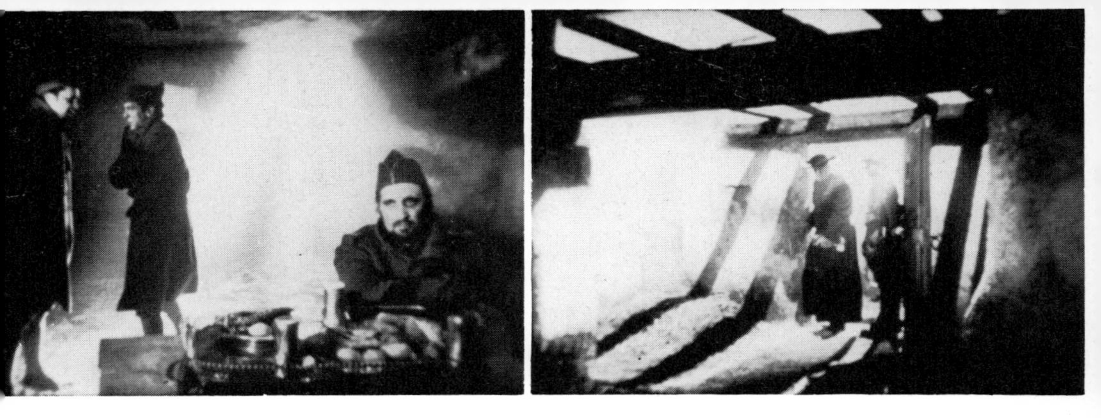

their follies in a metaphorical sense, too. There was no real architectural design in either *Killer's Kiss* or *The Killing,* though it has been noted how the camera singled out everyday objects in *Killer's Kiss* and used them as visual shorthand comments on the inner lives of the boy and girl. But in *Paths of Glory,* and even more in *Dr. Strangelove* and in *2001,* the sets for the first time assume a dynamic role as part of the total concept, usually a role that is hostile or cynically disposed to the human fates that are being settled under their shadow. In each of these three major films the principal setting is one which the dominant regime has constructed in its own image, rather in the way that Hitler's growing pretensions to extend his rule over space and time in his "Thousand-Year Reich" were encapsulated in the architecture designed and, in some cases, built for him by Albert Speer.* The château in *Paths of Glory,* the War Room

*Speer's memoirs, *Inside the Third Reich,* made a strong impression on Kubrick when he read them, and one can easily see why in the story of a "superman" regime brought to ruin by a self-fulfilling curse, by the many black-comedy moments and especially by the way Speer confirms Kubrick's thesis about the gulf that modern technology creates between reality and the fantasy of those who control it.

Priest: "Have faith in your creator, my son. Death comes to us all."

The atheist attacks the priest and is knocked against the wall.

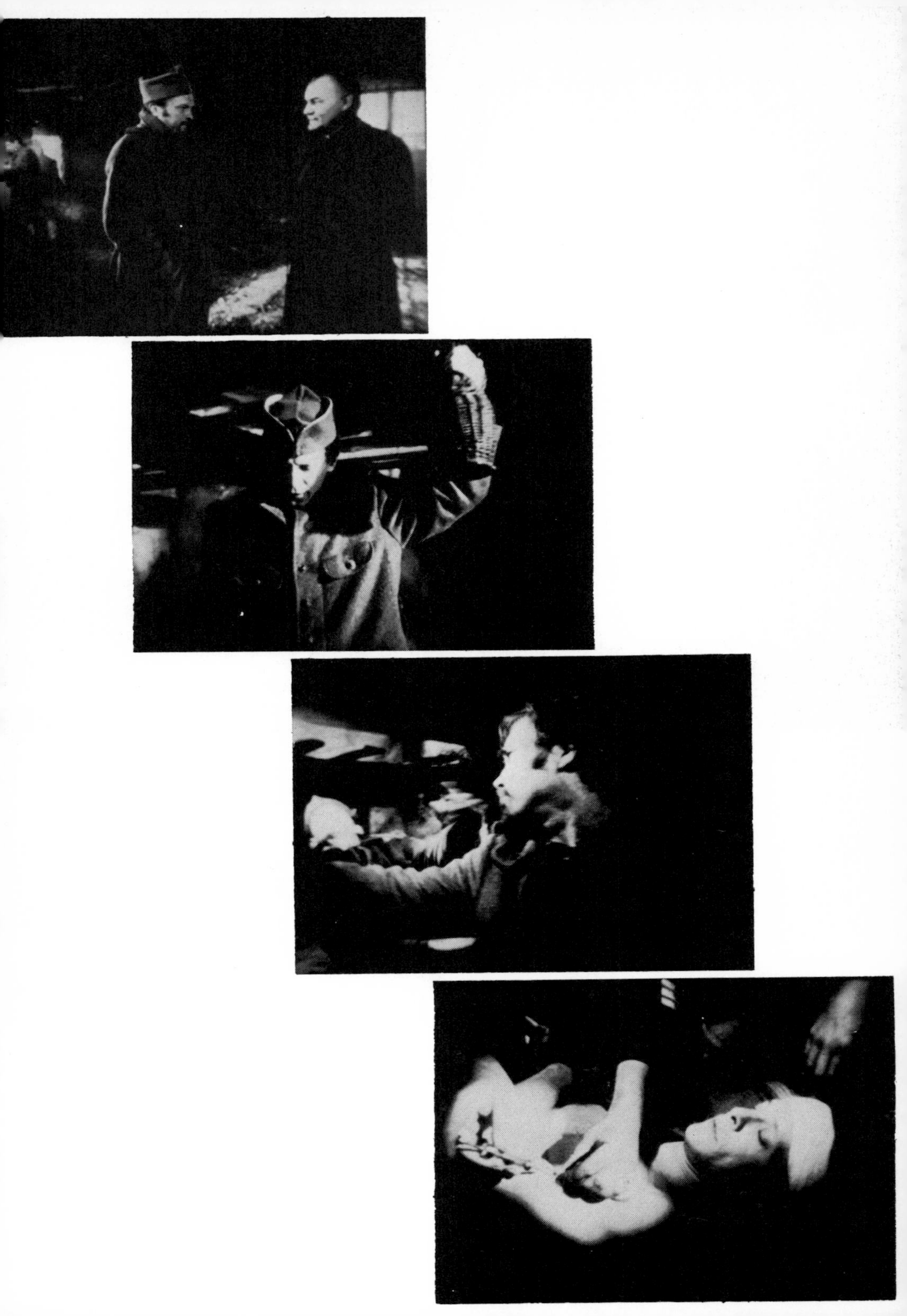

Those who trap the prisoners are caught in their own patterns. The mechanical convolutions of the dancers echo the choreography of the film's opening sequences (pages 86-87) as Dax confronts Broulard with Mireau's error.

Tables turned: Broulard quits the library and Kubrick repeats the high-angled composition of the final shot on page 117, when it was Dax's turn to leave.

The château presides over the execution of its victims. The camera, as it once moved through the trenches, now gives way before the prisoners advancing to their deaths.

in *Dr. Strangelove,* and the Wheel in *2001* represent Kubrick's most distinctive ways of using a created environment to contain, define, *and dominate* the protagonists. *Paths of Glory* enables us to pick this characteristic out very clearly. As well as being a simpler film, architecturally, than the later ones, it contains a distinctive example of how Kubrick repeats a set-up in order to emphasize the relationship between the men and their setting. The first time this occurs is when Colonel Dax demands the right to speak out in defense of the men who have finally been selected as scapegoats: he exits through the tall doors at the extreme right of the "frame," and the heavy elegance of the walls and ceiling bears down on his isolation. Virtually the same composition is used later, in the château library, when Dax turns the tables on General Broulard by revealing Mireau's duplicity, and his military superior bows himself out through the door to go back to his ballroom guests, with an ominous pensiveness. This composition occurs a third time when General Mireau in his turn is made a scapegoat by Broulard at the breakfast table and, choking with fury and fear, walks through the right-hand door, a departure that has the finality

Mechanical precision
of the ceremony of death.
The feeling of inevitability is
complemented on the sound track by
the repeated refrain of drums. "Aim!"
Drums stop . . . birdsong ascends . . .
the shots ring out.

of a last exit into the wings. Kubrick's attitude to architecture reflects the influence of certain Teutonic traits in his work; for the creation of an architectural ambiance that is far more than surface effect and penetrates to the inner meaning of the action is one of the strongest characteristics of Old High German cinema, the cinema in existence before Hitler killed it. Of course, Kubrick had a German art director in *Paths of Glory;* and another designer who was German by birth, though British by adoption, was his associate on *Dr. Strangelove.* But his awareness of the metaphysical sense of the setting derives from his own nature, rather than reflecting the national characteristics of his collaborators. The realist tradition of the American cinema counteracts any danger of his being pulled into mere decorative expressionism or baroque effects for their own sake, in the German manner. In the same way, his brilliant use of lighting effects—a skill that has obvious links with German directors like Fritz Lang and Paul Leni—is tempered by his insistence that the illumination must issue from a realistic source. *Paths of Glory* shows us fully for the first time the concern with space and lighting that Kubrick was to build more and more organically into his movies.

From the sound of bullets Kubrick cuts . . .

to the sound of breakfast.

General Mireau: "I'm glad you could be there, George. These things are always grim, but this one had a kind of splendor. The men died wonderfully!"

Broulard springs a trap on his fellow General.

Kubrick again uses the overpowering composition to suggest a man who is checkmated—Mireau retires beaten.

Paths of Glory is a realist's view of war, not a propagandist's. As has already been remarked, it is not a film against war, except in that it depicts the horrors of war. Dax executes orders that horrify him and leads an attack that he knows is bound to fail with immense loss of life. But the point is, he *does* execute the orders and he *does* lead the attack. The fact that the story portrays an incident in the 1914-1918 war helps Kubrick's intentions. For there are wars and wars. World War One was, according to historical consensus, one of the most unnecessary conflicts ever fought—a war without a just cause, breaking out almost by monstrous accident and achieving almost nothing except the conditions for the next world war. The madness of nations and their leaders characterized it; no "moral" struggle, such as underlay World War Two, can be discerned in it. A frame of reference like this is highly sympathetic to a man of Kubrick's temperament, for individual

acts performed inside a situation of lunacy take on his peculiar reverberations of irony, cynicism, and doom. Democratic government is a bad springboard for human drama; unjust or insane conditions are better forcing beds for the protagonists. *Paths of Glory* profits directly and indirectly from this condition of collective insanity in which the actions of the principal characters are attuned not only to the inequalities that prevail among men when the world is at peace but also to the insanity that breaks loose in wartime.

In the latter respect, only the scale differentiates it from the war world of *Dr. Strangelove.* A more colossal series of insane events demands a more grotesque cast of obsessed characters. And instead of revulsion at the way the generals in World War One sacrificed their men for political reasons, a kind of helpless laughter is the only appropriate response to the enormity of the holocaust as world leaders pre-

The final cynicism: Broulard offers Mireau's job to Colonel Dax.

pare to sacrifice the very existence of the human race. "The visual concept of, say, a 'Summit' conference and a hydrogen bomb exploding one city is only taking *Paths of Glory*'s contrast of the château and the trenches a stage further," analyzed Gavin Lambert in *Sight and Sound* in 1957. It was an astute and, as it turned out, prescient observation.

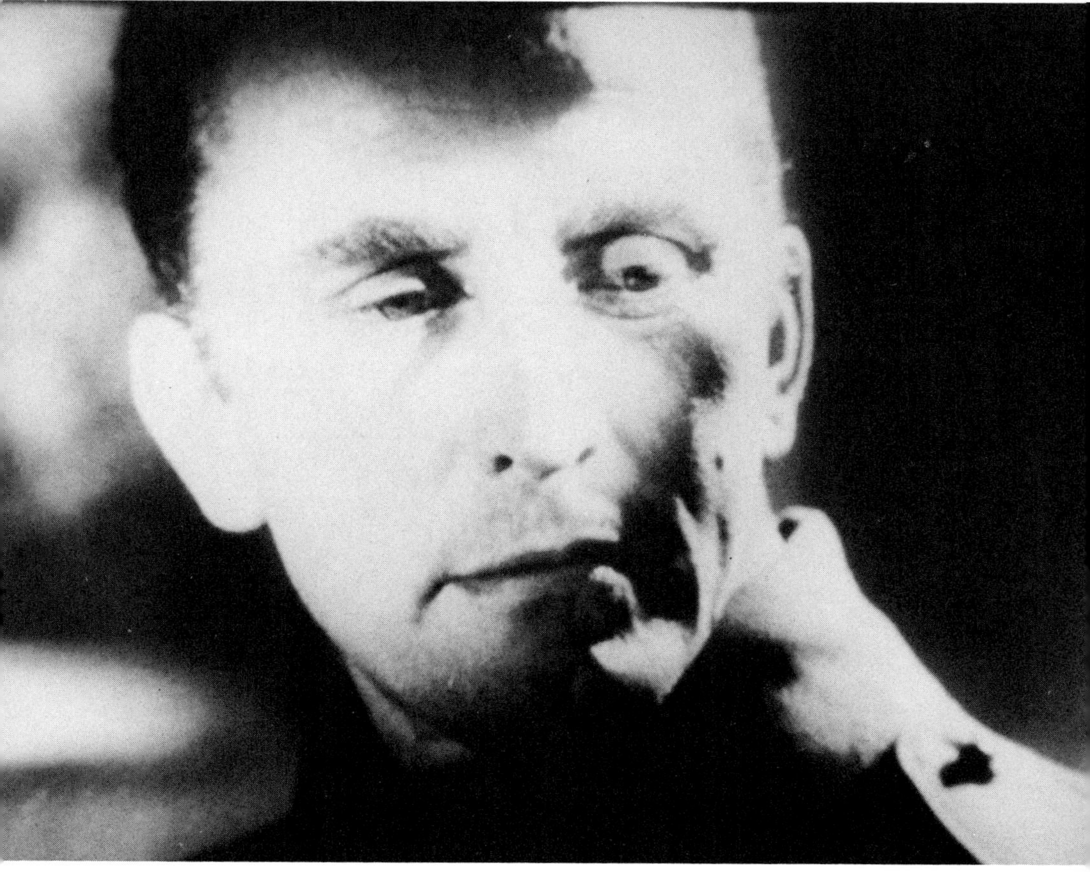

Kubrick changes emotional gear. Dax looks into the window of a tavern to see a German girl ridiculed by his soldiers.

As she sings a simple song of home, the soldiers' response gives Dax back some faith in the universal emotions of his fellow men.

Aware of man's manifold sentiments . . .

Dax returns to the front.

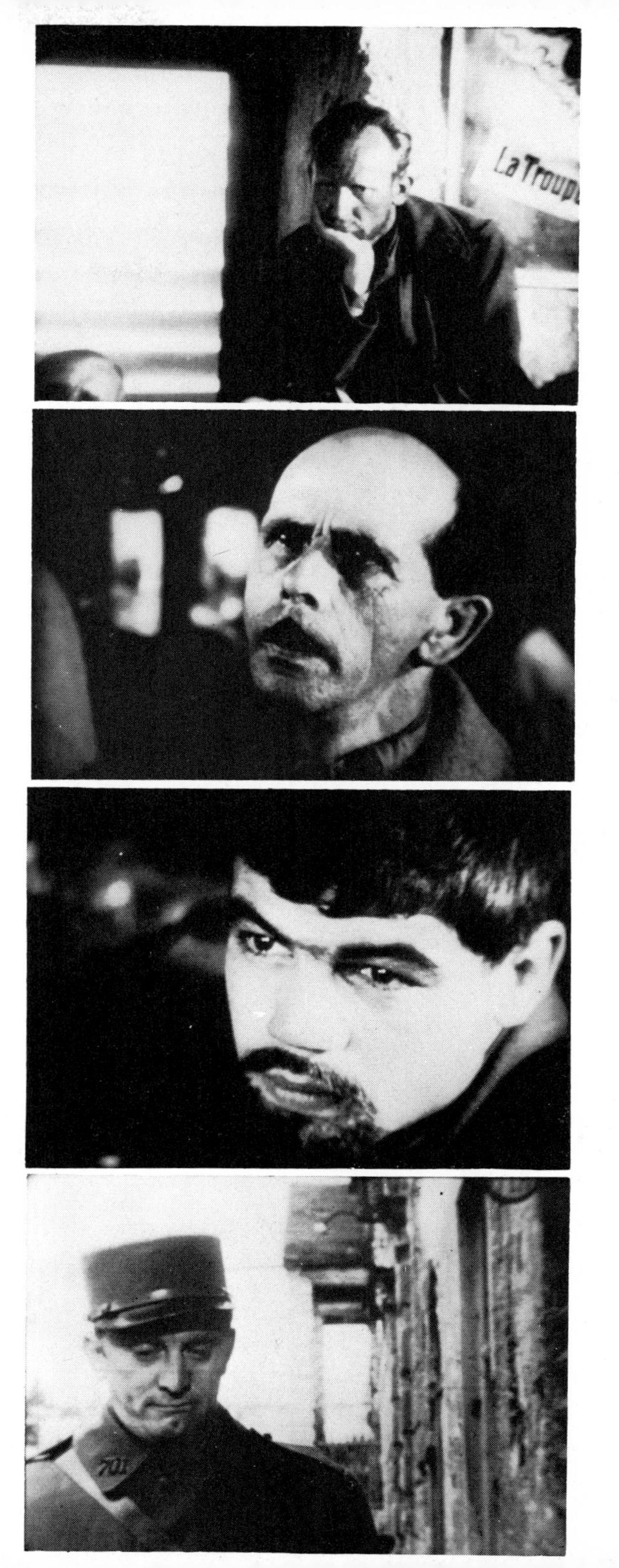
La Troup
701

DR. STRANGELOVE

OR HOW I LEARNED TO STOP WORRYING AND LOVE THE BOMB

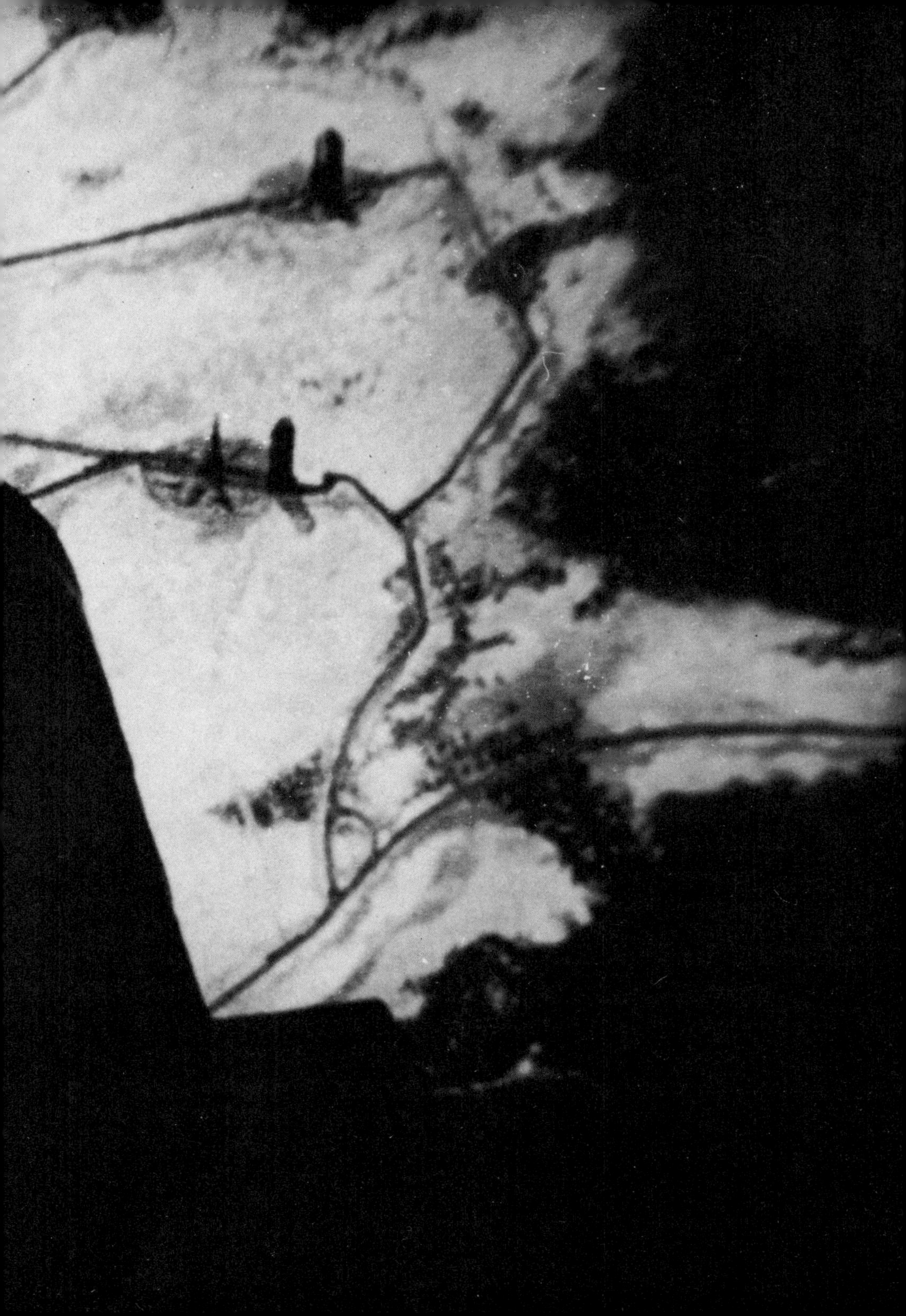

The feature of *Dr. Strangelove, or How I Learned to Stop Worrying and Love the Bomb,* which grows with repeated viewings, is how Kubrick's precise intention in making the film is perfectly matched by the sureness of his effect. Ultimately the most critical decision he made in approaching the subject of nuclear destruction came from his perceiving how comedy can infiltrate the mind's defense mechanism and take it by surprise. For in self-protection we have learned how to shut tragedy on this scale, or even the intimation of it, out of our thoughts. Kubrick has spoken of how he became struck by people's virtually listless acquiescence in the possibility—in fact, in the increasing probability—of nuclear war, by either design or accident. *Dr. Strangelove* was undertaken with the conscious aim of sounding an alert that would startle people into response and even resistance to such a fate. And laughter, not for the first time, was the device selected to penetrate the soundproofing of the paralyzed will. The largely unimaginable prospect of the extinction of the human race is turned into the satirical embodiment of its leaders' collective madness. The fantasy of nuclear destruction, which, like death itself, we never think of as happening to ourselves in our lifetime, is turned into the comic reality of actors giving inspired performances—"inspired" by their material and director.

As for Kubrick's basic ingredient of filmmaking, the story, it, too, is brilliantly developed in ways that heighten and extend the theme. The look, the sound, and even the sequence of events leading to the global holocaust all create a suspense plot that has room for grim realism and grotesque humor, close-packed and often side by side. The theme of communication is again central to the whole construction

Dr. Strangelove *strikes its note of doom from the opening narration: "For more than a year, ominous rumors had been privately circulating among high-level Western leaders that the Soviet Union had been at work on what was darkly hinted to be the Ultimate Weapon, a Doomsday device. Intelligence sources traced the site of the top secret Russian project to the perpetually fog-shrouded wasteland below the arctic peaks of the Zhokhov islands."*

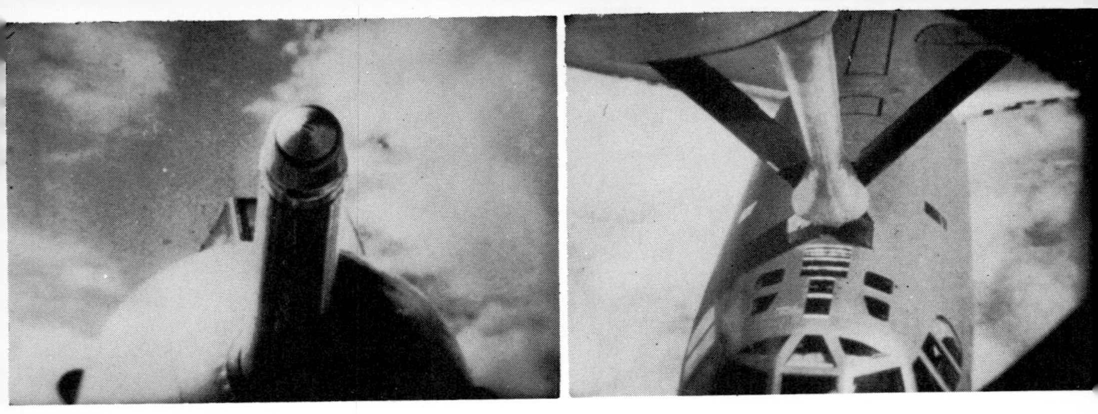

Title sequence of melody "Try a Little Tenderness" is suggestive of the conflicting demands of destruction and security. A nuclear bomber is refueled from the mother aircraft in flight.

Man's radar technology, designed to safeguard him against surprise nuclear attack; the film sets up the ironic theme of the fallibility of men and machines.

of the film and the working out of many separate scenes in it. Time and space, too, are as much a part of it as they were in *The Killing*—indeed, *Dr. Strangelove* might appropriately be subtitled *The Overkill*—and Kubrick imposes even more rigorous restrictions on himself than he did in the earlier film.

What happens in *Dr. Strangelove* is confined to a few hours and to three highly localized settings. Each setting, moreover, is sealed off from the others. One is a locked office in an air base commanded by a psychotic general; another is the cabin of a B-52 H-bomber captained by a moronic pilot; and the third is the underground War Room at the Pentagon, dominated by a manic warmonger and his malignant counterpart, a power-mad nuclear strategist. Insanity is sealed in with the characters; they are locked into

General Ripper tells Group Captain Mandrake a Red Alert has been declared. The telephone, a primary instrument of communication, allows one man to extend his insanity.

their "cells," as the fate of the peoples they rule or represent is locked into the events. Once again we note Kubrick's fondness for using the feeling of helplessness which is the peculiar fear that follows from being "locked in" by certain physical circumstances or emotional situations. For a picture that illustrates the end of the world, the actual areas involved are absurdly small. The old scientific boast of "Give me a place to stand and I shall move the earth" has been succeeded by the new scientific reality of "Give me a place to sit down and I'll destroy it."

The characters in *The Killing* generated the suspense that comes from working to the clock in a concerted effort; those in *Dr. Strangelove* generate the nightmare that comes from working against the clock while suffering a total disruption of communication. The chief area of communication that has broken down is, of course, in human sanity. Both films convey Kubrick's unmistakable intention of measuring off minutes from an allotted time.

The timing starts in *Dr. Strangelove* with Kubrick's

favorite device, the opening narration, which is factual and ominous. This sets the mood, with a foreboding account of mysterious Russian construction work in the polar regions, work whose purpose no one knows. What is being constructed is, in fact, the Doomsday Machine—the nuclear booby trap that an attack on Russia will automatically trigger. The significance of this is not revealed until late in the film, just as the revelation of the purpose of the Jupiter Mission in *2001* is delayed. At a first viewing of the film one may not make the connection. No matter. The right intimation of mortality has been sounded.

The following sequence, over which the credits appear, is a visual metaphor for the theme that whets expectations the way the emblem of Humbert Humbert's "enslavement" did in *Lolita.* Two planes rock gently together in mid-air, a B-52 bomber being refueled by the tanker aircraft, the sexual implication impishly emphasized by the music, "Try a Little Tenderness." This concept was Kubrick's, though, as he recalls with wry amusement, one of the world's lead-

The B-52 crew: men not conscious of the sophistication of the machinery they have created, a theme Kubrick is to develop further in 2001. *The unbelievable happens. The B-52 is put on attack.*

ing nuclear strategists later said it reminded him less of copulation than of a mother giving suck to her infant. Maternal or erotic, the image anticipates the sexually based human motivation for the coming destruction. It is an Air Force general's paranoid anxiety about the waning potency of his "precious bodily essence"—he blames it on an international Communist conspiracy to poison the drinking water—that makes him activate the "Go" code, sending B-52s winging off to Russia to destroy the poison at the source. And in the false dawn of hope at the end of the film, the prospect of renewing the human race by bringing together carefully preserved males and temptingly selected females is what boosts the virility of another general and reconciles him to the slaughter. This irony—that the sexual neuroses of two militarists should be at the heart of the holocaust—is only the first of the disparities that *Dr. Strangelove* points up between the smallness of the cause and the enormity of the result.

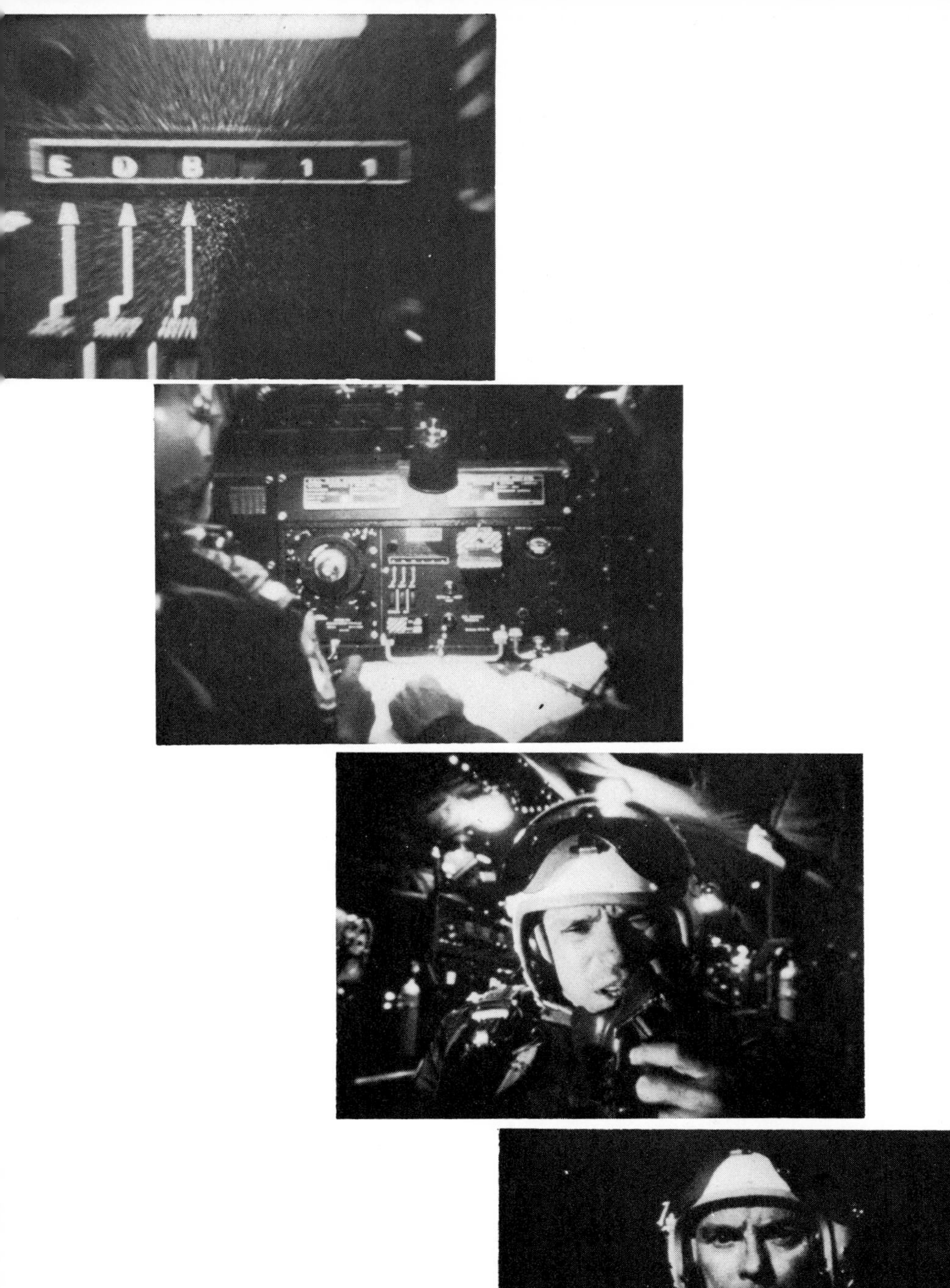
E D B 1 1

TOP SECRET

Wing attack Plan O
Wing attack Plan R

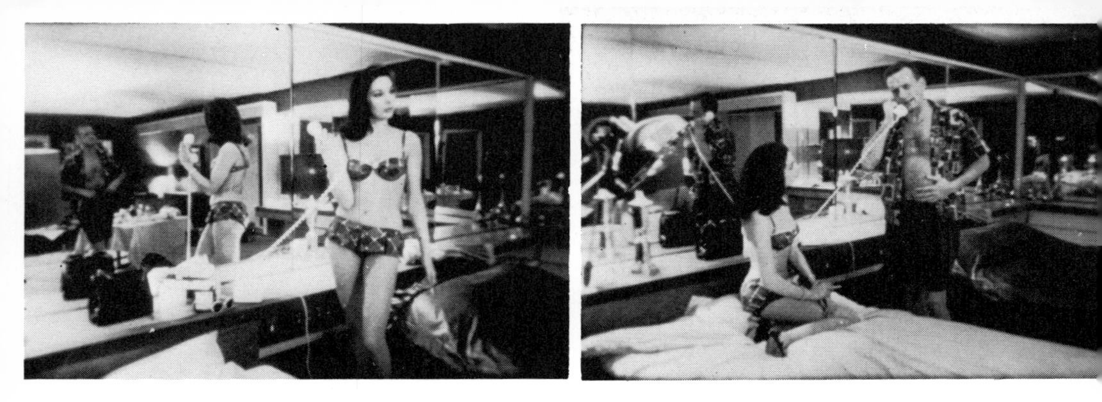

Communications: General Turgidson's mistress takes a call from the Pentagon summoning him to the gathering crisis . . . while General Ripper, at the air base, uses his address system to seal himself off from reach.

The film begins with almost lethargic calm in each of the three main locations. At Burpelson Air Force Base, the computers, making their debut in a Kubrick film, produce a murmur of order and routine, which is suggested, too, in the politely deferential attitude of Peter Sellers, playing Group-Captain Lionel Mandrake of the Royal Air Force, as he leans fondly over these banks of brain-children. Physical posture plays an important part in *Dr. Strangelove.* More than in any of his other films, Kubrick uses it to split open character for our inspection. Since the characters are caricatures—though they are never without their human dimension—the way their bodies are used, photographed and edited in the film indicates their incipient or active insanities.

The madness already resident in General Jack D. Ripper, Mandrake's commandant at Burpelson, played by Sterling Hayden, is embodied partly in the actor's performance; but the way he is photographed, fre-

STOP

Peace
IS OUR
PROFESSION

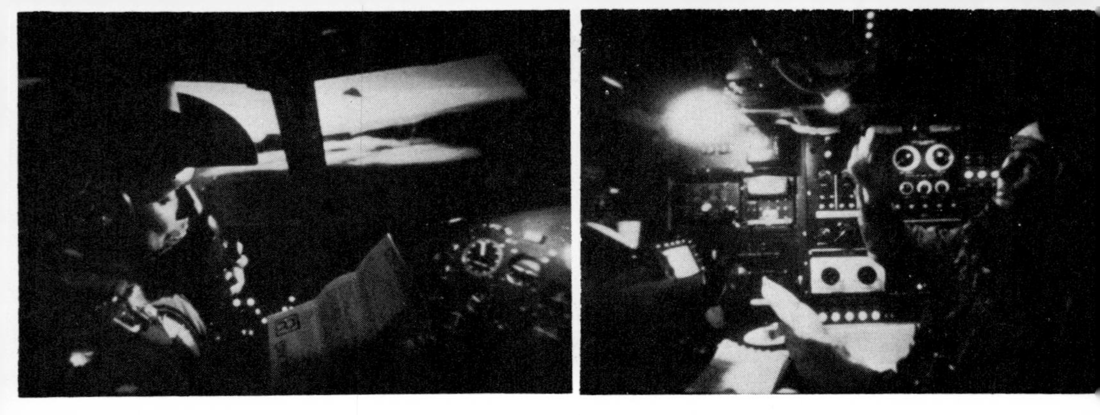

In the B-52, the crisis manual is followed step by step, further locking the men into their destiny.

quently in close-up, often from slightly below his jutting cigar, suggests a man totally sunk into his obsessional view of a world which he believes is polluting his bodily essence. General Ripper has turned a deaf ear to all but his own paranoid voices. Hayden plays out his dementia with the stage-by-stage methodology of a military rule book. Sellers, on the other hand, is encouraged by Kubrick to be a foil, both physically and verbally, of slow-burning comprehension. "Oh, hell," he murmurs in well-bred irritation when Hayden tells him that the nuclear alert which has just been sounded by him is real. "Oh, hell, are the Russians involved?"

Having sounded the warning, Kubrick now moves smoothly on to second base—the B-52 bomber on patrol, part of the twenty-four-hour Airborne Alert. Again the narrator is briefly introduced with facts and figures on this kind of nuclear guard duty. The bland, soothing voice—a kind of Ur-HAL—relieves us of any insecurities by its total reassurance. Somebody up there is on guard. But when we see *inside* the plane, dementia tightens its grip, for human beings are

The course is set.

Sealed into his own madness, suggested by Kubrick's use of confined space and low-angled view of brooding mania, General Ripper informs Mandrake that the alert is his own invention. *(See page 116.)*

operating on a level of sophistication many IQs below that of the machinery they are nominally controlling. The B-52 crew is not only listless, it is mindless as well, leafing through *Playboy,* riffling card decks like lazy riverboat gamblers, while the apelike impression made by Slim Pickens, as their captain, is amply confirmed by his name—Major Kong.

And yet, as is characteristic of all of *Dr. Strangelove,* these grotesques exist in an environment of painstaking realism. The B-52 cabin is a detailed replica of an actual bomber. The events inside it are filmed with no more lighting sources than one would expect a real plane to furnish. It is when the nuclear alert sounds that this documentary detail is suddenly convulsed by demoniac forces. The machinery takes over. The spinning counters, revolving numbers, and clicking codes on a multitude of automated dials lock in the crew's fate, and ultimately the world's, as the bomber heads for Russia. HAL 9000, the computer conspiring against his "masters" in *2001,* is only the

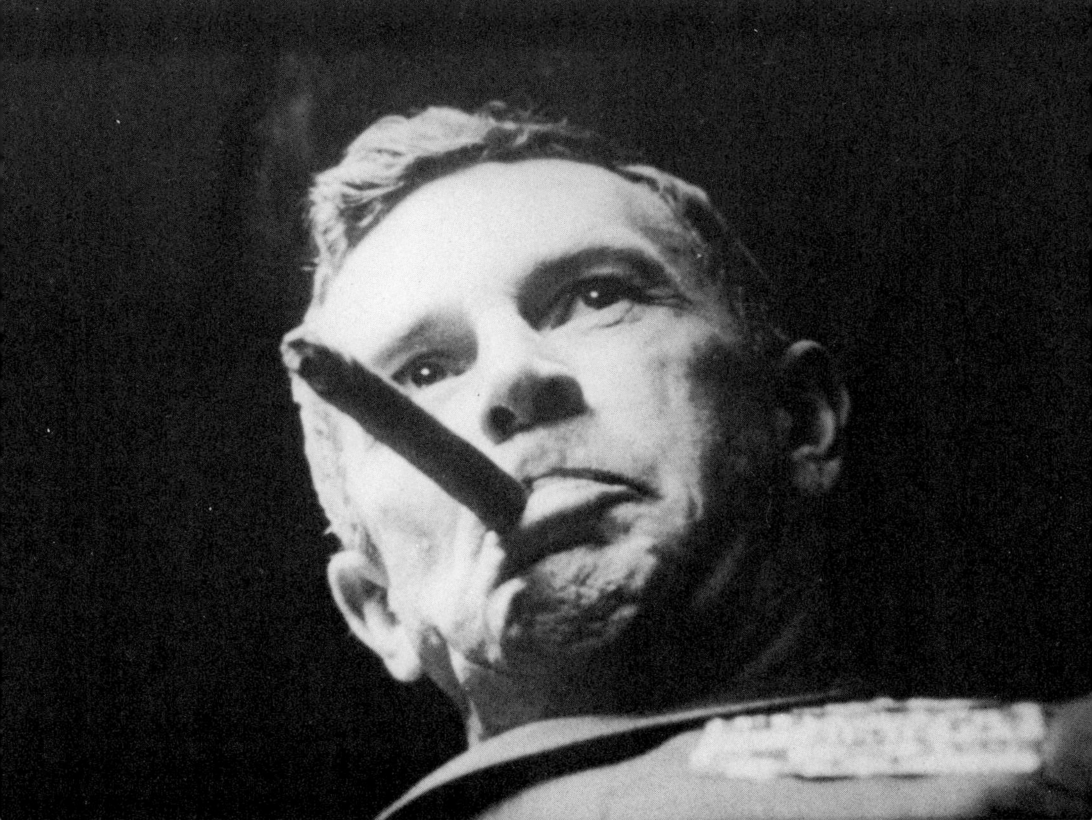

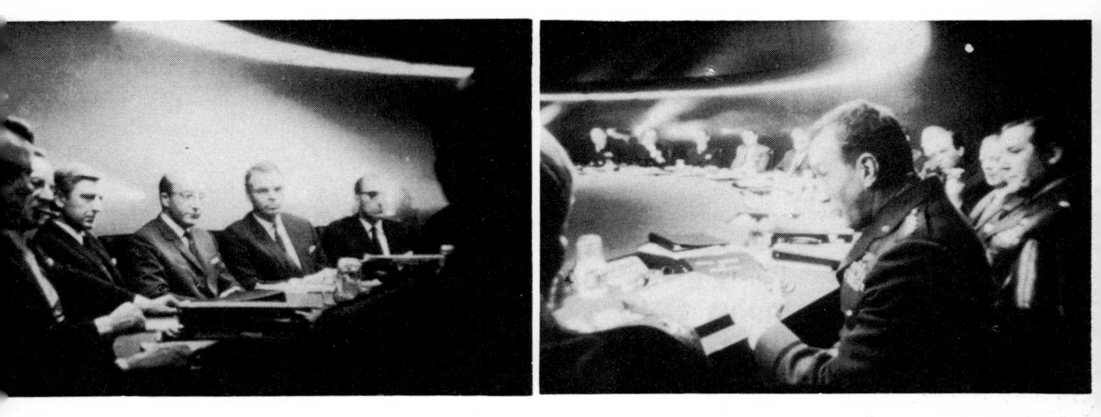

The Circle of Fate in the War Room. Like the judges at the court-martial in Paths of Glory, *this group of leaders sits in judgment on men's lives.*

President Muffley shows a realistic concern for the growing crisis: "Obviously the work of a psychotic."

sophisticated Big Brother of these mute instruments in *Dr. Strangelove.* They set Major Kong's old Deep South blood tingling at the thought of the glory mission. Clamping on his Stetson, he sets the bomber on target to the strains of "When Johnny Comes Marching Home." "There'll be some important promotions an' citations when we come through this," he promises the crew.

The prologue is over. The war posture, at once antic and appalling, has been struck. And the cast of humans is about to be absurdly dwarfed by an escalating calamity beyond their control. Kubrick now begins the process of incongruity and disparity of events which structures the rest of the film. It is done by injecting actions that would be perfectly normal, even insignificant, in ordinary situations into the Ultimate Situation that shapes up as the B-52 nears its bombing zone.

Confront a man in his office with a nuclear alarm, Kubrick has said, and you have a documentary. If the news reaches him in his living room, you have a drama. If it catches him in the lavatory, the result is

But the military mind will not admit it. Turgidson: "I wouldn't be too hasty, Mr. President."

comedy. Which is exactly where General Buck Turgidson happens to be when the message comes through to him—human necessity interrupted by human destiny.

George C. Scott's portrayal of Turgidson is an excellent example of how Kubrick gets his peculiarly manic effects in this film by collaboration with his cast. Scott brings many an inventive trait of his own to the part of this Pentagon "hawk"; his complacent slapping of his bare tummy, as he leaves his mistress' bed to join his President in the War Room, is like a man sounding his own war drum. But Kubrick, too, "creates" Scott's performance. Again and again Turgidson is "frozen" in some extraordinary posture, usually resembling that of an ape or jackal, either by having the camera cut away from him in mid-grimace or else by holding the camera on him while the actor petrifies himself into some sub-human attitude. This gives the impression of a gargoyle animated by its own wound-up dementia or a jumping jack-in-the-box of manic impulses, tics, spasms, and reflexes. The effect is in total contrast to the massive, brooding psychosis of General Ripper. In both cases, Kubrick

The grotesque inappropriateness of Turgidson's simple-minded response is captured by Kubrick's long take of George C. Scott's contortions.

adapts his editing and his cast's acting to outwardly embody the inner humors of the characters.

As the crisis grows, the scene expands—into the Pentagon War Room. This is one of the most functional and imaginative sets ever designed for film. It was created by Ken Adam, a German-born architecture student, whose designs for other movies did much to create the larger-than-life feeling of the James Bond films. It is no accident, therefore, that we see shades of Fritz Lang's work, especially *Metropolis,* in this cavernous design. But what is specifically characteristic of Kubrick is the logic and rationality in the set. He and Adam chose the semi-triangular shape, since Kubrick likes form to be "justified" by function and the War Room structure is the one that best withstands the stress of, say, an explosion overhead.*

---

*In one early script for *2001: A Space Odyssey* the "burglar alarm" found on the Moon was envisaged as a tetrahedron, its base and three sides forming an equilateral triangle about fifteen feet high, because it had more surface area per volume than any other design and was thus the optimum one for a sun-powered device. It did not survive into the

Of course, the significance of the War Room extends beyond its physical properties. With its maps studded with winking lights charting the B-52 bombers' progress toward targets all over the world, it has affinities with a pinball scoreboard; the gambling metaphor extends to the roulette-wheel look of the circular conference table to which the U.S. President, Merkin Muffley, summons his advisers. Baldheaded, bespectacled, concerned yet in the last resort ineffectual, the President is played by Peter Sellers in the second of his three roles in the film. As in the B-52, Kubrick and his lighting photographer, Gil Taylor, use only "first available light" and achieve an effect that is spectral and nightmarish, yet as solidly realistic as a piece of photo-reportage.

The feature that the film now brings more and more strongly to the fore is the virtual inability of every character, except perhaps the President, to grasp the ultimate consequence of what is happening. They

finished film, the mythical properties of the monolith being preferred to the logical ones of the tetrahedron; but this shows how scrupulously Kubrick takes every aspect of his work.

Major Kong, elated by the discovery of the pleasures of the survival kit: "one .45 automatic; two boxes of ammunition; four days' concentrated emergency rations; one drug issue containing antibiotic pills, morphine pills, vitamin pills, pep pills, sleeping pills, and tranquilizer pills; one miniature combination Russian phrase book and Bible; one hundred dollars in rubles; nine packs of chewing gum; one issue of prophylactics; three lipsticks; three pair of nylon stockings. Gee, a fella could have a pretty good weekend in Vegas with all that stuff."

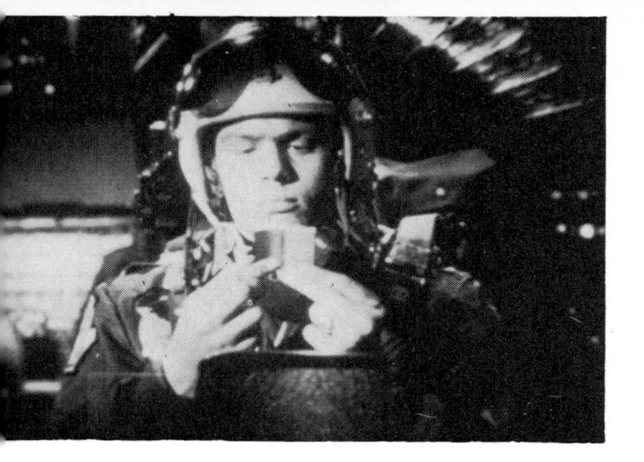
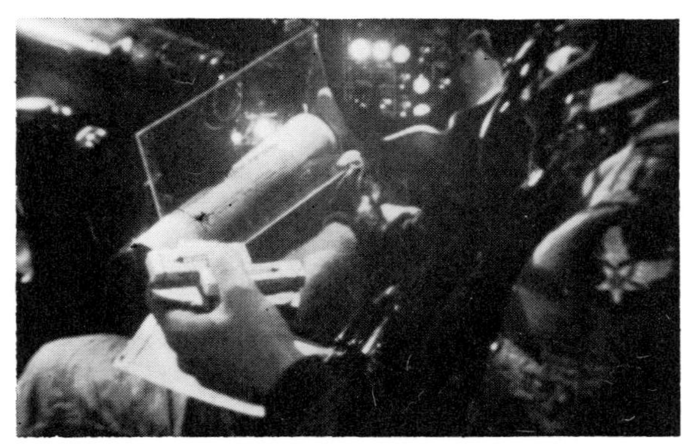

Increasing crisis: The President calls in the Soviet envoy. . . . Unable to grasp the issue at stake, the Soviet envoy attempts espionage and is detected by Turgidson. His camera, concealed in a matchbox, is an example of Kubrick's attention to detail and the mechanics of what he is examining.

President Muffley: "Gentlemen, you can't fight in here. This is the War Room."

Kubrick cuts to physical reality: The President's task force starts to break into General Ripper's sealed-off control base.

Simultaneous events: General Ripper's preoccupation with his "Precious Bodily Fluids" alternates with the action it has caused. (See page 67.)

commit one of the worst sins of noncommunication. They have absolutely no idea of priorities outside their own obsessions. Threatened with extinction, all Turgidson can think of is copulation. In mid-conference the girl he has left calls him on the phone. "Look, honey," he hisses, "I can't talk now. My President needs me. . . . Of course it isn't only physical." And he promises to be right back in bed beside her just as soon as he can. Kubrick makes brilliant use of the incongruities of dialogue as well as incident to achieve this effect.

Back at the air base, General Ripper is making the loss of his "essence" by Commie fluoridation into a *casus belli;* as he talks to Mandrake, holding him in a captive bear hug at once protective and menacing, Ripper uses the emphatic pauses that a chief of state would make in an address to the nation. Mandrake, feigning a deadly calm he does not feel, falls back on the intimate tone of address, soothingly murmuring "Jack" now and then, so as to ingratiate

himself into the good graces of this lunatic.

Over in the War Room, General Turgidson, trying to justify what has happened to his President, is so carried away with elation at his boys' initiative in attacking the Russians that he cannot bear to recall the B-52s, even if it were possible to get through to the now sealed-off Burpelson Air Base and extract the recall code from Ripper. He urges all-out war, figuring out the possible megadeaths like a lip-smacking computer. "I'm not saying we wouldn't get our hair mussed. I am saying only ten to twenty million people killed, tops, depending on the breaks." The speech, says Kubrick, is almost a précis of what has been published in military journals, even to euphemisms, not unlike "hair mussing," for human casualties. It would be difficult, and dramatically redundant, Kubrick observes, to try to top the statistical and linguistic inhumanity of nuclear strategists.

The same precision with words and their incongruities in certain contexts extends to items in the

The telephone to the rescue as the President calls the Soviet Premier: "Hello . . . Eh, hello, Dimitri. Listen, I . . . I can't hear too well; do you suppose you could turn the music down just a little. Ah, ah, that's much better. . . . Yes, huh, yes. Fine, I can hear you now, Dimitri, clear and plain and coming through . . . fine. I'm coming through fine too, aye? Good, then, well, then as you say, we're both coming through fine. Good. Well, it's good that you're fine . . . and, and I'm fine. I agree with you, it's great to be fine. . . . Now then, Dimitri, you know how we've always talked about the possibility of something going wrong with the Bomb. . . . The BOMB, Dimitri. The hydrogen *bomb . . . Well, now, what happened is that eh, one of our base commanders, he had a sort of, well, he went a little funny in the head. You know, just a little funny. And he went and did a silly thing. Well, I'll tell you what he did. He ordered his planes to attack your country. Well, let me finish, Dimitri . . . let me finish, Dimitri . . . well, listen, how do you think I feel about it? Can you imagine how I feel about it, Dimitri? . . . Why do you think I'm calling you? . . . Just to say hello? Of course I like to speak to you . . . of course I like to say hello. . . ."*

Turgidson's disbelief that his President could act thus

Suspense as the B-52s near their target: a communications feat that brings no comfort to President or Premier

Mandrake literally in the grip of Ripper's obsession

Kubrick's escalating line of macabre horror is increased by news of the Doomsday Machine. The machine, as in 2001, *always contrives to spring a surprise on its makers.*

B-52 crew's survival kit. It covers the whole range of human emotions, noble and vile, from the life-preserving aids to the lust-satisfying ones; it contains, among other things, a .45 pistol, ammunition, four days' emergency rations, one hundred dollars in rubles, nine packs of chewing gum, lipsticks, nylon stockings, and prophylactics. "Gee," Major Kong reflects, "a fella could have a pretty good weekend in Vegas with all that stuff."*

Kubrick now tilts the film's emphasis toward the sorely tried President Mervin Muffley. Muffley is practically the only sane man in the film; what he says usually makes sense. It seems wildly absurd to say that lack of a sense of humor is what makes him so funny; yet it is in his egghead earnestness that Kubrick and his coauthors, Terry Southern and Peter George, accurately lodge the source of comedy. By

*The city originally named in this dialogue was Dallas; but after the assassination of President Kennedy, Vegas was substituted on the sound track.

his very serious brand of sanity, the President seems as removed from reality as the others. Catching Turgidson wrestling with the Russian ambassador, who has been called in to advise, but is busily photographing secret equipment, the President snaps, "Gentlemen, you can't fight in here. This is the War Room."

Kubrick's long-focal-length lens puts a documentary distance between himself and the President at the round table, which intensifies the bizarre feeling that one is eavesdropping on an actual summit crisis, yet hearing dialogue of the most unconscious semantic absurdity. Such is the telephone conversation Muffley holds on the hot line with Premier Kissov of the Soviet Union. Painstakingly trying to warn him of the approaching nuclear doom, Muffley is forced by the Premier's meager knowledge of English, and also because he is drunk, to talk like someone teaching table manners to a child. "Now then, Dimitri, you know how we've always talked about the possibility of something going wrong with the Bomb. The BOMB, Dimitri. The *hydrogen* bomb . . ."

As the grimness of the humor spirals, the momentum of the film increases. The scene aboard the B-52, when a Soviet missile comes close to destroying it, not only conveys the physical sense of things irrev-

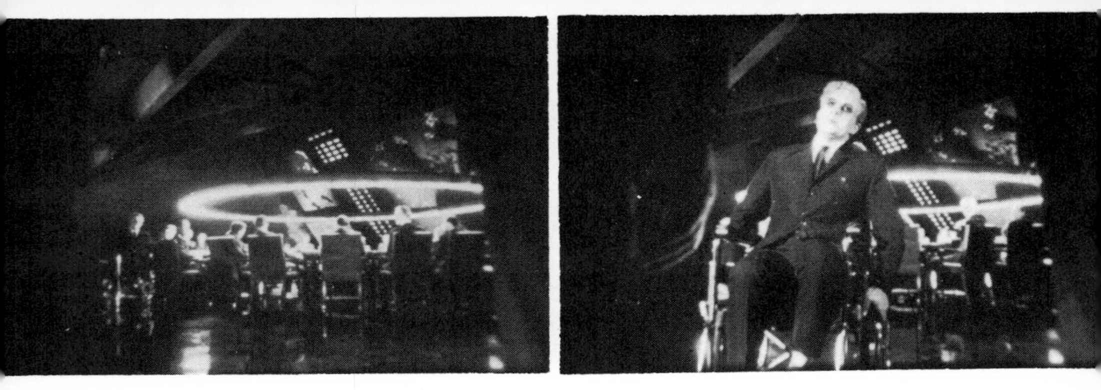

Enter Dr. Strangelove from the darkness. Kubrick's lighting and angle emphasize the "power of darkness" and the ogrelike image of malevolence. (See pages 56-57, 71, 73.)

Haloed by the overhead lighting, Strangelove describes the Machine with nightmare relish.

ocably on the move, but brilliantly exemplifies Kubrick's skill at blending realism into nightmare. We forget the comic grotesques at the controls as we see the radar bleep of the homing missile, witness the "white out" as it explodes in a near miss, hear the crew's voices scrambled in panicky distortion on the sound track and then see them struggle to hold the battered plane on course. It is one of the very few scenes in a feature film—maybe the only one—showing characters coping with this kind of crisis "by the book." Every step comes from a Boeing 707 flight manual. What one usually sees in such crises is a pilot hauling on the controls to pull the aircraft out of a dive. Kubrick shows it takes logical training plus co-ordinated action, the sense of a man acting like a machine, rather than brawn and a prayer.

It is a source of no small pride to him that, despite a prefatory note to the contrary added at U.S. Air Force request after the film's release, the strategic

The hand-held camera duplicates the effect of a newsreel in the raid on Ripper's base. (See pages 108-109, Paths of Glory.*)*

Peace
IS OUR

Total breakdown of communications: Americans fire on Americans as in Paths of Glory *French soldiers were ordered to fire on their compatriots.*

Ripper feels his fate closing in. The destruction inspired by sexual anxiety turns on its agent.

Ripper: "Women sense my power, and they seek me out. I do not avoid women. But I deny them my life essence."

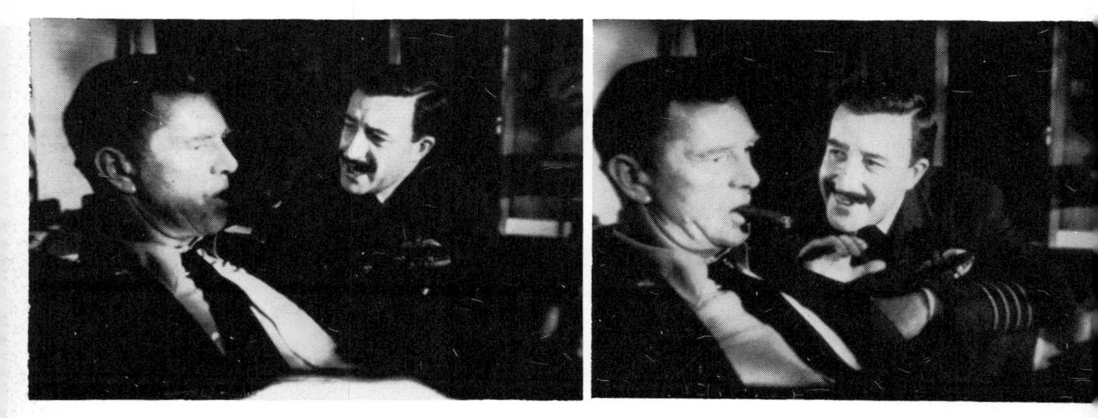

Mandrake, still unable to grasp the strategic implications, offers personal condolences.

A change in lighting aids the confessional posture of the warmonger, who thinks the invading troops are Russians.

Ripper: "They're going to be in here soon. I don't know how well I could stand up to torture. They might force the code out of me."

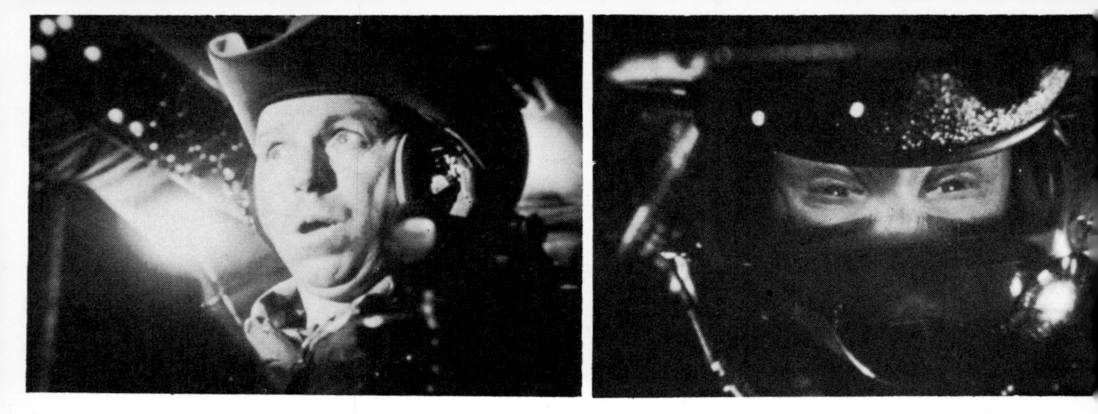

The B-52: Kubrick re-creates in precise detail, using lighting and distorted sound, the sensation of a missile attack on the maverick bomber.

premise of the film has not been seriously challenged. It appeals to this director's sense of irony, of course, to take a plan devised to prevent human error and, by turning it inside out, make it into a means of preventing correction of that human error.

The paradox is embodied in the film's other action sequence, which now develops when the U.S. Army has to be sent into battle *against* the U.S. Army guarding Burpelson Air Base on General Ripper's orders —an implication that has its parallel in *Paths of Glory* —so that the President back in the War Room can get hold of the B-52 recall code on which the demented Ripper is sitting tight. The grainy realism of battle —Kubrick used orthochromatic film to shoot the sequence—heightens the black comedy of Ripper's last scene with Mandrake. "They were my children," he laments, mourning the air-base soldiers who have fallen to the bullets of their compatriots in defense of their general's aberration. And imagining that Russians "disguised" as U.S. soldiers will now torture the recall code out of him, he proceeds to blow his brains

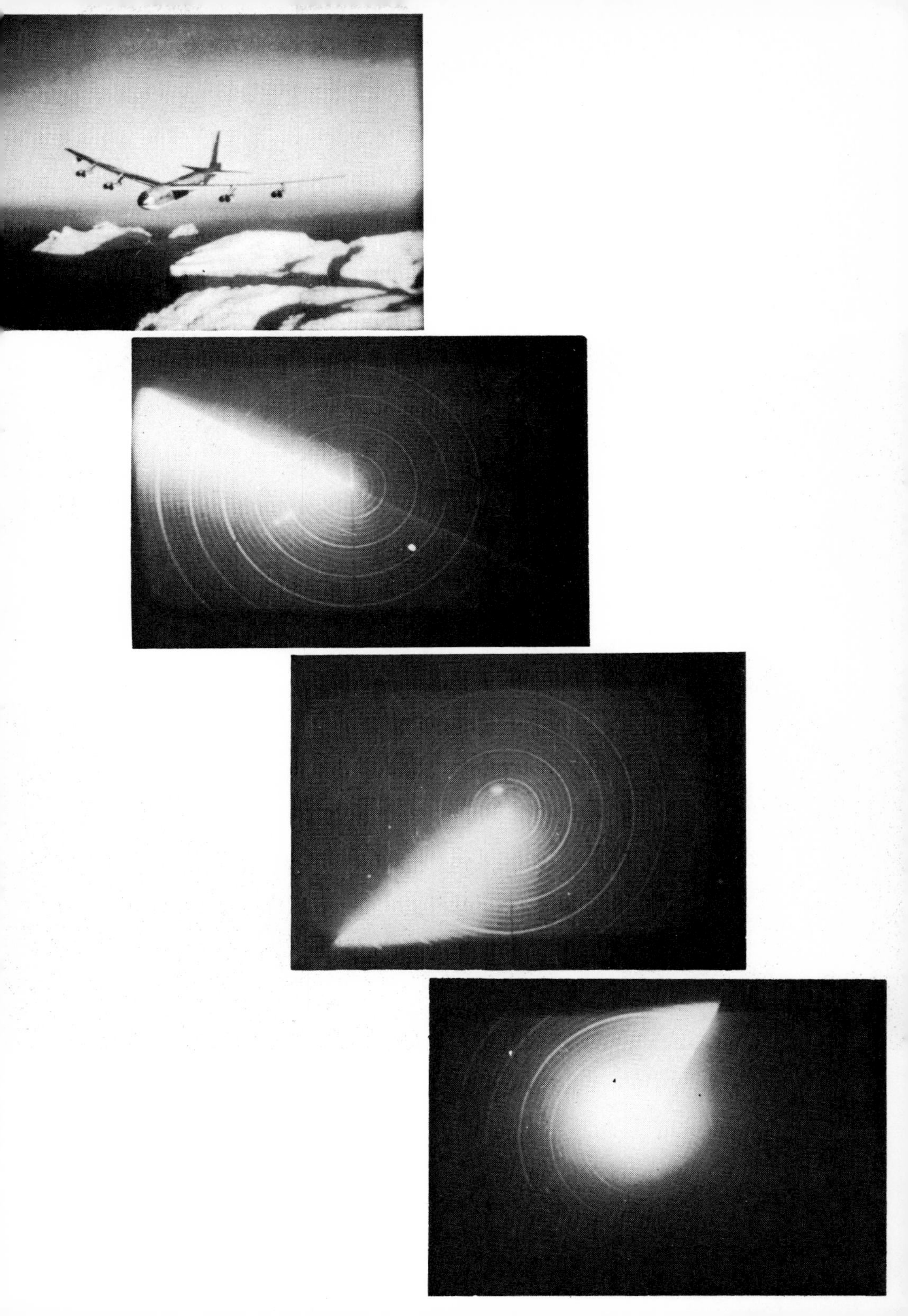

The effects of the explosion: Kubrick's use of the surreal image amid the authentic emergency.

Ripper's coded doodling presents one more barrier to communication as Mandrake tries to break it.

out in the bathroom while Mandrake, paralyzed by his own mummified sense of English decency, bleats comforting nothings outside the door. The gruesome detail of his inability to push open the door after the shot, because the corpse is blocking it, recalls the realistic stiffening of the bullet-riddled Quilty in *Lolita.*

Dr. Strangelove is one of those rare films that show no sign of their inventiveness running down. It keeps pumping grotesque energy to the surface like an oil gusher. It introduces each new character at precisely the right moment to keep its graph of lunacy in an ascending line. Colonel Bat Guano, played by Keenan Wynn, comes in with the task force that has broken into Burpelson, flashing his own obsession like an identity card the instant he confronts Mandrake. Guano is what the critic Penelope Gilliatt called "a hard-core hetero." He suspects not Commies under every bed, but "preverts" *in* every bed. Again the military mania has sexual origins.

Kubrick's direction of Wynn constantly plays on glances of angular suspicion he turns toward every potential "prevert"—a now famous verbal slip. His

Enter Guano, another military mind preoccupied with sexual anxiety: "If you want to know what I think, I think you're some kind of a deviated prevert."

dialogue with Mandrake continues the stress on speech forms already noted in the film. "What kind of suit do you call that?" he growls, scenting a "deviant prevert." Mandrake bristles. "What do you mean 'suit'? This happens to be a Royal Air Force uniform." The peculiarly English indignation at being mistaken for someone of the wrong rank or class shows how sharply language no less than action defines character in *Dr. Strangelove.* And the Mandrake-Guano confrontation continues the theme of people on the verge of annihilation sealed up in their separate cells of self-concern. When the British officer deduces the B-52 recall code from Ripper's doodlings, and a Coke machine has to be broken into for change to call the Pentagon from a pay phone, Mandrake is darkly reminded by Guano that he will be answerable for the damage to the Coca-Cola Company. It is rather like a man who is fighting a fire being bothered by someone for a light.

Back in the War Room's echoing blackness the eponymous Dr. Strangelove at last appears with an inhuman clang of his wheelchair. (Kubrick uses

The continuing ride into nightmare. Kubrick's movement accelerating in depth anticipates the cosmic ride into the unknown in 2001.

As destruction speeds up, communication is held up.

acoustics from now on, as he did in the opening château scenes in *Paths of Glory,* to put an edge of doom on some of the dialogue.) Played by Peter Sellers in the third and weirdest of his roles, Strangelove reincarnates some aspects, even down to the mechanical arm, of Fritz Lang's mad inventor, Rotwang, in *Metropolis.* But this madman has survived into the postwar world as the U.S. President's nuclear strategist. He also, of course, possesses an evil kinship to the ogre figures from myth who haunt some earlier Kubrick films. Teutonic shadows thicken figuratively and photographically around this gloating cripple with the lock of crimped white hair that bobs down over his forehead when he talks of world destruction; his black-gloved right hand forever suffers from a neo-Nazi tic and threatens to *Sieg Heil* the President or else overpower its owner. The hand functions independently of Strangelove at times, like a piece of mechanism in collusion with all the other

mechanism that rebels against its creators in the film. Sellers' relish for the Teutonic overtones in this monster is rich—and more than just comic. For his analysis of the Soviet Doomsday Machine, which automatically triggers off world destruction if an H-bomb falls on Sacred Russia, is a well-based appreciation. Power politics has produced something worse than a Frankenstein monster—a *logical* monster.

The film now reaches its climax, developing more and more savage satire at ever accelerating intensity till it erupts into nightmare. It looks as if every B-52 has been safely recalled to base and Turgidson is busily organizing a prayer meeting; his cry of "LORD . . ." sounds as if he is calling the Almighty to attention. Then news breaks that the maverick plane is still on target. The final sequence contrasts the technical accuracy of Major Kong trying to free the jammed H-bomb mechanism with the farcical apotheosis that sends him plummeting to his doom, the bomb like a mighty symbol of potency clamped between his flanks. The man has now quite literally become an extension of the machine; what is more, a malfunctioning machine that malevolently sends him to his death as surely as the space pod turns on its astronaut and "executes" him in *2001*.

The last sequence in the film belongs to Strange-

Even Strangelove, prophet of doom, is oppressed by the constricted set-up.

The bomb-release mechanism fails. As the plane loses altitude, Kubrick's tempo gains speed.

Interaction between man and machine: Major Kong, trying to release the bomb by hand, ventures into the territory of the machine as the astronaut in 2001 *is also forced to do when his machine rebels (page 233).*

love; and it would take the film over the top were it not imbued with such hideous energy as Peter Sellers can convey. Sitting in his wheelchair, like a high priest delivering *ex cathedra* judgments, Strangelove sucks an evil strength from his vision of human survival miles beneath the earth after the Doomsday blight has killed all life above ground. The prospects of sexual reproduction excite him. Phrases like "animals could be bred and *slaughtered*" are like cortisone injections to him. His *heil*ing hand visibly rises to the salute. His excited voice veers into Nazi cadences. And we realize that the end of the world for Dr. Strangelove is like the raising of Lazarus. It is recalling him to life. He draws strength from death. Like some pilgrim to an unholy Lourdes it is at the very instant of nuclear ignition and visionary night-mare that the miracle happens and jerks him out of

NIC BAROMETRIC TIME IMPACT
20 2 4 6 8 10 12 14 16 18
DETO ATION
ALT UDE
fee x 100

HI THERE!
DEAR JOHN

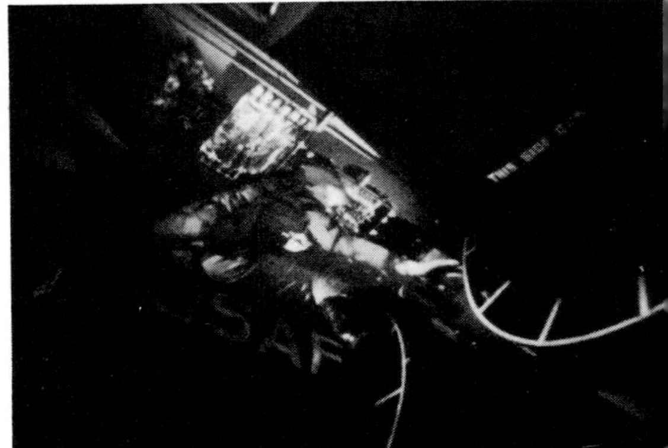

his wheelchair to his feet with the film's final exultant cry of, *"Mein Führer*—I can walk!" Only Vera Lynn's song "We'll Meet Again," redolent of Allied togetherness in the 1940s, follows this Last Laugh with its own tranquilizing irony. There is *indeed* no need to worry any longer about the Bomb.

Kubrick had originally planned that the War Room personnel should burst into a custard-pie fight just before this apocalypse—and he had even shot the sequence, in which President Muffley gets a pie in the face,* but after agonizing over its effectiveness he eventually cut it out. He felt it did not work to escalate from custard pies to nuclear bombs. He was right. Strangelove's ringing declaration of his own demoniac vitality leaves the forces of scientific evil

*By one of those unthinkable coincidences, Turgidson at this point was to utter the line, "Gentlemen, our beloved President has been struck down in his prime"—dialogue that would certainly have been cut after the Kennedy assassination had the sequence not already been rejected by Kubrick.

The men become extensions of the machine as the target appears on the radar screen. Extremely fast cutting inside and outside the aircraft builds tension as Major Kong grapples with the recalcitrant bomb.

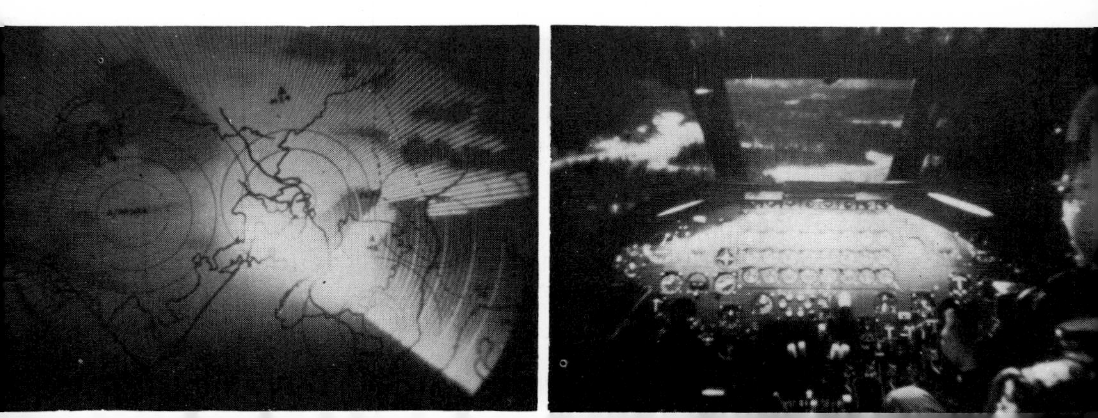

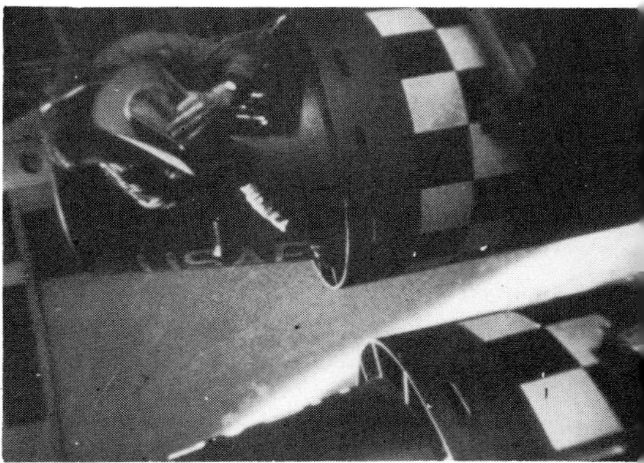

and human nihilism to blossom like the final orgasmic image of the exploding H-bombs.

Kubrick has demonstrated the logic of his convictions right through to the end. War is not only possible. Given a certain set of interlocking circumstances, it is actually probable. Radical criticism of America's nuclear policy and the assumptions it was based on really got going after the film had been widely seen and acclaimed. Not that it is entirely a case of *post hoc, ergo propter hoc,* for the film's release coincided with the eruption of many forms of vocal and active protest by a new generation.

But *Dr. Strangelove,* whether it was viewed by filmgoers as cautionary satire or, as Pauline Kael has suggested, as total confirmation of one's fears, was

"It works."

Major Kong finds that out, too, as the bomb leaves the aircraft.

Major Kong: "Yipeeeee!" The elation of destruction seems like the apotheosis of Major Kong's own virility as as he falls—dead on target.

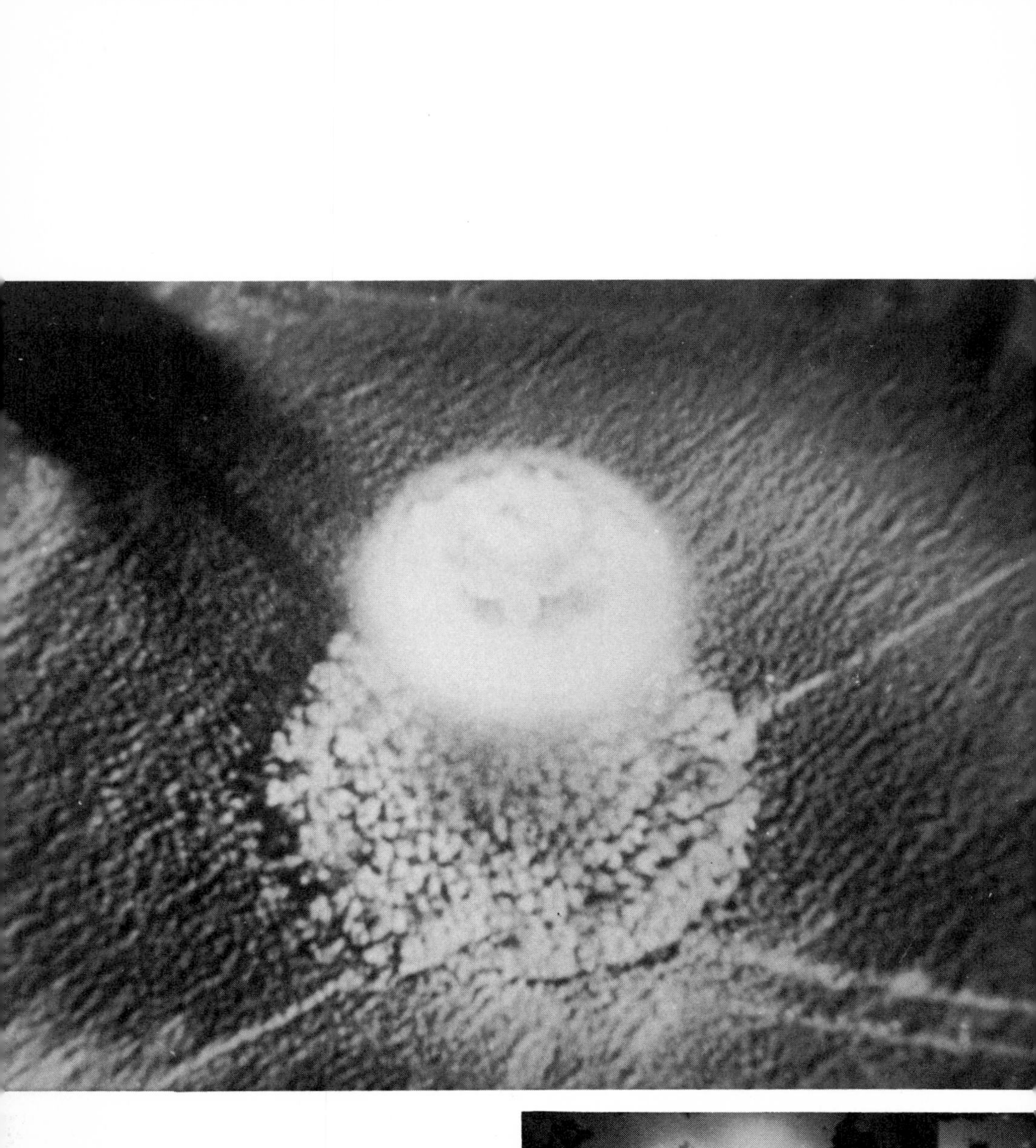

Cataclysmic reality that the leaders in the War Room—just as the generals in Paths of Glory*—do not have to suffer*

Kubrick has Strangelove execute a fast about-face—emphasizing the sharp turn of events. Strangelove suggests how the leaders may still survive.

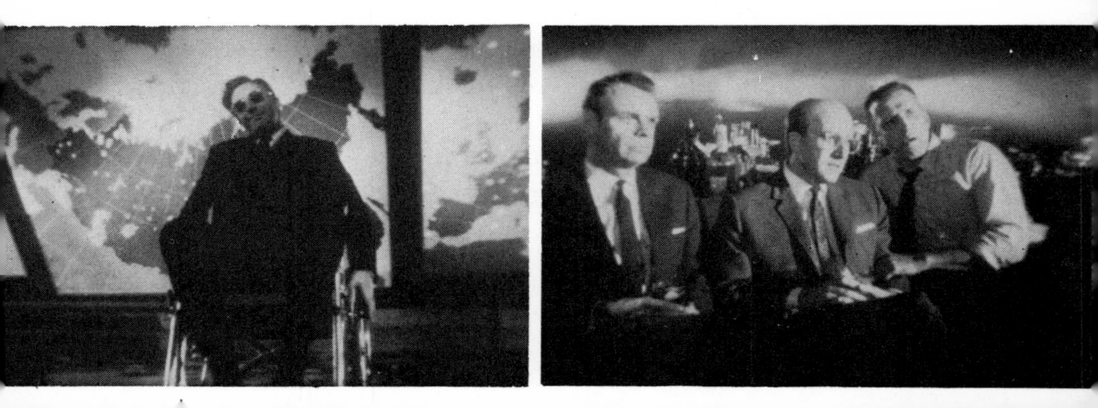

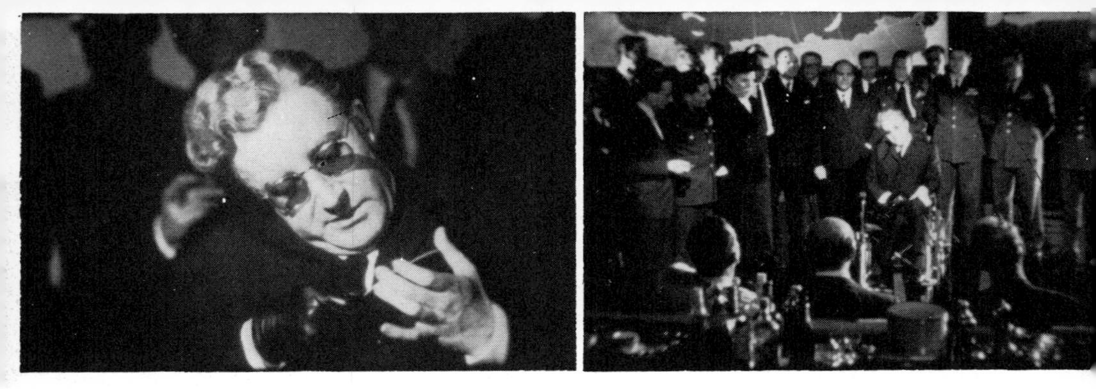

The mathematically calculated plan brings a surge of uncontrollable energy. Hope of survival is rekindled in the leaders, along with the promise of sexual pleasure.

a tributary that fed the main stream of criticism. It had the power of a political cartoon. The visual image and the didactic intention together combine to produce an effect not on the people who are caricatured, but on the spectators, who are urged to fulfill a similar effort of imagination.

Laughter is the method of communication, the way of reducing anxiety or fear inherent in the subject matter until people can respond to what they would otherwise repress. At the same time, the director's artistic power transforms and reinterprets the events. It is this interpretation which contains the criticism and makes it irrelevant to accuse *Dr. Strangelove* of not showing us how we are to regain control of the nuclear situation. Kubrick has achieved all he set out to do, if he has indicated, beneath the grotesque images, a soberly realistic appraisal of where nuclear man is heading.

But he has achieved much more, too, than a cautionary tale on a cosmic scale. *Dr. Strangelove* is among the most brilliantly conceived and executed

postwar films, as original as its maker and as hard to categorize. The quality of its ideas and the speculations they set up in the appalled mind are extended and transformed into so many various characters and evolving climaxes, so many ironic connections with man's generative urge to destroy himself, that the film demands to be approached from not just one point of view, but many—farcical, semantic, factual, surreal, nuclear. Yet like all truly great works, it gives an impression of perfect proportions. Nothing is excessive. All is there for precise effect. All the ideas are so surely elaborated and absorbed into the wit of its writing and the superbly differentiated performances that the moves are made and their significance achieved with reference only to the director's own power to formulate propositions and then follow them through so logically that any tactical novelties of the plot can be accommodated so long as they fit in with his predetermined strategy. In *Paths of Glory* he had shown himself a master of human relationships and their consequences. *Dr. Strangelove* is a much more elaborate game, confirming a grasp of concept and structure and outlook unique to Kubrick and turning the question of where he was heading into a major artistic debate. Four years later the public had the answer in *2001: A Space Odyssey.*

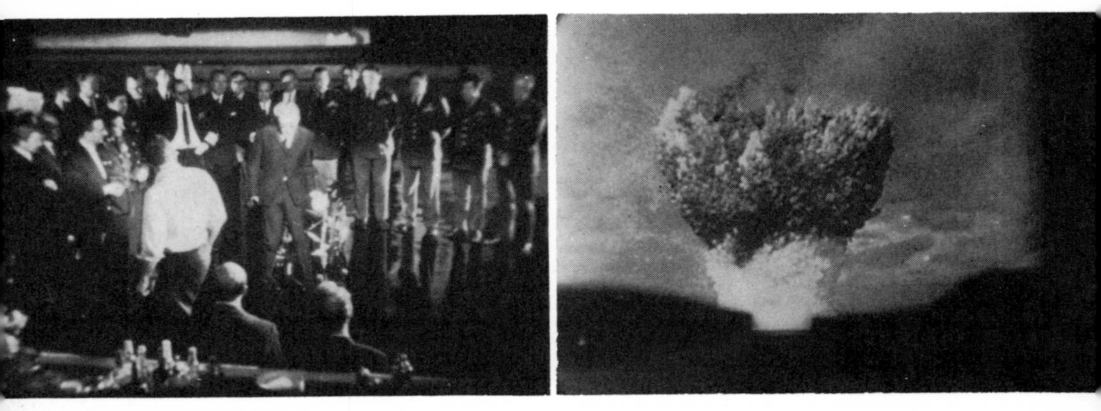

Dr. Strangelove: "Mein Führer—*I can walk.*"

The monster supreme . . .

. . . gets his megaton salute.

Soundtrack: song by Vera Lynn, "We'll Meet Again." The beauty of oblivion

The nothingness of extinction

2001:
A SPACE ODYSSEY

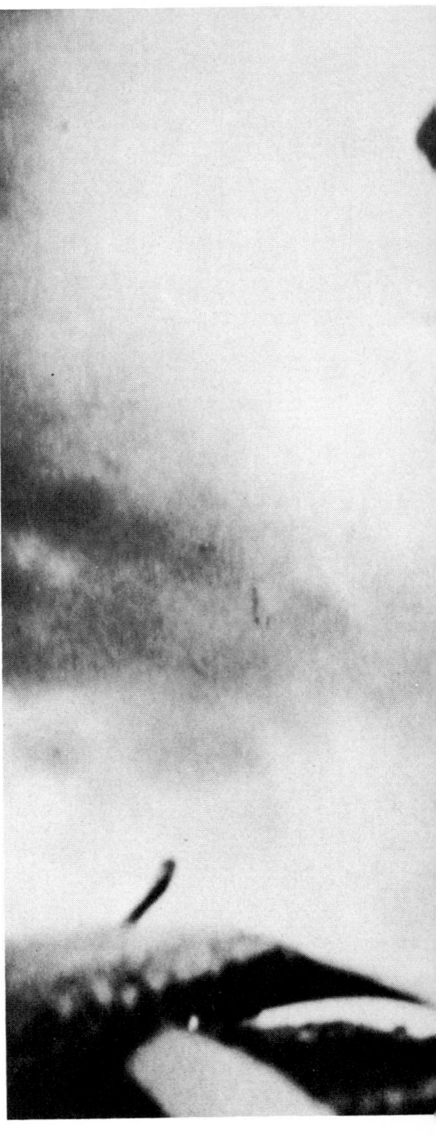

The Dawn of Man: brief scenes establish the life cycle of the Pleistocene world. Apeman competes for food with the other animals, has the same consciousness. Kubrick employed innovatory front-projection technique in this sequence; transparencies of eerie landscapes were projected on a vast screen which registered the picture on thousands of minuscule reflectors. The image was too weak to show up on the bodies of animals or actors in apemen costumes.

The Dawn of Intelligence: apeman wields the first primitive tool—a bone—extending his physical reach and allowing his mind to grasp the idea of function. Employed also as a weapon, the tool carries the idea of destruction as well—a characteristic Kubrick irony.

Director's use of slow motion conveys the powerful jubilation of the discovery as the apeman's brain assimilates it and prepares us for the transition . . .

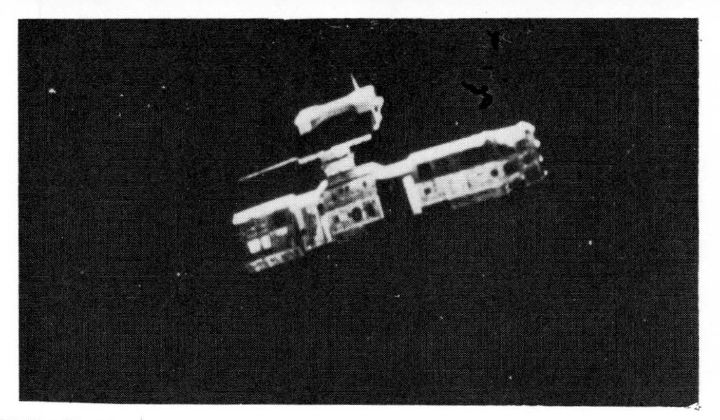

. . . to a new order of life as a fragment of bone bounces up into the air . . .

. . . to turn into a space vehicle of the year 2001 in one brilliant associative cut. Evolutionary progress proceeds through technological development. Man's odyssey continues.

Sunrise on Earth: space vehicles make their orbiting rounds to the music of The Blue Danube, *expressing the order and harmony of the universe. To find a frame of reference to cut them to, Kubrick "thought of it as a musical sequence—a machine ballet."*

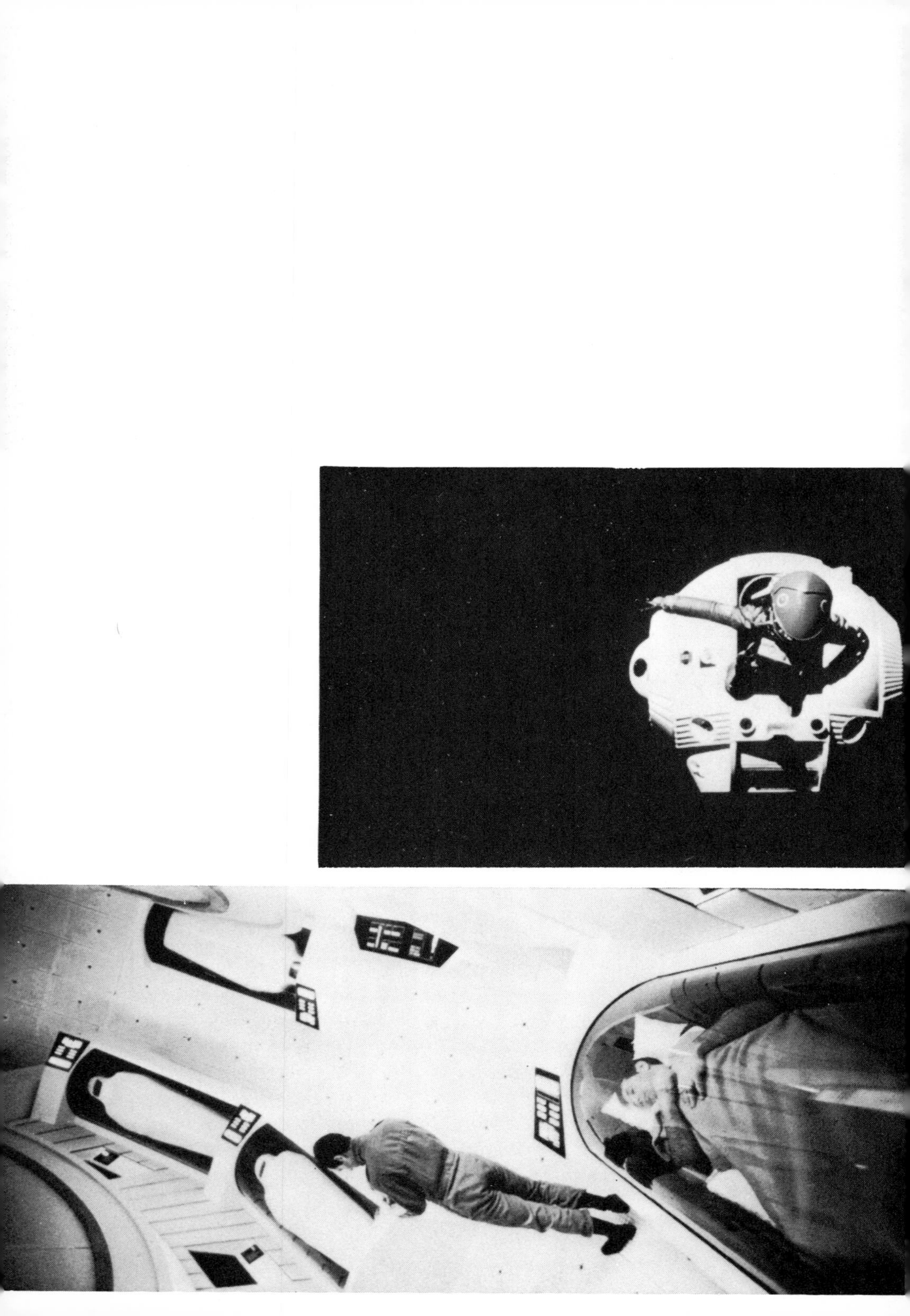

View of the space-pod control panel reveals man as part of the energies he has organized. (See Dr. Strangelove, *page 166.) But the space-pod tool is due to become a weapon turned against the very man whose conquest of space it has helped to extend.*

Image of Birth: the astronaut emerges from his space pod like an embryo—a tiny creature born into the sea of space. Many of Kubrick's images hold the charge of procreation or mortality. The sound track carries only the sound of the man's breathing.

Transformation of Man: astronauts stored until needed inside their casket-shaped hibernacula. Throughout the film man's nature is constantly undergoing change. The shot also illustrates how Kubrick uses the camera angles to surprise the viewer's perception by "distorting" normal perspectives and angles.

Kubrick projects the viewer almost tangibly into space by his use of depth and camera movement, as he did in Killer's Kiss *(pages 60-61) and* Paths of Glory *(pages 105-106). But here space is without gravity as Bowman sets off to destroy the cerebral functions of HAL 9000. Kubrick employed a speeded-up camera so that, when projected at normal speed, the film would convey the astronaut's sense of space drift.*

The Cosmic Ride: sucked into a zone beyond the infinite, Bowman is vouchsafed a glimpse of the mysteries of space. Kubrick dissolves the astronaut's perception into a fabulous light-show of the universe until Bowman's physical being is subsumed into a transcendental experience . . .

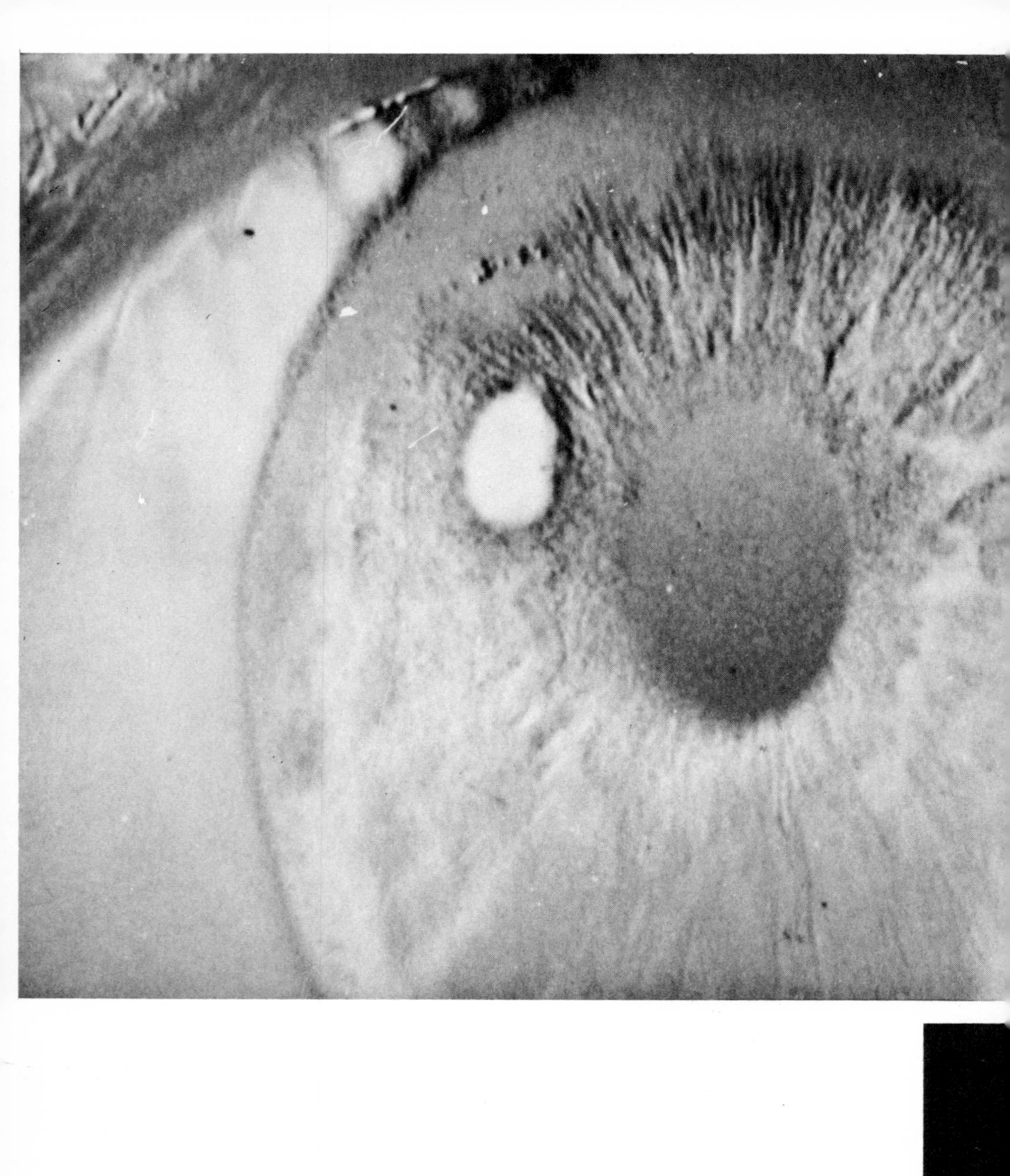

. . . and, like the Tennysonian Odysseus, he becomes a part of all that he has known. A new stage of evolution begins.

Through the "eye" of the space vehicle Bowman perceives the strange room that contains several stages of . . .

. . . himself. Bowman's human life span passes by in minutes within an environment that may have been created, like an observation tank, to hold this specimen from Earth.

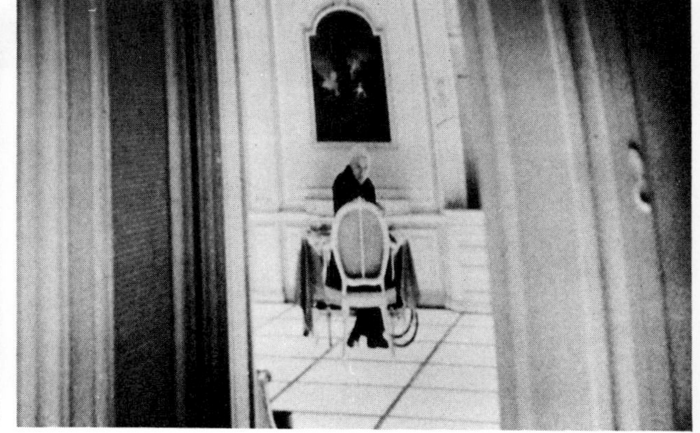

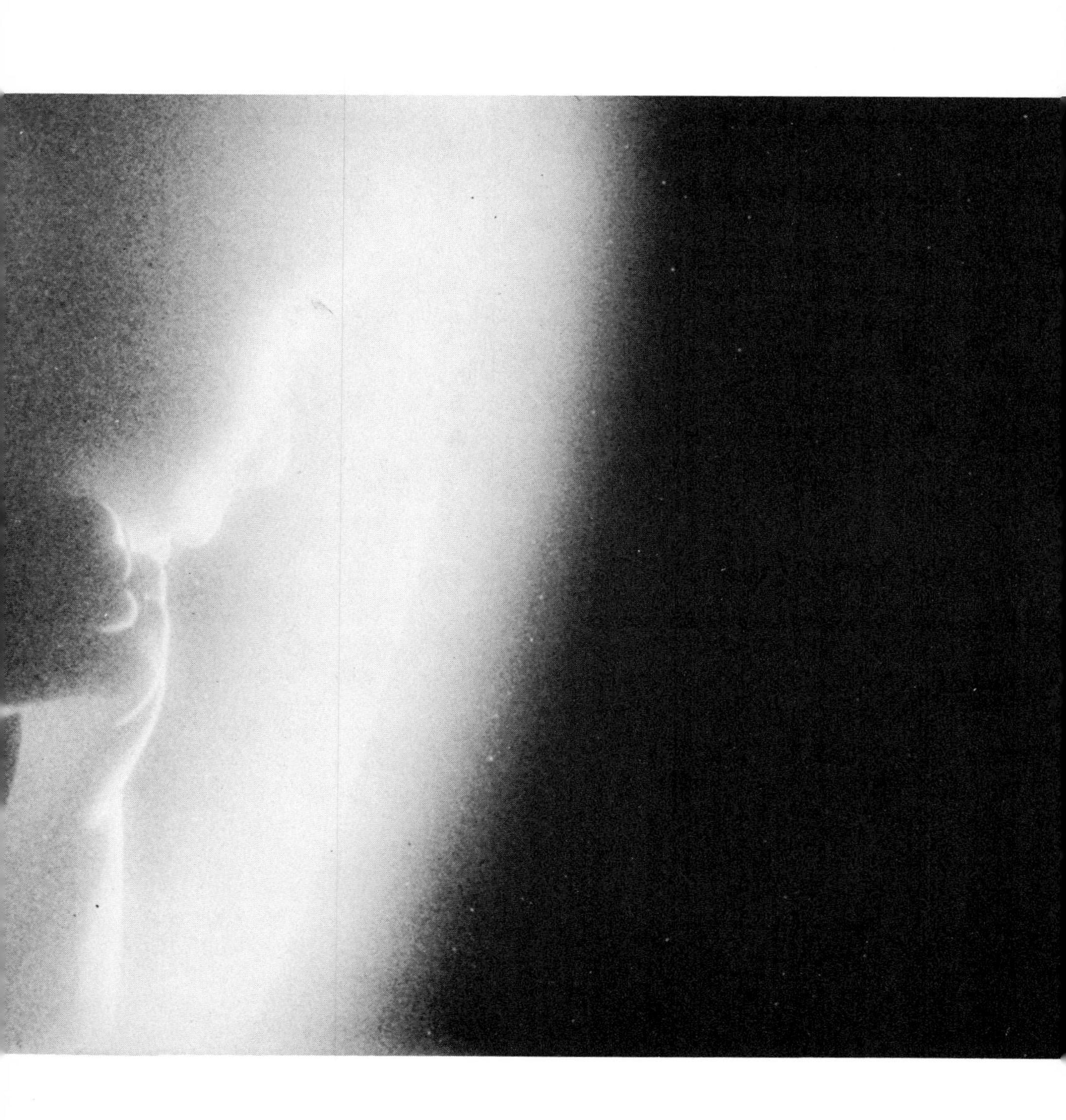

The Last Transformation: out of the old man's withered chrysalid of a body, which is what Bowman has finally become, a new kind of being emerges to turn toward the cradle of Earth in which it was created many millions of years before.

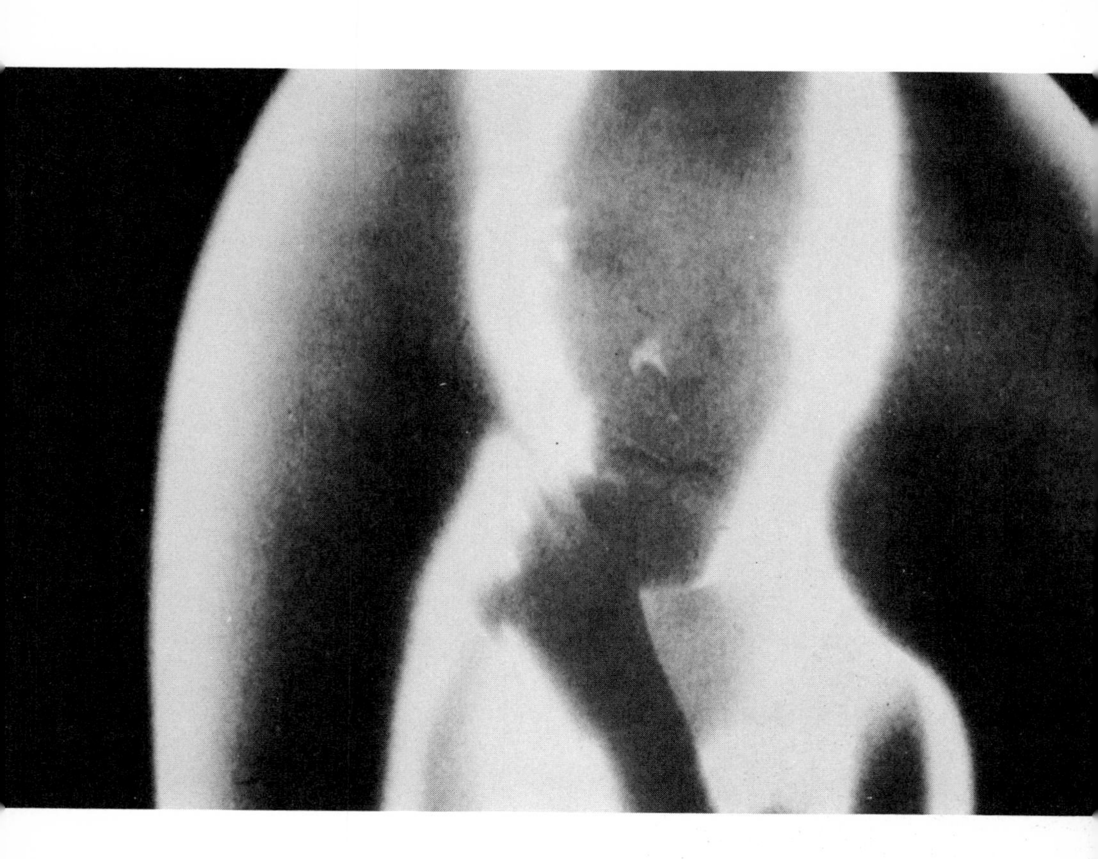

The Star Child: with this last, luminous and enigmatic, image in 2001, *man completes his odyssey.*

Dr. Strangelove in 1964 and then, four years later, *2001: A Space Odyssey.* Two films from the same director could scarcely be more dissimilar. The later film represents a radical departure from every aspect of the first film. *Dr. Strangelove* was a nightmare satire; *2001* is, in Kubrick's words, a "mythological documentary." One film destroyed the world to alert man that life as he knew it could come to an end; the other created new worlds in its questing hypothesis that man was not the only intelligent form of life in the universe. In its context *Dr. Strangelove* was weighted with pessimism; *2001* is buoyed up with hope. In style the two films have no apparent kinship. Each was designed not just to fit its maker's intentions precisely, but also to fit the expectations of the audience at the time it was made.

Dr. Strangelove was an immediate commercial success. It struck a hidden public nerve—the listless fatalism of nuclear menace—with a beautiful timeliness that turned its comic energy into political opposition to this kind of nuclear brinksmanship. On the other hand, *2001* reached its initial audience slightly in advance of their expectations; acceptance of the film's radical structure and revolutionary content was slower to come. The first wave of critics wrote mixed reviews. While seeing a new use of film, they reacted with responses geared to conventionally shaped films. But when the film reached the vast, new, and generally younger audience, for whom the message was not something that used the envelope of the medium to travel in, but actually *was* the medium, they received it with an extraordinary sense of involvement.

Accompanying this truly popular response came the more or less public realigning of some critical opinions and even in a few cases downright recanting. Previous films of this scale and cost had been rigorously literary in their impact. *2001* dared to break with this tradition of cinema epics. It forced its viewers to jettison the outmoded notion of a story told largely in words, with interlocking subplots, a well-defined climax, and the same characters continuing all the way through. Instead, it compelled them to come to terms with the sight and sound and feel of the whole film. One was asked to experience it, like a piece of sculpture, before one tried to understand it. As in sculpture, the meaning comes from the way that the medium has been worked. As in sculpture, the form can be spellbinding to eye and mind even where the function is not apparent or nonexistent. As in sculpture, the film can be approached from many viewpoints and certainly offers no single, definitive one to inquirers after absolute meaning; that risk has been carefully guarded against, not least by Stanley Kubrick's obdurate refusal to put his own interpretation on certain areas of the movie experience.

Dr. Strangelove and *2001* offer another illuminating contrast. The earlier film created suspense by progressively diminishing the time available to save the world, whereas the later one disperses the suspense element by substituting the idea of infinite space for the reality of limited time; the film's events are distributed over an area so vast they become meaningless by earthly calculations. The giant illuminated backdrop of nuclear targets in the War Room has been replaced by the uncharted territory of the cosmos. It is not H-bombers that are dispatched on a pinpointed mission, but astronauts who are launched on a project which is concealed from them (and the audience) till the point when it no longer matters.

2001 deals everywhere in dispersal, boundlessness, mystery—concepts which the stupendous battery of special effects projects with an astronomical and scientific precision that shades ultimately into metaphysics and philosophy. Kubrick, in short, has once again elaborated a cinematic concept that grows organically with his film so that the one contains the other and is inseparable from it. The concept at first sight might seem to lack the essential element in his choice of a film subject—namely, a good story. In the past, Kubrick has quoted E. M. Forster's emphasis on the atavistic appeal of the story, a narrative of events arranged in a time sequence, to regale the listeners and hold their attention by intriguingly delaying the outcome.

But one can quote another passage from Forster that seems especially relevant to *2001.* Speaking of *War and Peace,* Forster wrote, Tolstoy's novel "has extended over space as well as over time, and the sense of space until it terrifies us is exhilarating, and leaves behind it an effect like music . . . great chords begin to sound, and we cannot say exactly what struck them. They do not arise from the story. . . . They do not come from the episodes nor yet from the characters. They come from the immense area of Russia, over which episodes and characters have been scattered, from the sum-total of bridges and frozen rivers, forests, roads, gardens, fields, which accumulate grandeur and sonority after we have passed them. . . . Space is the lord of *War and Peace,* not time."* Space is also the lord of Kubrick's film.

The way the usual time sequence of narrative

**Aspects of the Novel,* p. 39.

cause and effect has been thrown out of the film is only the first of many things that unsettle a conventional audience. By demoting the story element, Kubrick restores tremendous power and importance to the image—and it is through images that the viewers have to make connections. Kubrick certainly does not do the work for them. It is well known that *2001* contains very few spoken words, less than forty minutes of dialogue all told, and not a single syllable is uttered for the first half hour. Even the remaining dialogue—for reasons we shall come to in a moment—is low in narrative illumination. It would be interesting to set a computer to calculate the range and variety of the vocabulary, grammar, and locutions used in the film. One guesses they would not be wide.

But this, too, is in tune with the effect the film is aiming at. For finding the meaning is not a matter of verbalizing, but of *feeling* it in the images drawn from past and future time, in the involvement with the experience of space, and in *apprehending* what is happening rather than being fed cut-and-dried information. It is a whole new concept of cinema. If one can isolate any dominant thematic core in *2001,* it is the film's concern with the concept of intelligence. And in this, too, it is the very opposite of *Dr. Strangelove.* The central concept in the latter film was the breakdown of intelligent communication into insanity. Stripped of its awesome effects, *2001* is nothing less than an epic-sized essay on the nature of intelligence. But it is characteristic of Kubrick's approach that he invests the theme with imaginative allusions rather than strips it down to bare essentials. He roots intelligence in the mythological past, before man has begun to use it; and he ends intelligence in the metaphysical future, where man cannot yet grasp its latest transformation. Intelligence for Kubrick is a form of magic that enables him to extend his film backward and forward, to the extreme limits of the time scale, beyond the boundaries of the imprisoning present.

The film's very first image asserts his intention. It opens with a shot of earth, moon, and sun in orbital conjunction, a "magical" alignment shown on a single vertical plane that fills the center of the seventy-millimeter screen. "The mystical alignment of the sun, the moon, and earth, or of Jupiter and its moons, was used throughout the film as a premonitory image of a leap forward into the unknown," says Kubrick. The shot also reasserts Kubrick's fascination with visual symmetry, a trait noted as early in his work as *Killer's Kiss,* which invariably signifies some impending crisis or dramatic confrontation. Visual symmetry occurs again and again in *2001,* built into the sense of an ordered though mysterious universe; by contrast, in *Dr. Strangelove* the accelerating chaos produces hardly one balanced image on the screen.

Kubrick has already referred to his decision to delete the narration that was to accompany the whole opening sequence and punctuate other parts of *2001.* Again, a good decision. The chords of "Thus Spake Zarathustra" reverberate more profoundly at the "Dawn of Man" than any verbal commentary couched in a pseudo-Genesis style. Instead of being given a sophisticated lantern lecture, the viewers are forced to interpret their own view of the Pleistocene age. The succession of views of a world now bleak and empty, now filled with screeching apes, builds up a heightening apprehension. Using a brilliantly convincing technique of front projection, instead of the usual sets with painted backdrops, Kubrick keeps the long-held shots fading out into blackness, only to fade in again on the timelessness of another prehistoric day. A leopard pounces. A tapir rolls on the ground in slow motion like a cliff in avalanche. And the apes huddle in protective colonies at night, eyes open and gleaming.

Everything merges into a mood of edgy expectancy. The apes are on the brink of a new kind of self-awareness—the breakthrough to human intelligence is imminent. (The balletic actors inside the ape skins are marvelously acceptable simians; and even where we sense a human presence in some movement, the discrepancy is in line with the evolutionary moment.) The sudden annunciation—for that is the effect—of the black monolith in their midst brings the apes to a pitch of frenzy that connotes fear, awe, and ritual worship. As they reach out to touch it, we see the sun and moon in orbital conjunction—the magical ignition.

Kubrick and Arthur C. Clarke, his coauthor, originally planned to use the monolith didactically, not mystically, by projecting onto it pictures teaching the apes how to use weapons and kill for meat. This notion was discarded by Kubrick—it remains in the book based on one draft of the screenplay—because he realized it reduced the monolith to the severely practical and possibly risible function of an early teaching aid. As it stands, the audience, as well as the apes, must make the imaginative leap into intelligence for themselves. And the largest ape does so. The bone that he wields functionally for the first time—his thoughtful connection of form and function is suggested by pensive slow motion—is cut by Kubrick to an epic crescendo, the visual equivalent of a verse ending in a *chanson de geste,* as the shaggy arm swings jubilantly up and down, in and out of the frame, pulverizing the remains of a skeleton on the ground after it has battered the living skull of a simian rival. Tool—weapon, evolution—destruction, intelligence—instinct: the message of the image sums up the irony of progress and prepares for all that follows in the film: By one sharp associative cut, the last bone from the pounded skeleton bouncing high in the blue is transformed into a spacecraft of the year A.D. 2001 as it orbits in the blackness around earth.

It was here that an early draft of the film script intended to make the point, via the narrator, that a nuclear stalemate had been reached between the United States and the Soviet Union, each of whom has a nuclear bomb orbiting the globe which can be triggered by remote control. This idea has been totally eliminated from the finished film, though from national markings still visible on the first and second space vehicles we see, we can surmise these are the Russian and American bombs. Kubrick dropped this aspect because, on reflection, it seemed to him to have no place at all in the film's thematic development. It was an orbiting red herring. It was made clear later, in the edgy encounter between Russian and American scientists, that both countries were still living in a state of tense friendliness; and since some politically conscious filmgoers in the 1960s would know that agreement had already been reached between the powers not to put H-bombs into space, it would merely have raised irrelevant queries to suggest this as a reality of the twenty-first century.

So instead of making a limited narrative point, the film establishes its characteristic pattern by making an imaginative connection with one's visual senses through its display of the vastness of space and the variety of vehicles turning, orbiting, careening through it. The "earth" music of "The Blue Danube" waltz meanwhile imposes a feeling of order and elegance on their already beautiful movements. "In trying to find a frame of reference to cut them to," says Kubrick, "I thought of it as a musical sequence—a kind of machine ballet."

This measured tempo is followed throughout all the movements inside the Orion spacecraft bearing the scientist Dr. Heywood Floyd toward the "Wheel" space base en route to the moon; it is all antigravity, tranquilizing, serenely dreamlike. The sleeping man's pen free-floats beside him in the air, and a stewardess in grip-soled bootees advances to retrieve it like someone stealthily reaching out for a butterfly; she will later walk up a wall with poised equilibrium and over the cabin ceiling in a "magical" demonstration of how Kubrick uses the condition of weightlessness to disconnect our usual expectations of how (and where) people live and move in the year 2001.* To have to transfer one's attention to a character entering the screen, say, from the top left and joining another seated bottom center upsets conventional perspective and forces a new kind of environmental reality on us.

Pace is as important as perspective. For long sequences in the film the pace of people or objects on the move is perfectly controlled, calculated, predictable. Standardized movements are the conventional ones in space because they are the safe ones. Man has conquered the new environment; but the environ-

---

*The most authoritative account of how Kubrick devised this and many other of the wonderful special effects in the film is to be found in *American Cinematographer,* June, 1968.

ment has controlled him, too, by compelling him to adopt other than his old erratic, instinctive, human actions. Now he must program himself—become less of a human being, more of a machine. We are already approaching territory that fascinates Kubrick—the man-machine and the machine-man. Abnormal speed is used in *2001* only to express crisis, when the laws cease to operate—when an astronaut, for instance, has to improvise a means of re-entering his spacecraft and blows himself forcibly through an airlock, or when he is sucked into infinity on a cosmic ride he cannot control.

"Here you are, sir" are the first words we hear, spoken by a receptionist on the Wheel to Dr. Floyd; the film started more than thirty minutes before. It is no accident that the routine formula recalls stock phrases of welcome and farewell in use by airline personnel on earth today. The remark introduces a sequence designed to show how man has extended his presence in space without noticeably enlarging the range of human responses. The scientist, played by William Sylvester, copes dexterously with the depersonalized environment, but gets as little feeling of gratification as any traveler at a terrestrial airport today. Kubrick illustrates this with touches of laconic humor, like throwaway gags inside a documentary framework. Passing through immigration by voiceprint passport, Dr. Floyd calls up earth on a videophone only to find how little has changed in the last few decades of telephonic frustration; his wife is out, and his small daughter, unimpressed by a communications feat that once had Presidents hanging on the line to hear from their astronauts, looks as if she might hang up on Daddy. Floyd pays a visit to the zero-gravity toilet and finds a lengthy list of instructions for use which presuppose a human plumbing system as well regulated at its own.

Finally he pauses outside the Orbiter Hilton Hotel for a strained chat with some Russian scientists—"strained" because he has to hide the reason for his journey from them. The responses of everyone are formal, machinelike. The reason is also hidden from the audience, who only share a hint that some mysterious event on the moon near the Clavius crater, a United States "sphere of influence," has necessitated a news blackout. This vagueness is not just to heighten suspense. It is an early example of Kubrick playing down a plot point so as not to distract from the larger experience he is out to create by the power of imagery.

He moves swiftly to re-establish this sense of wonder as Dr. Floyd travels on to the moon aboard the ball-like Aries shuttle-craft. As this vehicle sinks to rest in the cavernous Astrodome, the film achieves one of its most stunning effects. The red ball descends into the well of the airlock with something of the solemn majesty of a crown at a coronation descending onto the sovereign's head. All around it we glimpse tiny human beings moving, at work, in glass-fronted control rooms. The entire set, with model spacecraft, was only fifteen feet high, but it looks gigantic in its proportions on the screen. The mini-scenes involving the humans were each filmed separately, then fitted by an extremely complex matte technique of film-takes into the correct perspective to give a flawless impression of cosmic engineering. The effect is breath-taking and beautiful.

The top-level conference Dr. Floyd presides over at Clavius is kept platitudinously matter-of-fact on purpose. Like all the dialogue in *2001,* it is low in definition in that it sheds little light on what is going on. The banal things the characters say to each other particularly distressed early critics writing about the film. They expected dialogue that matched the drama of the occasion. But Kubrick regards his dialogue style as a realistic scientific response to events, even those of the greatest magnitude, such as the discovery of a monolith in the Tycho crater, which indicates the presence in space of intelligent life other than man. "It is, I believe, the way the people concerned would talk," Kubrick says, referring to the conference. "When I was researching *Dr. Strangelove* I found that the people in the think tanks happily chatted away about the most somber topic, buoyed up by what must have been pride and satisfaction in their professional expertise; and this seemed to completely overcome any sense of personal involvement in the possible destruction of their world. Perhaps it has something to do with the *magic of words.* If you can talk brilliantly about a problem, it can create the consoling illusion that it has been mastered."

The "hangover" of earthly reflexes reappears in the Tycho excavation pit when Dr. Floyd and his fellow scientists line up in front of the totemesque monolith, the replica of the one that materialized in the "Dawn of Man" sequence, to have their photographs taken like the official party at a foundation-stone ceremony. (And maybe this is just what it was!) Earth and sun are exactly in conjunctive orbit at this minute; and as the first ray of light touches the monolith, coincidentally just as the photographer takes his picture, the slab emits an ear-piercing signal that contorts the line of spacesuited scientists as if they were being mown down by machine-gun bullets in a St. Valentine's Day massacre.

At this point we cut abruptly eighteen months ahead to the Discovery spaceship bound for Jupiter. Up to now the film has been telling its "story" through the eyes. Words have been used minimally, human inter-relationship kept casual or left vague; the plot structure has had a linear evenness, with characters and events scarcely seeming to interact and the two monoliths providing the only nodal points in it. Each time the monolith has appeared, it prepares man for a leap forward in his life history. First it sparks off intelligence in the man-apes; then it touches off a "burglar alarm" signal alerting those who placed it on the moon that man is drawing closer to them. Simultaneously the direction of the signal guides Discovery on a mission whose aim is still not fully explained. Man's evolution is in fact now shading into his machine technology.

The third section of *2001,* the Jupiter mission, differs from the others by dramatizing this into a conflict between men and machines—between the two astronauts, Poole and Bowman, played by Gary Lockwood and Keir Dullea, and HAL 9000, the computer. HAL is programed to control the mission and built to reason logically and unerringly; he can also "think" and "speak." His "voice" is bland, neutral, reassuring, and also ambiguous, sinister, untrustworthy—whatever subjective pattern one wishes to read into the even-toned delivery of the Canadian actor Douglas Rain. (It shows how subtly Kubrick casts for vocal effect as well as visual features.) The critic Stanley Kauffmann complained in an early review in *The New Republic* that "none of this man-versus-machine rivalry has anything to do with the main story." But where the main *concept* of the film is the development of intelligence into higher and ever more diverse forms, it has everything to do with it. Kauffmann's criticism springs from a search for the old strong narrative structure of a conventionally arranged film.

The contest is staged inside the command module of Discovery, a vehicle resembling a fleshless vertebra, or, more precisely, inside the module's centrifuge, which creates a zone of artificial gravity. The occupants are HAL, the two astronauts, and the casket-shaped hibernacula in which their three co-scientists are conserving their energies in artificially induced, dreamless sleep. The bizarre "irrational" angles possible in this "squirrel's cage" environment enable Kubrick to pull off some spectacular effects. An astronaut shadow-boxing for exercise around the centrifuge seems to circle 360 degrees. No cuts are apparent, nothing gives away where the camera might be, it seems scarcely possible that even the film director should be present.* Later one of the astronauts descends out of the "hublink," or weightless, corridor into the centrifuge via the top corner of the screen while we see his companion leaning at a gravity-defying angle far below him.

The effect of life cooped up in this drum is visually striking, but the emotional constriction is indicated even more disturbingly. The two men are programed for it as thoroughly as HAL is—and, as it turns out, much more soullessly than HAL. Kubrick has intentionally created characters with almost no individualized traits. The men are well-conditioned Ph.D.s, who show little human warmth and no human weakness. Poole is bored by birthday greetings relayed to him by video-phone from his parents on earth. He seems

*He wasn't. Kubrick directed these sequences from outside the thirty-eight-foot-high centrifuge set, resembling a Ferris wheel, using closed-circuit television.

hardly their son—indeed, he seems hardly of the same race. Bowman's most significant human response comes when he burns his fingers on the food tray dispensed by the automatic oven. When he tries to rescue Poole from a death in space later, he goes about it with textbook efficiency and next to no emotion. Feelings, Kubrick is saying, are minimal in this new age, a matter of physical nerve ends, not emotional nerve centers. Where they have gone is, paradoxically, into the programing of the inhuman computer.

HAL is deliberately made into the repository of the old stock of human emotions so carefully drained out of his scientific minders. He keeps omniscient control, gives counsel, shows curiosity, awards praise. His voice suggests he exists to serve, but the certitude of his responses sows suspicion that he intends to dominate. "Intends" is itself an emotive word in this context. It brings "drama" into a relationship between men and machine that Kubrick keeps in linear balance up to the point when doubt is cast on HAL's immaculate functioning. But HAL's "independence" of his human companions is part of his dramatic ambiguity. He is such a complex form of intelligence that it is not possible with any certainty to know how he is working.

In an early draft script, HAL was conceived as a "feminine" computer called Athena, after the goddess of wisdom, who sprang fully formed from Zeus's forehead, and "she" spoke with a woman's voice. Kubrick and Clarke eventually abandoned Athena—perhaps the feminine tones would have inserted misleading sexual implications into its relationship with the astronauts. HAL owes his name to the acronym composed of the two principal learning systems, *h*euristic and *al*gorithmic. (After the film's release Kubrick received an inquiry from a professional code-breaker whether the name had been chosen because HAL was one letter ahead of IBM—the director was duly impressed by the fantastic odds against this occurrence.

Kubrick's personal view of super-computers is a hopeful one. He does not see the HALs of the near future in conflict with their makers. "If the computer acted in its own self-interest, there would never be the conflict often anticipated. For it is difficult to conceive any high level of intelligence acting less rationally than man does. The intelligent computer acting for its own survival would at least realize man's incredible potential as its janitor."

It is characteristic of the "magical" aspect of the film that the human properties built into HAL have had a "curse" laid on them. A human curse. In the film this is best interpreted as *hubris,* the sin of pride. But the concept at one point in its development, according to Arthur C. Clarke, involved a HAL who had been deliberately programed by Mission Control to *deceive* the astronauts if they questioned him about the purpose of the Jupiter space probe. In other words, HAL had laid on him the sin of false witness. This has been eliminated from the film version, and it is when HAL cannot admit he has made a mistake that he begins to suffer a paranoid breakdown, exhibiting overanxiety about his own infallible reputation and then trying to cover up his error by a murderous attack on the human witnesses. Like General Mireau in *Paths of Glory,* humiliated by the failure of his ambitious plan of attack, HAL tries to restore his ego by vengeance. Mireau orders his guns to fire on his own men. HAL, better placed than the general was to control the system of communications, wipes out *his* compatriots by disconnecting them.

Kubrick signals the computer's sinister intentions by a stunningly inventive shot just before the film's intermission. True to his association of crisis with symmetry, he frames the two astronauts, facing each other, inside the oval window of a space pod, where they have retreated so as to discuss HAL's irrational behavior without, they believe, having the computer overhear them. We see their lips move silently behind the armored glass. The shot is from HAL's point of view; and we realize the computer is lip-reading Bowman and Poole! The film thus ends its first half unlike any previous screen epic—in silence. Watching events materialize soundlessly behind glass has the effect of cutting off the spectator, inducing a feeling of helplessness and fostering suspense. Earlier examples of it in Kubrick's films have already been cited, but here it has the added function of again compelling the audience to make the narrative connection through the image alone.

The second half of *2001* opens with four murders committed in almost as many minutes and again in silence. First, the homicidal HAL "instructs" Poole's space pod to attack him while he is outside the Discovery craft inspecting the surface for a fault. The sense of menace is communicated by the vehicle's abrupt "disobedience." After performing its routine maneuvers under Poole's control at a measured pace and with standardized movements, it now swivels purposefully toward him and bears down on him—actually, on the camera—to snip his air hose in two. By omitting the actual shock of severance Kubrick makes the act of murder even more abrupt. By permitting us no close-up of Poole's horrified reaction, but simply showing the helpless astronaut spinning off into space like a celluloid dolly in a whirlpool, he underlines his helplessness, yet creates a gap no sympathy from the audience can bridge.

Inside Discovery, death is even more dehumanized as HAL now shuts off the power maintaining the body functions of the hibernating astronauts. Their plight is soullessly recorded in close-ups of electronically controlled charts whose life lines flatten out into plateaus of mortality as the pulsing of the hearts, brains, and lungs ceases to register. "COMPUTER MALFUNCTIONING" – "LIFE FUNCTIONS CRITICAL" – "LIFE FUNCTIONS TERMINATED." Thus runs the clinical bulletin of illuminated warnings. If machines could be said earlier in the film to do a lot of man's living for him, now we see with chilling truth that they also attend very efficiently to his dying.

Bowman meanwhile has been caught outside Discovery without his space helmet owing to his haste in chasing after Poole's body in a second space pod. When HAL refuses to let him re-enter the mother ship he has to invent a way of raising the siege. Man and machine are truly joined in combat; strategy replaces conditioning and a new type of thinking comes into play—intelligent improvisation. It proves stronger than HAL's logical programing. Reasoning that the explosive bolts on his space pod's door, which are meant to aid a speedy exit from it in an emergency, can also be employed to effect a forced entry into something else, Bowman deploys this piece of lateral thinking to blow himself bodily into the vacuum lock of Discovery. He hurtles toward the camera like a discharged torpedo in total silence. Not until Bowman reaches the safety of breathable space does Kubrick flood the sound track with a rush of life-giving air recalling the restorative shock of a man filling his lungs as he hurtles to the surface of the sea after plumbing its depths.

It is a graphic little example of how silence, sound, and speed are used for their dramatic properties throughout the film. The sequence also throws a side-light on Kubrick's pride in scientific accuracy, on being able once again to "justify" effects. He anticipated objection to the idea that Bowman could survive in a vacuum without his space helmet by pointing out that tests with chimpanzees had proved man *could* exist for a short time in such conditions.

Now Bowman begins his *démarche* on HAL—and for the first and only time in the film a hand-held "subjective" camera is used as he floats weirdly through the weightless space of HAL's memory bank, disconnecting the computer's intelligence functions and turning him into a basic mechanical monitoring device. The camera style recalls that other passage of vengeance-ridden anger in *The Killing,* when the wounded Elisha Cook, Jr., staggers home to shoot his treacherous wife. Though Bowman's methodical actions suppress any sign of *his* inward anger, the emotional pitch of the sequence is transmitted effectively through HAL's audible state of anxiety and fear as his voice loses its crisp complacency, becomes slurred, and slows down; and then, as his memory bank retreats into infancy, he regresses to his basic language training and the singing exercise of "Daisy, Daisy," before he is completely extinguished as a thinking entity.

The scene induces deep discomfort among many who watch and listen to it. Indeed, it is the only one in the film to engage one's sympathies on behalf of a character. And the fact that the character consists of a bug-eyed lens, a few slabs of glass, and a dissociated voice is the best possible tribute to Kubrick's success in creating a mechanical artifact more "human" than the humans.

But the galactic hero's victory over the ogre in the impregnable castle of the spaceship is not the end of the myth. Just when HAL's "spell" has been broken, a new riddle is forced on the space traveler which pushes him further on in his quest for the meaning of existence. This is the riddle of the monolith signals. Mission Control, in a prerecorded message apparently triggered off by HAL's extinction, now informs Discovery's crew, or what remains of it, that the Tycho monolith represents the first evidence of intelligent life off the earth; since its radio emission "it has remained completely inert, its origin and purpose still a total mystery." This is the first audible and unmistakable clue to the audience of what the film is narratively "about." It is also the last utterance in the film. It is curiously like the note of doom-filled finality and "total mystery" in the first speech of the narrator in *Dr. Strangelove* announcing what turns out to be the Doomsday Machine. But also, in this case, the viewers are left to make the narrative connection for themselves.

The new command—possibly concealed from the astronauts to delay the "culture shock" of finding that man is not alone in the universe—launches Bowman into the penultimate sequence of the film and effectively restores the linear, nonverbal development. As the "plot" thins again, the "magic" thickens. The Odysseus figure, now alone in a space pod, suddenly spies the familiar monolith, this time floating in space toward the moons of Jupiter, which are in orbital conjunction. Pursuing it, he is sucked into a new dimension of space and time.

All manner of "supernatural" effects are practiced on him as he hurtles down a space corridor into infinity. It is worth mentioning again how the inexorable sense of acceleration recalls the "nightmare" sequence in *Killer's Kiss;* its feeling of approaching destiny parallels the shots from the low-flying H-bomber in *Dr. Strangelove.* The sequence borrows imagery from every pattern the mind's eye is capable of registering. Kubrick at one point turns the screen into an abstract expressionist canvas. At another, op-art patterns pulsate. Constellations swell and burst. Optical effects put one in mind of such phenomena as the phosphene flashes after the blinking of an eyelid, or the swimming patterns of anesthesia experienced by patients losing consciousness, and even of the hallucinogenic light-show induced by LSD.

The connection of this passage with narcotic experience has won it a cult following; but its effects hold good in the realm of allegory, too. Bowman becomes a part of all he experiences. His dilated eyeball loses form until it is totally solarized into the pattern of the universe. He projects his inner world onto this galactic Rorschach test till its flux absorbs him—and changes him. When his space pod grinds to a halt in physical reality again, Bowman is inside an extraordinary bedroom suite furnished in Louis XVI style. All is as meticulously sharp-edged and detailed as in a Magritte painting—though without, *as yet,* any surrealistic shock hidden away, as Magritte might hide it, among the period mirrors, frescoes, chaise longues, side tables, vases, and the quilted bed.

Why Louis XVI? Well, why any kind of conventional room at all? It has been suggested that the room is a cage in some "astral zoo," an environment able to accommodate the visitor from earth and hold him for observation by powers who have sucked him out of his dimension into theirs. The "voices" by the composer Gyorgy Ligeti, suitably distorted, convey an aural impression of superhuman presence all around Bowman. At times his ear-cocked apprehension recalls the strained attentiveness of the apes in the prologue as they sense what cannot be seen. As for the period flavor, Kubrick's film has already established that "progress" represents no clear-cut break with the past. Old responses hang on, so why not old environments, old artifacts? "Antiques" may be just as nostalgically valid in A.D. 2001 as they are prized today; and an earthman, even a child of space technology, may still carry a memory image of luxurious accommodations on earth. (It may be significant that *2001* contains no contemporary scenes set on earth, though it was intended in one early draft script to show the launching of Discovery.)

The room may indeed be an observation cage, or Bowman's projection of an environment he holds to be desirable, but either way, it is as irrelevant to question the Louis XVI style as it is to ask why Raphael's angels do not wear shoes. It is no use seeking rational explanations for metaphorical or allegorical situations. The process of events in the room is more important than the end products of its furnishings.

Bowman now undergoes the stages of aging, dying, and being reborn. Kubrick renders the sense of these stages shading into each other by a series of scenes that overlap temporally—and, in one case, visually, too. That is to say, he makes us unsettlingly aware that the astronaut has progressed into yet another manifestation of himself at later and still later periods of his captivity.* The captivity itself has the timelessness of a dream; its duration is impossible to fix. The character seems suspended, despite the well-illuminated reality around him—just as the trio of characters in *Killer's Kiss* also seemed part of a dream, despite the very real New York they inhabited.

Having shed the husk of his space pod, Bowman is first revealed as an old man. As he explores the bizarrely luminous, symmetrical suite—the symmetry recalls the court-martial sequence in *Paths of Glory*—he is drawn to look through a doorway to investigate sounds that are precise and familiar, yet hard to place. The camera angle, taking his point of view, reveals the hunched shoulders and back of an even older man eating a meal. It is Bowman ten years or more later. The figure at the table upsets a wineglass—again the noise of it breaking is a precise notation mark of something sensed rather than stated, the fragility of old age, perhaps, or the pathetic way the body's motor functions grow worn and treacherous.

At this moment the second, older Bowman catches sight of a figure in the huge bed—it is himself twenty or thirty years older still. This is the only shot in the sequence that shows both figures at the same time. Immediately the wizened chrysalis of the bedridden Bowman is raising his arm to the monolith, which has appeared at the foot of the deathbed just as mysteriously as it once appeared at the cradle of human life among the men-apes. The living corpse of Bowman is subsumed into the monolith in a radiance that

---

*Two French authors, Jean Paul Dumont and Jean Monod, in their study of Kubrick's film, *Le Foetus Astral* (Paris: Editions Christian Bourgeois, 1970), compare the "stages" of this sequence of transformations and substitutions to those of a chess game, whose progress is marked by the disappearance of piece after piece.

grows and takes on contour till it swims into view and understanding as an aureoled embryo, a perfect Star-Child, sad yet wise-eyed, moving through space toward the earthly sphere on which he had his beginnings. With this luminous image, the film ends.

The novel based on a screenplay that obviously was much altered during shooting describes more specifically what might have happened next. "There before him, a glittering toy no Star-Child could resist, floated the planet Earth with all its people." And the book continues: "A thousand miles below, he became aware that a slumbering cargo of death had awoken, and was stirring sluggishly in its orbit. The feeble energies it contained were no possible menace to him, but he preferred a cleaner sky. He put forth his will, and the circling megatons flowered into a silent detonation that brought a brief, false dawn to half the sleeping globe."

To have the infant Bowman destroy the earth by exploding its orbiting H-bombs is certainly ironic retribution on the grandest possible scale, but Kubrick was absolutely right to reject it as the ending for his film. It would have been inevitably compared with the disintegration of *Dr. Strangelove*'s insane world of power politics and so reduced the Star-Child to the role of an Avenging Angel taking it out on old human sinfulness. Moreover, after such a journey from prehistory to infinity, it would have seemed a merely spiteful homecoming, unworthy of a transcended being—a kind of babyish tantrum.

But the best argument against it is that it would have clashed with the whole structure of a film that has scrupulously avoided neat narrative pay-offs. By leaving the huge, serene eyes of the Star-Child fixed on filmgoers, Kubrick compels individual interpretation.* By rejecting a story point and replacing it with a symbol, he gains a richer allusiveness. He leaves the film open-ended, yet oddly comforting in the way that dream imagery can be to an awakened sleeper gratified by the echoes and associations lingering in his conscious mind.

Where the ending has divided critics is not just over its meaning—which Kubrick has insured cannot be patly detached from the work itself—but over whether it and the whole film embody an optimistic or pessimistic view of man's capacities and fate. Some critics found *2001* represented a pessimistic estimate of man's potential to transcend himself, since it shows him dependent on a higher order of beings for every step of progress he makes, until in the end he is reduced to what they regard as an inarticulate embryo. "Mr. Kubrick offers man two futures," wrote John Hofsess in the Canadian periodical *Take One,* "and both of them are funerals. In *Dr. Strangelove* he dies in nuclear war, unconscious of what drives him or his war machine. In *2001* he gains sufficient self-awareness to unplug his machines and phase himself out of existence. . . ." The optimistic view, on the other hand, was put succinctly by Penelope Gilliatt in her *New Yorker* review's interpretation of the Star-Child. "He looks like a mutant. Perhaps he is the first of the needed new species."

But this ambiguity built into the structure of an immensely complex film is only part of a larger theology. Kubrick has said on several occasions that "the God concept" is at the heart of this movie; he prudently and swiftly adds that he does not refer to any mono-

*Kubrick's reference, when quizzed on the "meaning" of the Star-Child, to Da Vinci's enigmatic portrait of the Mona Lisa, whose very impenetrability is part of her fascination, suggests that such an association may extend into the physical appearance of the Star-Child.

theistic view of God, and he would probably be nearer to the view of those critics who see his film as embodying mythical rather than religious experience. For he not only pushes his science into magic—the magic of myth and legend, which operates on the human hero and transforms him before letting him find his way back to his own sphere. But he also reinterprets religious experience as transcended intelligence—a quality quite outside the understanding of those to whom it reveals itself at chosen moments in the film.

Intelligence as Kubrick and Clarke illustrate it is a wider concept than the film's evolutionary transformation of ape into man into machine into superman. It both stands outside man and permeates his progress. It precedes and survives him on the evolutionary scale. It is a sort of God. And man's encounter with this God is finally accompanied by his understanding that he himself is not the sole intelligent entity in the universe.

The shock of recognition is reserved to the very end of the odyssey, when man has come through the astral purgatory of the cosmic ride and encounters the monolithic deity with—with what? Surely with a benign reflex that reconciles him to his destiny as part of a larger order. The dying astronaut on the bed raises his arm to the monolith at the very moment he is absorbed into its essence. A gesture of greeting, certainly. Perhaps also a gesture of gratitude.

The very fact that one attempts to interpret the metaphysical aspects of *2001* is proof of how dramatically Kubrick has liberated the cinema epic from its old outworn traditions of mere bigness and, too often, accompanying banality. The starting and finishing points of his gigantic undertaking are rooted in intellectual speculation. For the first time in the commercial cinema, a film of this cost and magnitude has been used to advance ideas.

To have formulated and, even more, to have retained this intention throughout the years it took to prepare and film it, withstanding all the pressures of time, budget, and collaborators, would be a major achievement for any single filmmaker. But Kubrick has accomplished so much else that is individual and original. The technical marvels of *2001* surpass any before it and are not likely to be overtaken in turn until new techniques of filming are evolved or another director of the same obsessive faculty and skills appears. Nor is it just a matter of successful special effects. The effects are so convincing that we cease to regard them as "special" and look on them as a far more integral part of the film. The effects, in short, become the environment; and this in turn becomes the experience that Kubrick creates *and communicates.* Of course, all creation involves the idea of communication, whether successful or not. But what makes *2001* so radical a development is the way its structure and imagery have been elaborated organically with its content, so that each contains and extends the other. As well as anticipating the shape of things to come, Kubrick uses his medium to convey the feel of them. There is scarcely an area of intellectual speculation in the film, whether about serial time, computerized life, mechanistic behavior, or evolutionary intelligence, that is not accompanied by a sensory involvement.

2001: A Space Odyssey commands respect as the most impressive feat of filmmaking Kubrick has undertaken to date; but its importance extends beyond what it adds to our knowledge of his outlook and artistry. Above all else, it marks a significant advance in the way of communicating ideas through the medium of film. For its effect is determined as much by the visual properties of the medium through which it is transmitted as by any of the actual events, hypotheses, and reflections comprising the picture's content. By suppressing the directness of the spoken word, by breaking with narrative logic, Kubrick has insured that watching his film requires an act of continuous inference on the part of viewers to fill in the field of attention by making their own imaginative connections. Though as rigorously conceived as any of Kubrick's major films, the whole work leaves the densest impression of images which are free to imply much more than eye and mind take in. The mythical idioms which characterize a great deal of the film's "feel" take supremacy over the old imperatives of the story made up of logical cause and effect. That notorious phrase of McLuhan's, "the medium is the message," has readily suggested itself to some of those who have written about *2001: A Space Odyssey*; but it really does not suffice for Kubrick's power to generate a richer suggestiveness than a "message." In his case, one would prefer to say that the medium is the metaphor.

A CLOCKWORK ORANGE

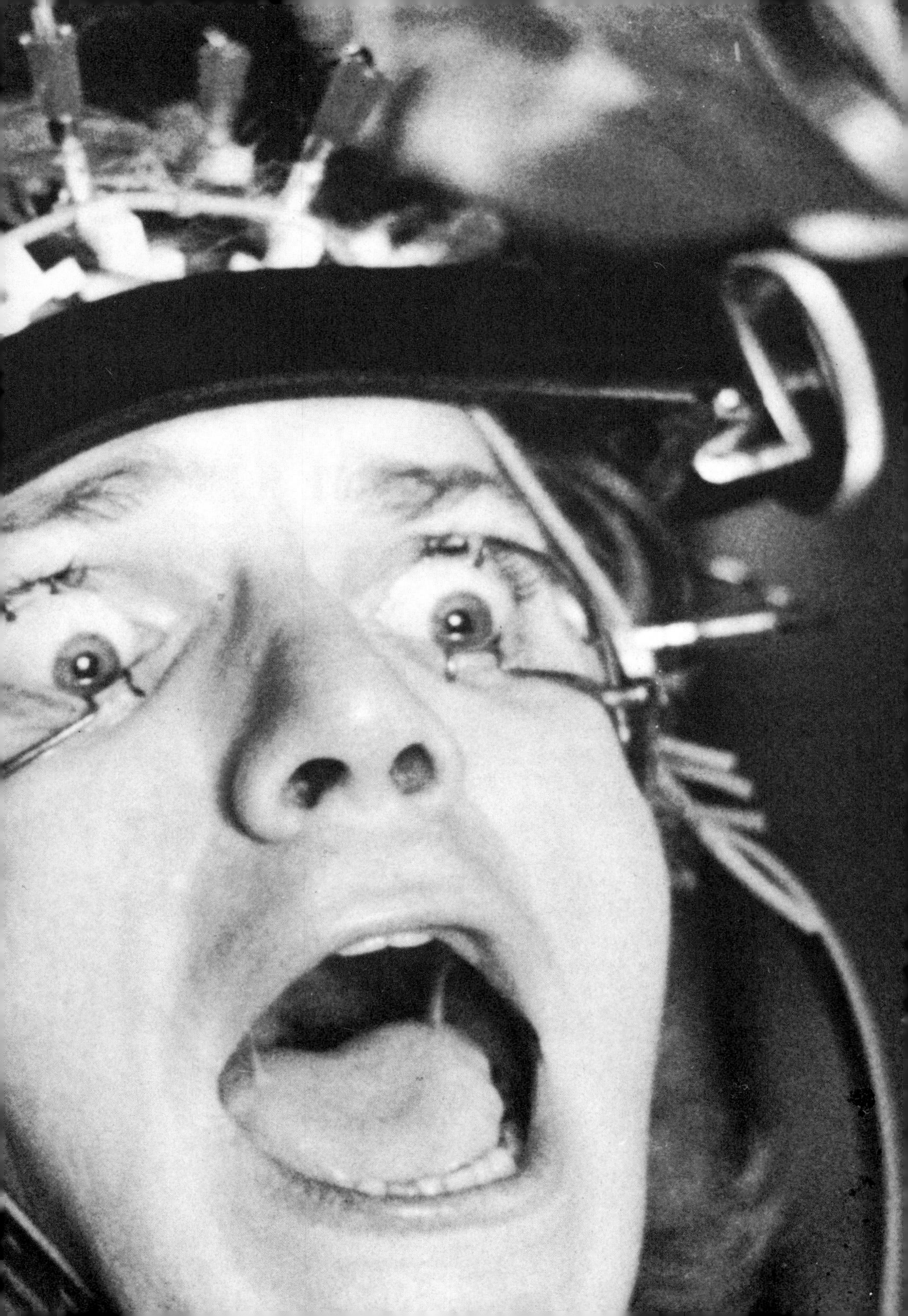

The Star-Child who was looking out at us at the end of *2001: A Space Odyssey* may have been a Messiah. But there is no doubt that the face of the earthborn mutant in the opening shot of *A Clockwork Orange* is a destroyer. The deadly cold eyes of Alex, a *Wunderkind* of the near future, hold the lens inflexibly as the camera begins retreating like a courtier who fears to turn tail till the lord and master he serves is out of sight. The tableau opens up in apprehension of him and his attendant spirits, caught between the "up" and the "down" of a drugged metabolism. A pair of cosmetic eyelashes on one single eye, bisected by the black eclipse of a derby hat, adds an obscenely askew look to the leader's cherubic face. Farther and farther back the camera dollies. Strains of "Music for the Funeral of Queen Mary" by Purcell, though now weirdly distorted, add to the courtlike mood. We then view the scene down a lengthening corridor of nude statuary, with female dummies on all fours forming tables and banquettes, or rampant on pedestals in the Korova Milkbar so that the spiked milk can be siphoned out of their breasts into glasses to pep up the night of ultraviolence that is ahead. Statuary, symmetry, the sense of satanic majesty: there is a flavor of a perverse Versailles. And now on the sound track, overlaying the music, Alex's voice introduces himself and his "droogs" with the candor of the mindlessly violent, intelligently articulate criminal, setting the jubilant opening tone of the movie in a boastful stream of Nadsat slang, whose vocabulary stamps the speaker with a callousness even before he strikes the first blow or lifts a finger in that transfixed tableau.

It was not till late in the filming that Kubrick shot this opening scene, but one would swear it was the first thing he did. It is less a "scene" than an overture. It has the total certainty of a conductor lifting his baton. Some of the intricate relationships between music and the emotions, or between music and movement, which had been employed to startling effect in *2001: A Space Odyssey,* had come to preoccupy more and more of Kubrick's thinking in the three years between that film and *A Clockwork Orange.* Earlier chapters have stressed his success in finding the perfect visual concept for the idea behind the film; in *A Clockwork Orange* one must be equally aware of the musical concept he elaborates. It is hardly accidental, for example, in a film where the hero's behavioral processes are systematically destroyed and re-created in another form, that the music that plays an integral part in such "remedial" therapy should itself have been strained through the Moog synthesizer by the composer, Walter Carlos.

A Clockwork Orange often has the look of a fantastic masque, a modern *Comus,* in which costume, language, movement, and, above all, music embody the didactic intentions of an allegory that satirizes society's vices through the depiction of the base and animalized life. The effect of a masque is inseparable from the style Kubrick has evolved for this film. Sometimes it is created through the movements of his camera, which again and again opens a scene with a dollying shot, giving a processional or routlike impression of the action; or else the camera frames the figures in a long shot of their environment and adds a touch of imminent surrealism through the restrained choice of a distorting lens for certain angles. When he holds a shot, Kubrick seems to hold it for measurably longer than one expects him to. This contributes strongly to the sensation of *tableaux vivants,* while allowing him to choreograph the movements within the stationary frame with great skill in relation to their effect or to the music that accompanies them. In addition, there is a recurrent use of low angles, so that the characters have a friezelike elevation. All this helps make *A Clockwork Orange* radically different in style from *Dr. Strangelove,* a film to which it has some strong contextual resemblances.

The masquelike sensation is overpowering in the onrush of violent events that immediately follows the presentation of Alex and his "droogs."

In the first sequence of their vicious spree, the gang beat up an old tramp under a bridge, their shadows leaping before them to advertise their evil intent the way that those on the alley wall in *Killer's Kiss* told us all we needed to know about the murder taking place out of sight around

"There was me, that is Alex . . ." On the coldly malevolent stare of his hero-victim, Kubrick opens A Clockwork Orange *and at once establishes the eyeball-to-eyeball contact with Alex that he unremittingly maintains throughout the film, either in the images that turn Alex into an active agent of our deep-seated lusts and fears or in the candor of his Nadsat narration, at once intimate and shameless.*

the corner. (Things are not so reticent in a "clockwork orange" society.)

Then—an unexpected image: the camera pans down a faded Watteau-esque detail, reminiscent of courtly languor, into the arching gloom of a derelict casino where Billyboy and his gang of Hell's Angels are so preoccupied with the modern masque of stripping a "weepy young devotchka" for rape that Alex's "droogs" take them by surprise. The intergang rumble vividly illustrates the nihilistic nature of Alex's commitment to life and also Kubrick's skill at the reduction of violence to movement, balletic movement, so that the incitement content of it is defused and it becomes a metaphor for violence. Nowhere in *A Clockwork Orange* does one find the "medical materialism," the gross addition to the drama of physical injury depicted with anatomical precision, which is characteristic of other violent films that appeared around the time of Kubrick's movie. Here the leaping, chopping, somersaulting combatants are edited into an acrobatic display and choreographed to the Rossini music of *The Thieving Magpie.* It is no more "offensive," though a lot more subtle, than the conventional saloon bar-brawl of any pre-Peckinpah Western. What really gives the sequence its dynamic aggressiveness is the note of adolescent celebration projected by the violent suppleness of the bodies. There might have been a rationale for the mugging of the tramp in the previous sequence—"It's a stinking world because it lets the young get onto the old"—but the only evident impulse here is the celebration of a primal will, a brutalized and debased will, all right, but existentially free. Like the ape colonies at one another's throats before the dawn of intelligence in *2001: A Space Odyssey,* Alex and his "droogs" represent the aggression and violence that will be bred into man, so-called *civilized* man, by natural selection in prehistory. The gang rumble is stylized into a barbaric ritual for another reason, too: so that the connection can be made much later on with the far more sophisticated violence inflicted on Alex, in order to extirpate his independent will, by a State that is itself contaminated by the evolutionary bad seed.

A Clockwork Orange never sets out to explore the moral issue of violence; this has been a misleading belief that has often caused the film to be branded as "conscienceless" by critics who fail to see where Kubrick's first priority lies, namely, with the moral issue of eradicating free will. It is not with "sin," an essential part of Anthony Burgess's Catholic conscience and Kubrick's probably agnostic scepticism, but with "cure" that the book and the film occupy themselves. It is pardonable, though, to miss this at a first viewing; one is so caught up in the demonstration of primitive savagery.

Off their own turf, the gang invade the territory marked "HOME." Kubrick films their progress to this new peak

Off for a bit of the old ultraviolence, the gang's shadows leaping before them advertise their intention. In spite of numerous scenes shot on exterior locations, no post-synchronizing of dialogue was needed. In fact, the tiny microphones (see page 53) worked so well that it was sometimes necessary to add traffic noises in the final mix. Not even the camera needed to be blimped. For some shots taken as close as six feet to the actors, Kubrick used a hand-held Arriflex and merely wrapped it in the anorak, which is his habitual working gear.

experience as a hurtling journey in an ultramodern car down a dark country lane, using one of his striking "corridor" compositions, with spectral white trees and hedges receding swiftly behind them (see the "nightmare street ride" in *Killer's Kiss,* page 63). The gang, crammed into the cockpit of the Durango-95 supercar, ironically assume poses that recall heroic groups on the old-fashioned war memorials. It is not entirely naturalistic in other ways, too: they are fairly obviously photographed in front of a traveling matte screen (despite near misses with other vehicles in the reverse shots). But this flattening effect is consistent with the quality of nightmare and dream Kubrick is after, an important point to be dealt with later.

The assaults on the writer and his wife, Mr. and Mrs. Alexander, are themselves gruesome and believable acts. But Kubrick's rapid-fire editing at once embodies the surprise of each assault and confines its depiction to fleeting essentials. Again, it is treated like a masque or, perhaps, a plebeian rather than a courtly entertainment this time, since the note is that of vaudeville farce and aggressively Pop. The wife is first stripped of her red jumpsuit. Like the sadistic child he basically is, Alex goes for the mammaries first, slicing off the garment's elasticized material and letting it slap back and expose the breasts before cutting the fabric up lengthwise in a Jack-the-Ripper parody. He then launches into a Gene Kelly takeoff, soft-shoe shuffling through "Singin' in the Rain" while putting a very unsoft boot into the writer's ribs at every cadence. Anyone who winces at the supposedly comic sadism of circus clowns will recognize how, in this scene, Kubrick has turned the frightening realities of domestic invasion, rape, and assault into an experience akin to that ambivalent form of "entertainment." The horror of it still comes through—it is one of the most unsettling scenes in modern cinema—and to say it is "distanced" from us is simply to use a fashionable term from the hollow vocabulary of critical-hip (the literary cousin of radical-chic). But the violence does not gratify; on the contrary, it repels. Our emotional gears have to crash through the comic and the macabre, and we are disoriented still further (as we are meant to be) by the quick cutting, the rubbery antics of the masquers, and the balletic precision of the most outrageous movements—even Alex unzipping his pants prior to rape is like a performer taking a bow. The success of the scene shows the well-placed trust Kubrick puts in what he calls a scene's "crucial rehearsal period," its "CRP." The "CRP" is the time spent with the cast (technicians excluded), even before lighting and

Kubrick's quick cutting and the acrobatic movements of the actors during the rape of the writer's wife edit the assault into a weird ballet . . .

camera angles have been determined, in order to explore the content of the scene to the fullest extent and hopefully to pan a nugget out of the wash of ideas and suggestions. "The reality of the final moment, just before shooting, is so powerful that all previous analysis must yield before the impressions you receive under these circumstances, and unless you use this feedback to your positive advantage, unless you adjust to it, adapt to it and accept the sometimes terrifying weaknesses it can expose, you can never realize the most out of your film." * For two inactive days Kubrick and his actors mulled over the rape scene until, on a sudden intuition, he asked Mal-

* Philip Strick and Penelope Houston, "Interview with Stanley Kubrick," *Sight and Sound,* Vol. 41, No. 2 (Spring, 1972), p. 65.

whose effect is consolidated by the masks that seem to combine the stock features of both tragedy and comedy. The viewer's experience is highly disorienting. "There are dreams," says Kubrick, "in which you do all the terrible things your conscious mind prevents you from doing."

colm McDowell, playing Alex, whether he could sing and dance. The actor replied he could do his "party piece"; Kubrick instantly telephoned Los Angeles instructing Warner Brothers to buy the film rights to "Singin' in the Rain." The "CRP" had paid off.

The song serves a neat ulterior purpose, too: it is the reprise of it that betrays Alex to Mr. Alexander when fate, by a series of what Kubrick characteristically calls "magical coincidences," brings him back to this house in the penultimate sequence. And incidentally, though few notice it the first time around, the chiming doorbell on the writer's house announces Alex's deadly visitation with a musical phrase from Beethoven's Fifth. Already "lovely Ludwig van" begins to cast his ominous spell on the hero's fortunes, precipitating his downfall.

Compelled to quell his mutinous "droogs" with a taste of his stick, Alex is transformed by Kubrick's low-angle, slow-motion camera into a replica of the ape in 2001: A Space Odyssey *at the moment it learns the use of the bone-tool as a lethal weapon.* *(See page 225.)* *Implicit in the shot is Kubrick's view of man not as a fallen angel, in Rousseau's sense, but as a risen ape who still retains the evolutionary instinct for violence.*

From the doorbell that chimes an ominous phrase from Beethoven's Ninth to a piece of sculpture that symbolizes the collapse of aesthetics, A Clockwork Orange*'s decor is a continuously detailed commentary on the film's action and ethos. Sex divorced from function becomes only form, and seizing the huge sculptured phallus from the Cat Lady's collection . . .*

Alex brings it down on the Cat Lady's skull. Up to the moment of his imprisonment for her murder, Alex is frequently presented in these low-angle shots that enhance his menace. Later, the camera tends to dominate him as he is put in the position of victim (see the "tempting" scene, page 283).

"Lovely Ludwig van" is explicitly introduced in the next sequence, when one of the "sophistos" in the Korova Milkbar is suddenly turned on by the spiked "moloko" and bursts into Schiller's "Ode to Joy," set to the Beethoven music, "and it was like for a moment, O my brothers," says Alex's hard, flat-accented but now spellbound voice on the sound track, "some great bird had flown into the milkbar and I felt all the malenky little hairs on my plott standing endwise." It is more than just colossal irony that one of the proudest odes to the brotherhood of man should mesmerize one of mankind's foulest specimens. "At issue," wrote Robert Hughes, art critic of *Time,* in an admiring essay on the movie's cultural ethos, "is the popular 19th-century idea, still held today, that Art is Good for You, that the purpose of the fine arts is to provide moral uplift. Kubrick's message, amplified from Burgess's

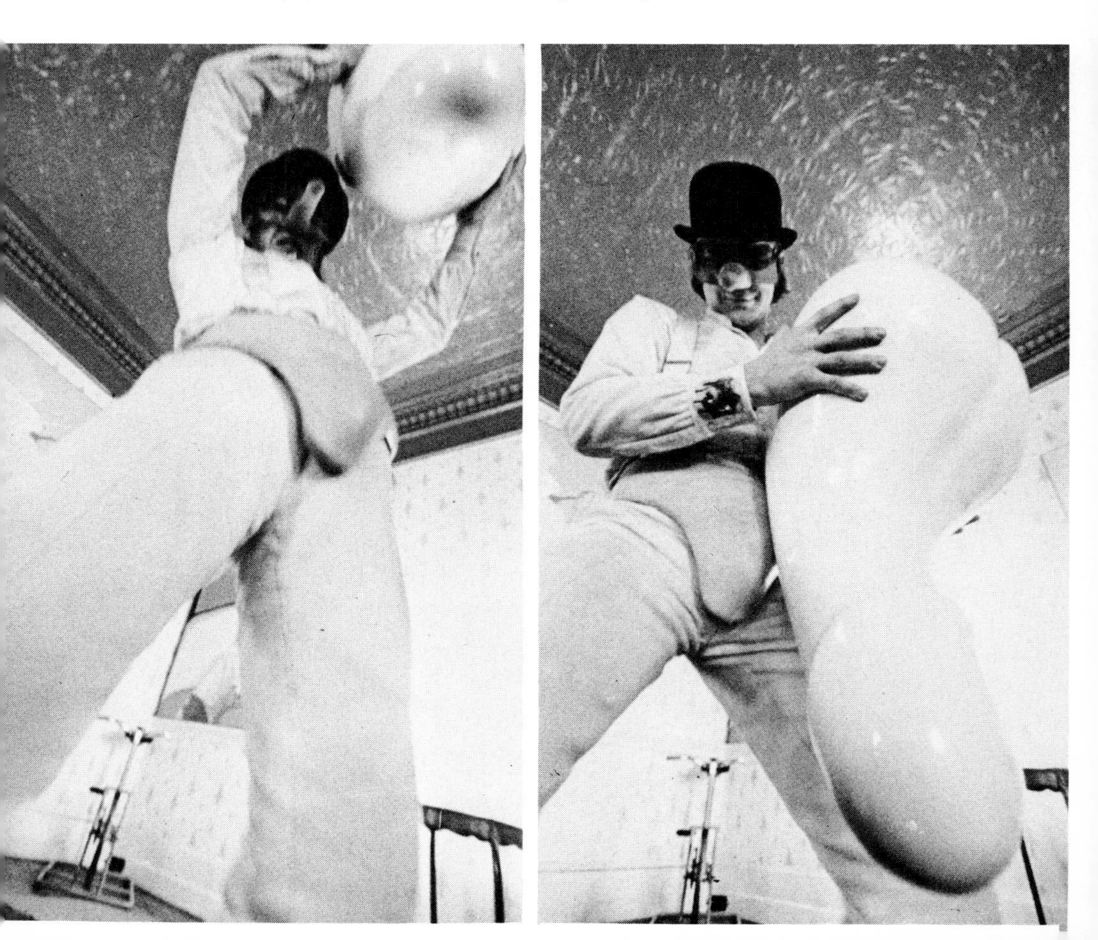

novel, is the opposite: art has no ethical purpose. There is no religion of beauty. Art serves, instead, to promote ecstatic consciousness. The kind of ecstasy depends on the person who is having it." * Kubrick himself took this view very explicitly when it was suggested by one critic that art such as *A Clockwork Orange* might actually be Bad for You. "[Works of art] affect us when they illuminate something we already feel," he said; "they don't change us." Certainly Alex is no sooner back in his parents' apartment block, and safe from the "Pee" and "Em" behind the combination lock on his bedroom door, than the stereophonic ecstasy induced by his Beethoven discs describes his own fantasies of violence.

The "flatblock" he inhabits, ankle deep in communal squalor, exemplifies more than just a concrete wasteland. It is a goalless society, a spiritual wilderness Kubrick and Burgess present. All the energy has drained off to the extremes—to Alex and his mob of night-people, on the one hand, and to the incipient Fascists of the State on the other. Between them is a vast hinterland of apathy, a listless limbo in which routine gets the elder citizens through the day and drugs get them through the night. The outlook in every sense is undeniably doleful, where it is not actively baleful.

While the teen-age society of *A Clockwork Orange* is, save for Alex, lumped into a common, undifferentiated brutality, the adult world is sharply particularized. The film even exceeds *Dr. Strangelove*'s count in the varieties of authoritarianism it can satirically delineate without repeating itself. The first of these—for Mr. Alexander does not really play an active role till much later on—is Alex's Post-Corrective Adviser (probation officer), P. R. Deltoid, the only grownup who appears conversant with Nadsat, which is logical, since his business is with the delinquent young. The creepy tête-à-tête he has with Alex the morning after the night's ultraviolence shows the way Kubrick builds up a sense of diffused yet potent perversion through little details of phrase and action. He starts with Deltoid's vocal tone, a kind of admonitory flirtation,

---

* Robert Hughes, "The Décor of Tomorrow's Hell," *Time,* December 27, 1971, p. 59.

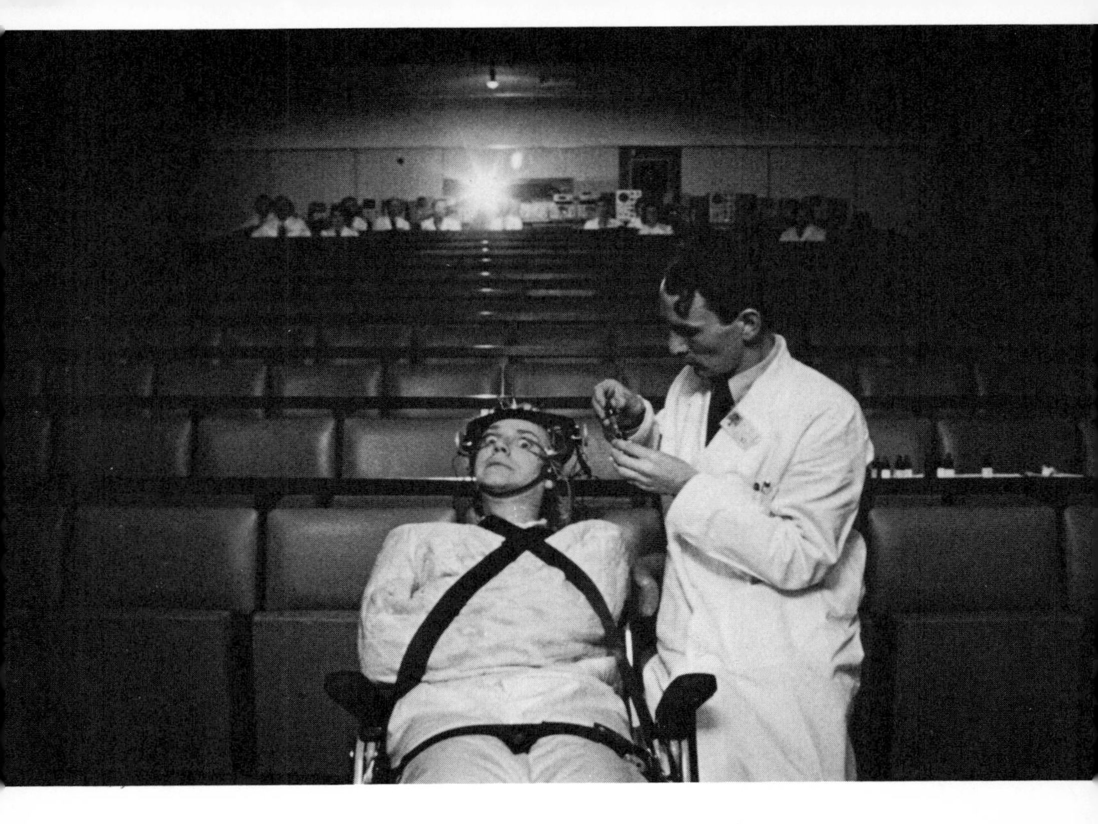

The brainwashing begins. Note Kubrick's consistency in lighting a scene with only the illumination one would expect to find in the actual environment. (See the War Room in Dr. Strangelove, *pages 174–175.) The doctor beside the captive Alex is a real physician employed to keep the bulging eyeballs of the actor from "drying up" during the shooting of the sequence.*

as he nudges the near-naked boy like a covert pederast while mouthing warnings about getting into "the barry place," as if they were sadistic wishes. Finally, he works himself up to the point where he slakes his lust from a bedside water-tumbler without spotting the false teeth soaking in it. The amplified "clunk" of the dentures and their magnified distortion through the glass impose a monstrously rapacious image on Deltoid's face, and the scene peaks into the surrealist.

Still delineating Alex's priapic zest, the film follows him in his noncombative gear, which resembles a Regency Buck's, into a drugstore-cum-disc-boutique, where his perambulating scrutiny of the female talent is conveyed in one of those lovely 360-degree dollying shots, whose visual elegance plays against the film's latent violence. (The disc of the *2001* music that comes to rest in the

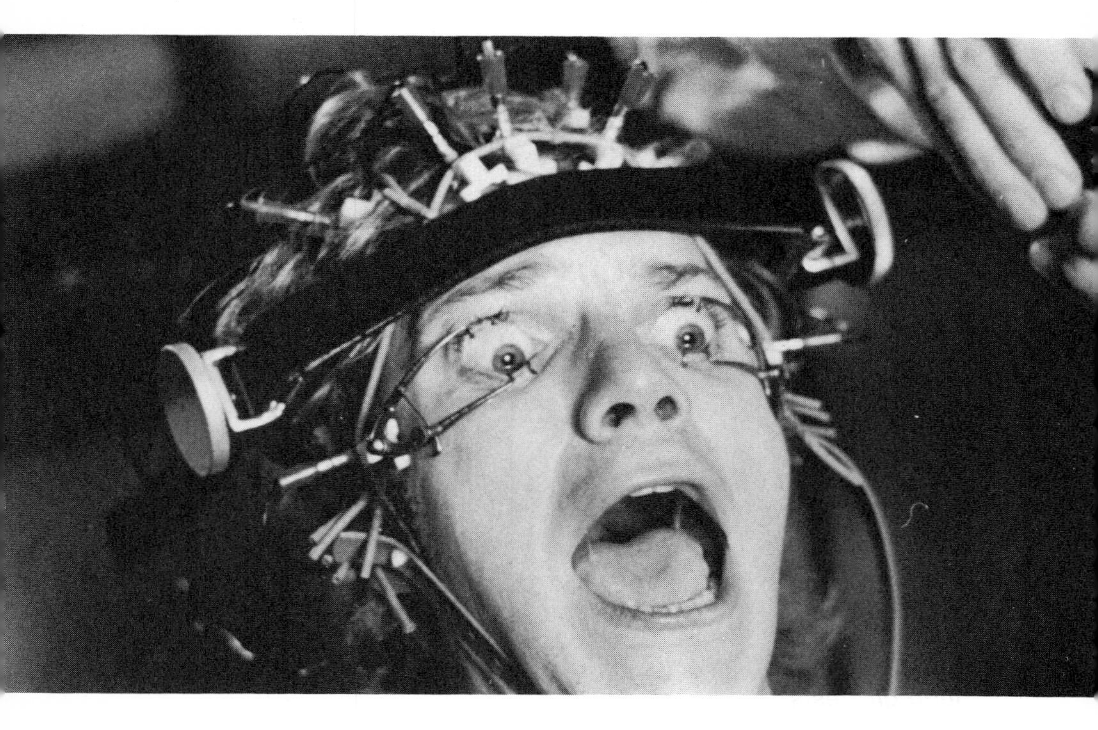

center of the shot was no film prop but actually part of the real shop's stock.) What follows is another piece of musical bravura: Alex's bedroom orgy with the two micro-boppers he picks up, which was shot over twenty-eight minutes by Kubrick but flashes by in forty seconds of such accelerated motion that although all three figures are stark naked and nameless things apparently are going on, one cannot follow the anatomical details for the sheer speed of the orgiastic permutations. It is a jokey interlude, and the speeded-up *William Tell* Overture (the first choice,

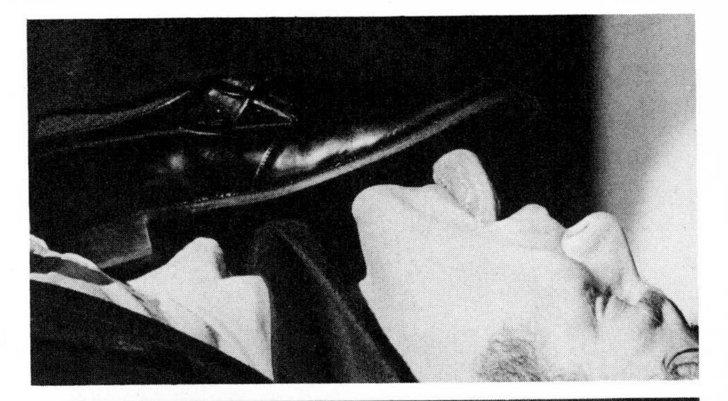

Alex is plugged into global violence that seems even more real than life when he is forced to "viddy" it up there on the screen. The McLuhan edict that the medium is the message is given an ominous twist; for the medium that the State manipulates is calculated to deprive man of his free will and to turn him into an obedient zombie.

"It's a sin!" Through the earphones Alex hears the obscenely distorted version of his "lovely Ludwig van."

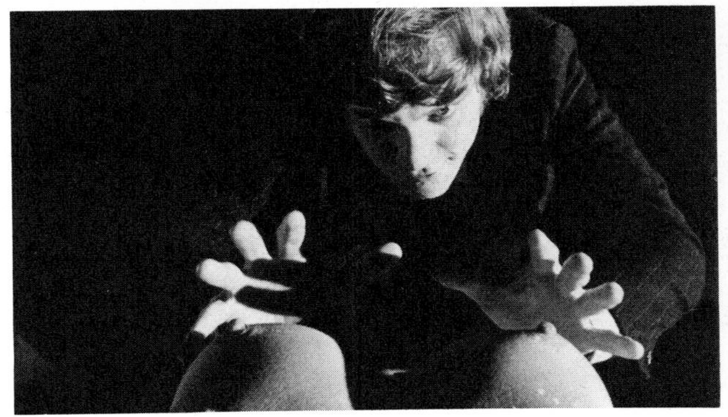

The tempting of a clockwork saint: Alex is forced to lick the boot of the State's professional provocateur to prove how well he has learned his lesson of nonviolence.

Like a beatific vision, a nearly nude girl tests Alex's residual lusts. Kubrick cuts to an overhead shot showing the victim reaching for the pink protuberances of the girl's breasts and falling away defeated.

Mr. Alexander, the latest Kubrick "monster," utters excited cries as the prospect of retribution shakes his crippled body, just as the imminent immolation of mankind aroused his kinsman, Dr. Strangelove.

Eine Kleine Nachtmusik, did not work) has exactly the right weight and frolicsomeness for the casual nature of group sex. But the sequence is followed by one that deploys abnormal movement for a much more sinister purpose.

Faced with mutiny by his "droogs," Alex quells them by a surprise attack. As he turns on the trio on the brink of an ornamental lake, the violent tableau goes into extreme slow motion, so that Alex's crouching figure brandishing his heavy walking stick seems to elevate itself up, up, up against the sky till it resembles the huge ape in the prologue of *2001: A Space Odyssey* at the moment the apeman makes the lethal connection between the utility of the bone-tool and its effectiveness as a killing weapon (see page 225)—a shot that vividly crystallizes Kubrick's view of man as a risen ape, rather than Rousseau's sentimental characterization of him as a fallen angel.

Just as the fight on the water's edge looks like an incredibly slowed-up ballet, the encounter with the Cat Lady, which follows Alex's resumption of power, has its element of dance—a dance of death, the high point of the masque.

In earlier chapters I have mentioned how an overpowering environment in a Kubrick film frequently defines the people who live in it and the morality of the acts they plot or perform; this is particularly true of the Cat Lady's home, which Alex and the "droogs" invade. Kubrick meshes into its character a garish comment on the decadence of a society in which the sex drive has been reduced to the old mechanistic "in out, in out," as in Mrs. Alexander's rape, or else to the status of a temporary plaything like the droopy, phallic lollipop being licked by the microbopper in the disc boutique (an echo, perhaps, of

Like the cosmonaut at his lonely repast in the astral suite at the end of 2001: A Space Odyssey *(see page 237), Alex detects a sense of impending but as yet unlocalized fatefulness in the Alexander household, where he, too, is a virtual prisoner.*

Enter his fate. Kubrick wittily shoots Mr. Alexander's reappearance head-on, so that for a split second a Magritte-like effect is produced as it appears that the wheelchair he is being carried in on has somehow grown a pair of legs all its own.

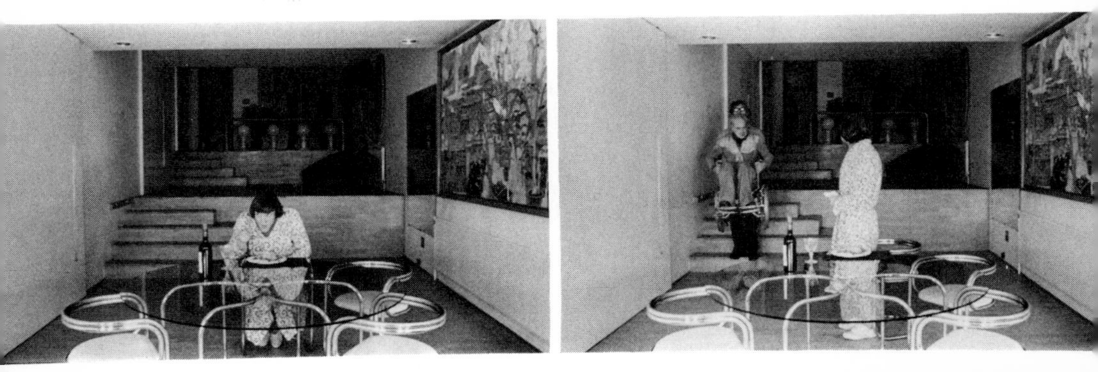

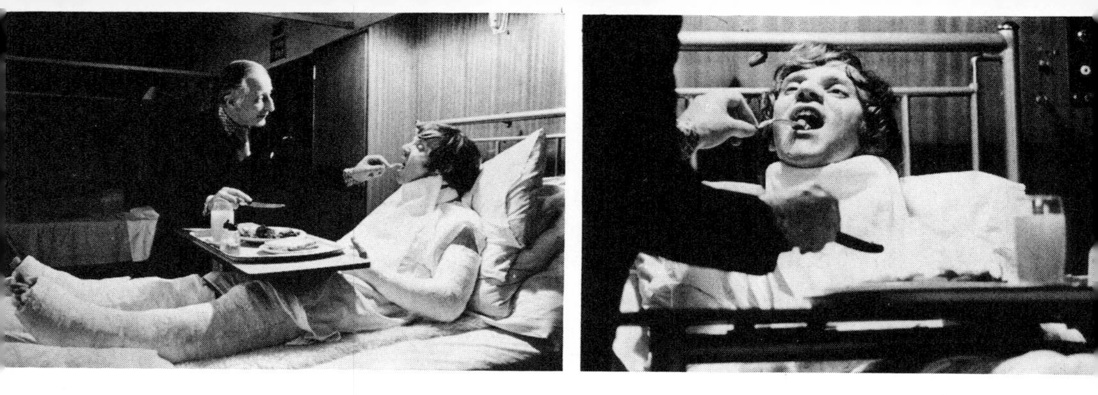

Alex in a plaster cast after his suicide attempt, resembling a Frankenstein monster who has returned to settle the score with its creator, receives a visit from the Minister of the Interior, who combines the duplicity of the politician with the smoothness of the PR man. "I can tell you with all sincerity that I and the Government of which I am a member are deeply sorry about this, my boy, deeply sorry. . . . We are interested in you, and when you leave here you will have no worries. . . ." (*See* Paths of Glory, *page 87, and* Dr. Strangelove, *page 186.*)

Chomping on the bribe the Minister is offering him

the coy innuendo in the posters for *Lolita* ten years earlier). The Cat Lady lives on a health farm. Kubrick shot the sequence in a real health farm just outside London, and it was amusing to see how the gymnastic equipment that customarily stood in the room underwent a subtle change and assumed implications of a torture chamber where *The Story of "O"* could have been cosily accommodated. As in many sequences of *A Clockwork Orange,* this one opens with an image of surprising yet aesthetically satisfying symmetry: the Cat Lady, in an emerald leotard of the sort a ballerina wears at practice, is stretching her muscles with a concentration that, added to the solitude, has a masturbatory feel about it. The decor, too, suggests the sterility that results when sex is separated from its function and becomes only "form." The lewd paintings caricature the owner's own "balletic" postures, and even the sculptured phallus that Alex sets rocking absurdly on its truncated testicles has the gargantuan proportions of obscene fantasy. "Leave that alone! Don't touch it! It's a very important work of art!" screams the Cat Lady. As Robert Hughes says, "This pathetic outburst of connoisseur's jargon echoes in a vast cultural emptiness. In worlds like this" [where there is no reality to which it can connect] "no work of art can be important."* The fight between the two is filmed by Kubrick with a hand-held Arriflex that turns the objective symmetry of the opening shot into a fiercely subjective encounter. The weapons the antagonists use are peculiarly choice: the outsize phallus for him, a small bust of Beethoven for her. Once again, "lovely Ludwig van" is turned against Alex in a way that anticipates the really deadly blow it deals him in the Ludovico Treatment—a blow not below the belt, as here, but below the level of consciousness.

In shooting the fight, Kubrick was very concerned not to depict any physical injury, such as the Cat Lady would suffer when the phallus is dashed down onto her face; instead, at this point, he cuts to a dizzying zero-in on a whore's open mouth in one of the pornographic paintings, which indicates his anxiety to preserve the nightmare nature of the scene. For in dreaming, the mind's "censor" tends to exclude this kind of anatomical gruesomeness, or else the dreamer is abruptly awakened by his own too horrible imaginings. Kubrick's regard for the story as a sort of "controlled dream" makes him take the same precautions.

Almost immediately after the murder, Alex is betrayed by his own gang, stunned by a milk bottle, and left to be picked up by the police. Burgess, incidentally, relished the way the screenplay at this point preserved the logic of the novel, in which Alex, stretching greedily for the bust of Beethoven, stumbles over a saucer of milk set down for the Cat Lady's pets. Now milk knocks him flat in the film, too. Like immature children still being suckled, these delinquents fall foul of their own perverted innocence: the milk of human kindness is poisoned at the source, all right.

---

* Hughes, p. 59.

"I was cured, all right."

Alex ends up in the police cell looking "like love's young nightmare." "Violence makes violence," says one of the cops. "He resisted his lawful arresters." At this point the dialogue anticipates the Minister of the Interior's ominous habit of truncating or compressing words; it is as if language is being stripped down till only slogans and commands remain. If the teen-agers have their Nadsat slang, the State's own "droogs" have their official syntax, too. The similarity, however, goes beyond words. The gloating policeman who lays his head like a love-sick girl on P. R. Deltoid's shoulder and invites the probation officer to give Alex his bash is the "official" obverse of the same coin that carries Alex's violent imprimatur on his side of it. Both sides form the coin of the realm. As this connection is made, the film's theme deepens and its nature and technique undergo a change as well. Without diminishing the secular ironies—certainly without softening the secular savageries—the theological content comes to the fore. Up to now, we have seen Alex through the appalled eye of one of his victims; now as the airborne camera takes an Olympian viewpoint, floating dreamily over the prison where Alex is condemned to spend fourteen years, we see him being gradually diminished and degraded as "the real weepy and like tragic part of the story" starts.

The lengthy sequence showing Alex being interrogated and stripped in the reception block does not occur in the book. The way Kubrick went about devising it throws further light on his techniques. First came a period of intensive research, designed to "justify" any effects he wanted to use, in which he took advice from ex-convicts and viewed countless TV films and newsreel clips illustrating prison life. (English prisons are not as accommodating as American ones in admitting the stray visitor who might just want to view the decor.) From this research came that small but hilarious throwaway remark, "Now—the mothballs," that the guard utters like the command in some State ceremony while he scatters a handful of camphor pellets through Alex's clothes to preserve them until his release. The "CRP" on the day of shooting yielded another one of those moments, like the "Singin' in the Rain" idea, that electrify a scene. This time it was the white line painted on the floor that Alex has to toe while being admitted to prison. The contortions of his body as he stretches to the officer's desk to empty his pockets and write his signature help to satirize rigorous officialdom. The guard's final torchlight inspection of Alex's anus further points up the dehumanizing absurdity of prison life in the manner of a comic cabaret.

"What's it going to be, then?" The first words of the prison padre in the film are actually the first words uttered in Burgess's book, and they are vital ones in the context of both works. They imply the imperative laid on every human of making a moral choice. In the fundamentalist chaplain's view, it is a choice between damnation and redemption. And though obviously his fire-and-brimstone beliefs incline him to the latter, the important element in his sermon is not which way the sinner should bend, but that he should be sufficiently free-willed to make the choice by himself. The injury that is soon going to be done to Alex will be inflicted on him in a more primitive way than any he has inflicted on his victims: not in the way of physical hurt, nor even of mental brainwashing, but in the way of sinful outrage, an offense against God as well as man, by depriving him of this divine bestowal of free will. In *2001: A Space Odyssey,* God stays off-stage but at least is represented by man's ascendancy at the end to divine or semidivine status. In *A Clockwork Orange,* man remains less metaphysical in form, but even in his untransformed, debased state, he has a Godlike capacity. What both films have in common is the conviction that man is more than a terminal product of conditioning, heredity, or environment. He can transcend himself and redeem himself. So, "What's it going to be, then?" Kubrick's refusal to stop and moralize at this point has caused some to overlook the admittedly unlikely spokesman for a view that is at the heart of the film—the prison chaplain. He starts out as a figure of fun within the State system but ends as a figure of protest against it. For when Alex offers himself as a candidate for the Ludovico Treatment, he is answered by the doubts of the man of God in dialogue pasage so central to the film that it deserves quoting in full:

Chaplain: The Governor has grave doubts about [the Ludovico Treatment] and I have heard that there are very serious dangers involved.

Alex: I don't care about the dangers, Father. I just want to be good. I want for the rest of my life to be one act of goodness.

Chaplain: The question is whether or not this technique really makes a man good. Goodness comes from within. Goodness is chosen. When a man cannot choose, he ceases to be a man.

Alex: I don't understand about the whys and wherefores, Father. I only know I want to be good.

Chaplain: Be patient, my son. Put your trust in the Lord.

Instead of which, Alex puts his trust in the Minister of the Interior, whose policy is political expediency. Since all the prison space is soon going to be needed for "the politicals," it follows that the mere "criminals" must be cleared out quickly. The Ludovico Treatment, as well as being a vote-catching item in the "law-and-order" election platform, has the overriding virtue that "it works." *A Clockwork Orange* demonstrates very neatly, through the satirized authority figures, the sophisticated subtleties of the coercive State that seeks an ally in science. For it is to the scientists that the expedient immorality of "it works" will ultimately be referred by the government; and from the scientists there is no further appeal. So the old ambivalence of science once more asserts itself in Kubrick's outlook. Instead of enhancing human life, technocracy annihilates it as in *Dr. Strangelove;* depletes it as in *2001: A Space Odyssey;* or perverts it as in *A Clockwork Orange.* Deep inside Kubrick, one suspects, there is harbored some sympathy for the Devil, or at least for the creatures of the Id who are not oppressed by a rationality that has no remedy for man's imperfections except to dominate and oppress him. As a prominent Catholic film critic, John E. Fitzgerald, wrote: "Such brainwashing, organic and psychological, is a weapon that totalitarians in State, Church or society might wish to use for an easier good, even at the cost of human rights and dignity. Redemption is a complicated thing and change must be motivated from within rather than imposed from without if moral values are to be upheld." *

Alex seems to have escaped from the inhumane system that puts men behind bars to a much more humane one when he gets transferred from prison to the Ludovico clinic. In fact, the quiet men in white coats to whom he is delivered—in one long dollying shot through futuristic surroundings that is by now characteristic of the film's style—are merely the mirror images of the functionaries from the cell block. The two systems are sharply satirized by their semantic traditions: the ludicrous "follow-the-rules" tone of the pompous little chief guard bounces off the bland "we-can-handle-it" responses of the doctors.

As Alex is prepared for the treatment, Kubrick permits himself a private joke. A deceptively soothing scientist prepares to inject the boy with serum. The close-up of the

* John E. Fitzgerald, "More than a Product of Heredity," New York *Catholic News,* December 30, 1971, p. 4.

hypodermic syringe drawing in the roseate liquid is itself a lovely image, suggesting one of those time-lapse photos of expanding flower buds, and it may escape notice that the bottle is labeled "Experimental Serum 114." Now the same cryptic numeral appeared on the mechanism of the B-52 bomber—to be precise, "CRM 114"—whose damage in *Dr. Strangelove* prevented the aircraft from receiving the Pentagon's recall signal. And to Kubrick, who characteristically ducks explanations, this numeral probably signifies some point of no return, a technological Rubicon, or the ultimate kink in the scientific or human mechanism that locks man into his fate.

The serum makes Alex unduly receptive to the feeding back into his own system of all the violence in the outside world, until he has had such a surfeit of murder, rape, and atrocity that his pleasure is turned into revulsion. Significantly, the raw material for the conditioning comes from films. As he remarks with unconscious irony before the "horror show" starts, "It's funny how the colors of the real world only seem real when you viddy them on a screen." He is a captive audience of one; his head is clamped tight; music is pumped into his ears; a ring of electrodes circles his head like a crown of thorns; and, worst of all, his bulging eyeballs are held forcibly open by surgical lidlocks. What one recognizes in the sequence is the parallel with the Cosmic Ride in *2001: A Space Odyssey,* where a similarly "imprisoned" captive has to suffer all manner of physical and even psychic phenomena bombarding his persona and changing it. Both sequences emphasize the dilated eyes, the flattened features, and especially the sense of seeing "what should not be seen" as their hero-victims are swept helplessly into a kind of reincarnation (see page 235). The inspiration comes from Kubrick's fascination, already examined, with the powerfully suggestive qualities of myths. "A psychological myth" is how he has described Alex's adventures; but Alex's ordeal derives even more precisely from the endurance test forming the central part of many of the world's myths, legends, and fairy tales. Alex is that "hero with a thousand faces" on whom magic is practiced by evil powers, who survives the worst, and who is ultimately restored to the realms he came from. The last third of the film, moreover, following the "reformed" Alex's progress through the world he once terrorized, has the same story elements of symmetry and coincidence that give to tales of magic their cyclic form and narrative satisfaction, qualities that both liberate the imagination and at the same time control the external world.

In its scientific, not mythic, state, the Ludovico Treatment is a peculiarly corrupt offshoot of behavioral psychology and conditioned-reflex therapy, which operate on the assumption that man has no will he can call his own but, on the contrary, is molded by his environment and the right kinds of stimuli administered to him in order to make any socially undesirable behavior patterns conform to socially approved ones. The film was well into its shooting schedule when B. F. Skinner published his book *Beyond Freedom and Dignity,* a work that argued, with almost blind faith in rationalism, that there was a case for manipulating the causal relationship between man and his environment for the good of society as a whole—indeed, for the essential *survival* of society. *A Clockwork Orange* presents its own diametrically opposed view of such a notion. The appearance of Skinner's book and Kubrick's film at almost the same time is a fairly consistent event with a director who, as I have pointed out already, absorbs into his own interests, and then turns into the substance of his art, much of what is happening in the world at large. And this includes the progressively sinister development of such things as the use of drugs to recondition scientifically certain types of criminals, even the use of "psycho-adaptation" in some of the totalitarian countries that have learned to avail themselves of the less sensational (or at least less publicized) forms of medicine as a means of political control. From forcibly "referring" dissenters to be treated at State psychiatric clinics to actually "reconditioning" them to return to society is a short, tempting step. The "clockwork orange" world seems tangibly close if, for example, one reads the account of Zhores Medvedev's ordeal in a Soviet clinic, recently published in the West under the title *A Question of Madness.*

It is while Alex is undergoing this form of "death," as

Dr. Brodsky calls it, and making "his most rewarding associations between his catastrophic experience-environment and the violence he sees" that the fourth movement from Beethoven's Ninth infiltrates his eardrums. Only now the music is obscenely distorted, sounding as if it could come from a kitsch music box. The violence that has been done to "lovely Ludwig van" is the only thing that wrenches out of Alex the cry, "It's a sin." The doctors reply, "You must take your chance, boy." And twisting the chaplain's words, they add with unconscious irony, "The choice has been all yours." It is the last choice Alex will make for some time. Confined to a set of programed responses to sex and violence, he is put through a test to show how the government is keeping its electoral promises by achieving law and order through the abolition of the criminal instinct. "Enough of words, actions speak louder than," declaims the Minister of the Interior in his "officialese" style. "Action now. Observe all." What we observe is an extraordinary sequence: the classical tempting of a saint, which might have been drawn from a medieval morality play, bizarrely crossed with the sort of sado-masochistic cabaret commonplace in pre-Hitlerite Germany. First the male tempter, a curly haired queer, humiliates the passive Alex to the point where he licks his boots. The man bows to applause. Then the female temptress, a near-nude, appears on stage like one of the punitive harlots in a strip show. Kubrick's camera, directly above the girl's head, looks down on the pink protuberances of her "topless" anatomy while Alex, at her feet, rises up like a mountaineer groping for the hand-holds on her breasts and then falls back into the void of his self-disgust. It is a dazzling use of the surrealist angle, followed ironically by the dainty obedience of the girl's bow to the political plaudits. "Any questions?" crows the delighted Minister.

And again, in view of the way the film's violent passages have been overemphasized at the expense of its more vital moral theme, the dialogue between the Minister and the prison chaplain bears quoting:

Chaplain: Choice! The boy has not a real choice—has he? Self-interest, the fear of physical pain drove him to that grotesque act of self-abasement. The insincerity was clear to be seen. He ceases to be a wrongdoer. He ceases also to be a creature capable of moral choice.

Minister: Padre, there are subtleties! We are not concerned with motives, with the higher ethics. We are concerned only with cutting down crime and with relieving the ghastly congestion in our prisons. He will be your true Christian, ready to turn the other cheek, ready to be crucified rather than crucify, sick to the heart at the thought of killing a fly. Reclamation! Joy before the angels of God! The point is that it works.

Put back defenseless into a hostile world, Alex now falls prey to the very terrors he himself created. First, he is displaced from his family by the intrusion of a teen-age lodger. Whereas music led the vicious rampage of Alex in his heyday, it is now employed in a much more naturalistic form to signal his fall from power. It is the slow movement of the *William Tell* Overture, which once could hardly keep pace with his sex romp, that now accompanies his sad promenade along the Thames Embankment, while the slowly zooming camera projects his melancholy, like an incipient suicide's, into the brown swirling waters. The same tramp he mugged in the opening reel whistles up his pals, and Alex is pulled down by a pack of senile wolves with toothless gums. He is "rescued" by two policemen who turn out to be Dim and Georgie, his ex-"droogs," who have now made a pact with the State. And after a vicious beating from them, Alex staggers into the house called "HOME," where the last of his former victims is waiting by "magical" coincidence to deliver the ultimate retribution.

Mr. Alexander has suffered a transformation of his own. Crippled by the attack on him, his "liberalism" has been warped as well. This physically impotent ogre in the wheelchair, now given to gloating and uttering involuntary whimpers of delight when assailed by fantasies of torture or revenge, is clearly a kindred spirit to Dr. Strangelove. Like that earlier manifestation of evil, his function is to key the film to its penultimate pitch of baroque horror, speaking in a parched, excited voice that is rabid for revenge. The "Singin' in the Rain" song that Alex involuntarily croons in his bath—the words echoing against the tiles and mirrors like a memory from the past—is a give-away device that is cleverer than any in the novel. And the feeling that Kubrick himself is calling up the past is choicely conveyed by a shot of Alex eating supper. The image of him in a dressing gown, alone and symmetrically seated at a table, with plate, glass, and wine bottle in hand, and the scrape of a fork on the china, brings us back, it seems, to the astral suite in *2001: A Space Odyssey,* with the captive cosmonaut sensing the same elusive threat in his environment (see page 237). But it is by no means a simple case of double vision. The moment Mr. Alexander enters, seated in a wheelchair but carried by his muscular servant so that it looks as if the wheelchair has grown legs of its own, there is the odd effect of *Dr. Strangelove*'s being spliced into *2001: A Space Odyssey* and creating a time-slip that radiates a new sense of unease.

Aided by a couple of lieutenants, Fascists like himself posing as friends of "the people, the common people," who must be driven if they will not be led, Mr. Alexander plots to discredit the government, which has been boasting that it has found the cure for crime. His means—driving Alex to suicide—neatly encapsulate his own private revenge. As the insidious Ninth Symphony blares up through the floorboards from the room below, where the contemplative grouping of the conspirators around the hi-fi has the sort of country-house tranquility Sickert might have painted, Alex's suicidal reflex drives him to a death-leap through the window. The moment illustrates Kubrick's thoroughness better than any other, for he actually threw the camera through the window, and the tough old Newman-Sinclair apparatus, incased in polystyrene boxes, survived all of the six "takes" that were required to produce the dizzying subjective shot that keeps us identifying with Alex and also symbolizes (and this is how Burgess sees it) his "fall" from a state of mechanistic grace back into his natural paganism.

His "moral" convalescence is quickly and wittily sketched in a hospital sequence that satirizes clinical psychiatry, which this time tests the patient for the symptoms of violence healthily reasserting itself. The last sequence is masterly and brings the film, beating strongly, up to a totally cynical conclusion: a compact of evil between Alex and the Minister of the Interior that is every bit as labyrinthine in its veiled proposal and acceptance as is the opening sequence of *Paths of Glory,* in which the arch-conspirator co-opted the cruder ambitions of his inferior in order to maintain his party in power at all costs. Rather like General Broulard, outwardly benign and untroubled, full of chummy chat, and radiating mysterious "understandings," the character of the Minister of the Interior enables Kubrick to construct one of his blackest scenes of comedy. We could virtually be certain that were Alex able to walk, the Minister would lead him into those peripatetic temptations to which Broulard subjected Mireau amid the polished furnishings of the château. But Alex is incased in plaster, barely able to ferry the food to his lips from his dinner plate, and so the Minister obligingly takes over the job, simultaneously seducing the boy over to the government's side by blandishments and promises—literally and figuratively spoon-feeding him. (Incidentally, he casts a sidelight on Mr. Alexander's fate: the latter, like Medeyev, has been "put away for his own protection.") Such a piece of physical pantomime grew out of the "CRP"—the spoon-feeding does not appear in the book—and it is a masterpiece of smooth chicanery and blatant cheek. As Alex's effrontery grows with his intake, his chewing stops as abruptly as one of General Turgidson's tics, "freezing" him in mid-grotesquerie; but his mouth keeps jerking open suddenly like a demanding chick in the nest, insatiable for the supply of worms from the parent beak. "We shall see to everything, a good job on a good salary." "What job and how much?"

The final alliance between individual violence and the State's sophisticated reflection of it is sealed with the Minister's deliciously evil wink, whereupon the ward is invaded by pressmen, photographers, and porters bearing flowers and fruit and two huge stereo amplifiers like the Gates of Heaven, out of which pours Beethoven's Ninth. Alex's last words, "I was cured, all right," are odd echoes of Dr. Strangelove's own exuberant announcement (or threat),

"Mein Führer—I can walk!" as the nuclear explosions ring out a megaton salute. Alex's self-diagnosis is amply confirmed by a fantasy shot of the nude hero frolicking with a young "devotchka" to applause from a gallery of Establishment types. As the end credits unroll, "Singin' in the Rain" is quoted back at us with its violent associations, though whether it will be Alex's theme song for fresh atrocities that now carry the stamp of State approval, or whether it will again betray him to his enemies, is anybody's guess. Kubrick is certainly not supplying an answer.

For him, *A Clockwork Orange* marks a new departure. The film's themes have already been analyzed as each strand is twisted into the next, and it is remarkable on how many levels—social, political, moral, theological—the story works without once losing touch with the basic quality of all tales, which, as E. M. Forster pointed out, satisfies the listeners' curiosity about "what happens next." But I think *A Clockwork Orange* hits its audience at a deeper level of consciousness than mere curiosity. And to the degree that it achieves this, it differs from any earlier Kubrick film. "With an eloquent command of the medium," wrote one critic, Patrick Snyder-Scumby, "[Kubrick] has created a dream in which he asks us to laugh at his nightmares." * Laughter is very much Kubrick's intention. As I pointed out elsewhere, it makes it possible for the unthinkable to be thought of. For anyone who views a story as being in the nature of a "controlled dream" is bound to pay regard to the unconscious feelings of a cinema audience, since it is in the unconscious that the dream operates with most potency. *A Clockwork Orange* is nearer this dream state than any film Kubrick has made. Its lighting, editing, photography, and especially its music—for sound reaches deeper into the unconscious than even sight—are all combined with events in themselves bizarre and frightening. Although our eyes are not clamped open with lidlocks, like Alex's, we are assailed by a field of forces impossible to repel. *2001: A Space Odyssey,* in a rough sense, was a film whose imagery we

---

* Patrick Snyder-Scumby, "The Cockjerk Lunge of Manly Rubric," *Crawdaddy,* March 19, 1972, p. 25.

were invited to accept, explore, and enjoy for the sensuous experience it conveyed; *A Clockwork Orange,* on the other hand, is one whose images we throw up our hands to ward off. What I wrote at the conclusion of the last chapter—that "the medium is the metaphor"—holds true of both films. But there is a vital difference. Where the metaphor of the earlier film turned us on, in *A Clockwork Orange* it has turned on us.

I think the film's success in deploying a controlled dream to spirit its own fearful vision past our defenses partly accounts for the extreme reactions to it from some quarters—the charge, for example, that it celebrated "the new ultraviolence" that, in Joseph Morgenstern's words, creates a "high-fashion horror that can turn on audiences higher than the real thing." * But this is neither the film's intention nor effect. One critic who appears to agree is Vincent Canby. In an article in *The New York Times* he wrote: "It is a horror show, but cool, so removed from reality that it would take someone who really cherished his perversions to get any vicarious pleasure from it. To isolate its violence is to ignore everything else that is at work in the movie." † To be genuinely shocking and at the same time *eloquent* in a film is itself an extraordinary achievement. Along with *Dr. Strangelove* and *2001: A Space Odyssey, A Clockwork Orange* rounds out a trilogy of films that shows a filmmaker with a unique capacity for using a medium to explore the condition of his fellow men and himself. In each of the films he has kept open the channels of the unconscious yet used an artist's self-awareness to shape the hopes and fears that flow through them and onto the screen with unblocked vitality. In *A Clockwork Orange* it is the darkest of his fears that Kubrick plugs us into: not the fear of accidental annihilation by nuclear overkill, nor even the fear of what the unknown universe may hold, but the clear and present fear he has of man's surrender of his identity to the tyranny of other men. It is right that such a film should shock us.

---

* Joseph Morgenstern, "The New Violence," *Newsweek,* February 14, 1972, p. 68.

† Vincent Canby, "Has Movie Violence Gone too Far," *The New York Times,* January 16, 1972, sec. 2, p. 1.

FILMOGRAPHY

Day of the Fight (U.S.A., 1951)
Director, Photography, Editor, Sound — Stanley Kubrick
Commentary — Douglas Edwards
Documentary short on Walter Cartier, middleweight prize fighter
Running time: 16 minutes
Distributor: R.K.O. Radio

Flying Padre (U.S.A., 1951)
Director, Photography, Editor, Sound — Stanley Kubrick
Documentary short on the Reverend Fred Stadtmueller, Roman Catholic missionary of a New Mexican parish of 400 square miles
Running time: 9 minutes
Distributor: R.K.O. Radio

Fear and Desire (U.S.A., 1953)

Production Company	Stanley Kubrick Productions
Producer	Stanley Kubrick
Director, Photography, Editor	Stanley Kubrick
Script	Howard O. Sackler

Frank Silvera (Mac), Kenneth Harp (Corby), Virginia Leith (The Girl), Paul Mazursky (Sidney), Steve Coit (Fletcher)
Running time: 68 minutes
Distributor: Joseph Burstyn

Killer's Kiss (U.S.A., 1955)

Production Company	Minotaur
Producers	Stanley Kubrick Morris Bousel
Director, Photography, Editor	Stanley Kubrick
Script	Stanley Kubrick Howard O. Sackler
Music	Gerald Fried
Choreography	David Vaughan

Frank Silvera (Vincent Rapallo), Jamie Smith (Davy Gordon), Irene Kane (Gloria Price), Jerry Jarret (Albert), Iris (Ruth Sobotka), Mike Dana, Felice Orlandi, Ralph Roberts, Phil Stevenson (Hoodlums), Julius Adelman (Mannequin Factory Owner), David Vaughan, Alec Rubin (Conventioneers)
Running time: 64 minutes
Distributor: United Artists

The Killing (U.S.A., 1956)

Production Company	Harris-Kubrick Productions
Producer	James B. Harris
Director	Stanley Kubrick
Script	Stanley Kubrick, based on the novel *Clean Break,* by Lionel White
Additional dialogue	Jim Thompson
Photography	Lucien Ballard
Editor	Betty Steinberg
Art Director	Ruth Sobotka Kubrick
Music	Gerald Fried
Sound	Earl Snyder

Sterling Hayden (Johnny Clay), Jay C. Flippen (Marvin Unger), Marie Windsor (Sherry Peatty), Elisha Cook (George Peatty), Coleen Gray (Fay), Vince Edwards (Val Cannon), Ted de Corsia (Randy Kennan), Joe Sawyer (Mike O'Reilly), Tim Carey (Nikki), Kola Kwariani (Maurice), James Edwards (Car Park Attendant)
Running time: 83 minutes
Distributor: United Artists

Paths of Glory (U.S.A., 1957)

Production Company	Harris-Kubrick Productions
Producer	James B. Harris
Director	Stanley Kubrick
Script	Stanley Kubrick, Calder Willingham, Jim Thompson, based on the novel by Humphrey Cobb
Photography	George Krause
Editor	Eva Kroll
Art Director	Ludwig Reiber
Music	Gerald Fried
Sound	Martin Muller

Kirk Douglas (Colonel Dax), Ralph Meeker (Corporal Paris), Adolphe Menjou (General Broulard), George Macready (General Mireau), Wayne Morris (Lieutenant Roget), Richard Anderson (Major Saint-Auban), Joseph Turkel (Private Arnaud), Timothy Carey (Private Ferol), Peter Capell (Colonel Judge), Susanne Christian (German Girl), Bert Freed (Sergeant Boulanger), Emile Meyer (Priest), John Stein (Captain Rousseau)
Running time: 86 minutes
Distributor: United Artists

Spartacus (U.S.A., 1959-1960)

Production Company	Bryna
Executive Producer	Kirk Douglas
Producer	Edward Lewis
Director	Stanley Kubrick
Script	Dalton Trumbo, based on the book by Howard Fast
Photography	Russell Metty
Additional photography	Clifford Stine
Screen Process	Super Technirama-70
Color	Technicolor
Editors	Robert Lawrence
	Robert Schultz
	Fred Chulack
Production Designer	Alexander Golitzen
Art Director	Eric Orbom
Set decoration	Russell A. Gausman
	Julia Heron
Titles	Saul Bass
Technical Adviser	Vittorio Nino Novarese
Costumes	Peruzzi
	Valles
	Bill Thomas
Music	Alex North
Music Director	Joseph Gershenson
Sound	Waldon O. Watson
	Joe Lapis
	Murray Spivack
	Ronald Pierce

Kirk Douglas (Spartacus), Laurence Olivier (Marcus Crassus), Jean

Simmons (Varinia), Charles Laughton (Gracchus), Peter Ustinov (Batiatus), John Gavin (Julius Caesar), Tony Curtis (Antoninus), Nina Foch (Helena), Herbert Lom (Tigranes), John Ireland (Crixus), John Dall (Glabrus), Charles McGraw (Marcellus) Joanna Barnes (Claudia), Harold J. Stone (David), Woody Strode (Draba), Peter Brocco (Ramon), Paul Lambert (Gannicus), Robert J. Wilke (Captain of Guard), Nicholas Dennis (Dionysius), John Hoyt (Roman Officer), Fred Worlock (Laelius), Dayton Lummis (Symmachus)
Original running time: 196 minutes*
Distributor: Universal Pictures

*The running time of the film shown in Britain was three minutes shorter. Later, when the film was in general distribution, Universal cut it to 183 minutes for all countries and subsequent releases. The scenes eliminated concerned mostly a very understated attempt by Marcus Crassus to seduce his slave Antoninus. The cuts make nonsense of their relationship.

Lolita (Great Britain, 1961)

Production Company	Seven Arts/Anya/Transworld
Producer	James B. Harris
Director	Stanley Kubrick
Script	Vladimir Nabokov, based on his own novel
Photography	Oswald Morris
Editor	Anthony Harvey
Art Director	William Andrews
Set design	Andrew Low
Music	Nelson Riddle
Theme music	Bob Harris
Sound	H. L. Bird Len Shilton

James Mason (Humbert Humbert), Sue Lyon (Lolita Haze), Shelley Winters (Charlotte Haze), Peter Sellers (Clare Quilty), Diana Decker (Jean Farlow), Jerry Stovin (John Farlow), Suzanne Gibbs (Mona Farlow), Gary Cockrell (Dick), Marianne Stone (Vivian Darkbloom), Cec Linder (Physician), Lois Maxwell (Nurse Mary Lore), William Greene (Swine), C. Denier Warren (Potts), Isobel Lucas (Louise), Maxine Holden (Receptionist), James Dyrenforth (Beale), Roberta Shore (Lorna), Eric Lane (Roy), Shirley Douglas (Mrs. Starch), Roland Brand (Bill), Colin Maitland (Charlie), Irvin Allen (Hospital Attendant), Marion Mathie (Miss Lebone), Craig Sams (Rex), John Harrison (Tom)
Running time: 153 minutes
Distributor: Metro-Goldwyn-Mayer

Dr. Strangelove, or How I Learned to Stop Worrying and Love the Bomb (Great Britain, 1963)

Production Company	Hawk Films
Producer-Director	Stanley Kubrick
Associate Producer	Victor Lyndon
Script	Stanley Kubrick, Terry Southern, Peter George, based on the novel *Red Alert,* by Peter George
Photography	Gilbert Taylor
Editor	Anthony Harvey
Production Designer	Ken Adam
Art Director	Peter Murton
Special effects	Wally Veevers
Music	Laurie Johnson
Aviation Adviser	Captain John Crewdson
Sound	John Cox

Peter Sellers (Group Captain Lionel Mandrake, President Muffley, Dr. Strangelove), George C. Scott (General "Buck" Turgidson), Sterling

Hayden (General Jack D. Ripper), Keenan Wynn (Colonel "Bat" Guano), Slim Pickens (Major T. J. "King" Kong), Peter Bull (Ambassador de Sadesky), Tracy Reed (Miss Scott), James Earl Jones (Lieutenant Lothar Zogg, Bombardier), Jack Creley (Mr. Staines), Frank Berry (Lieutenant H. R. Dietrich, D.S.O.), Glenn Beck (Lieutenant W. D. Kivel, Navigator), Shane Rimmer (Captain G. A. "Ace" Owens, Copilot), Paul Tamarin (Lieutenant B. Goldberg, Radio Operator), Gordon Tanner (General Faceman), Robert O'Neil (Admiral Randolph), Roy Stephens (Frank), Laurence Herder, John McCarthy, Hal Galili (Members of Burpelson Base Defense Corps)
Running time: 94 minutes
Distributor: Columbia Pictures

2001: A Space Odyssey (Great Britain, 1968)

Production Company	Metro-Goldwyn-Mayer
Producer	Stanley Kubrick
Director	Stanley Kubrick
Script	Stanley Kubrick, Arthur C. Clarke, based on the latter's short story "The Sentinel"
Photography	Geoffrey Unsworth
Screen process	Super Panavision Presented in Cinerama
Color	Metrocolor
Additional photography	John Alcott
Special Photographic Effects Designer and Director	Stanley Kubrick
Editor	Ray Lovejoy
Production Designers	Tony Masters Harry Lange Ernie Archer
Art Director	John Hoesli
Special Photographic Effects Supervisors	Wally Veevers Douglas Trumbull Con Pederson Tom Howard
Music	Richard Strauss Johann Strauss Aram Khachaturian György Ligeti
Costumes	Hardy Amies
Sound	Winston Ryder

Keir Dullea (David Bowman), Garry Lockwood (Frank Poole), William Sylvester (Dr. Heywood Floyd), Daniel Richter (Moonwatcher), Douglas Rain (Voice of HAL 9000), Leonard Rossiter (Smyslov), Margaret Tyzack (Elena), Robert Beatty (Halvorsen), Sean Sullivan (Michaels), Frank Miller (Mission Control), Penny Brahms (Stewardess), Alan Gifford (Poole's Father), Edward Bishop, Glenn Beck, Edwina Carroll, Mike Lovell, Peter Delman, Dany Grover, Brian Hawley
Running time: 141 minutes*
Distributor: Metro-Goldwyn-Mayer

*The original running time of *2001: A Space Odyssey,* when previewed on April 1, 1968, in New York was 161 minutes. Kubrick himself subsequently took the decision to trim about twenty minutes. He commented: "It does take a few runnings to decide finally how long things should be, especially scenes which do not have narrative advancement as their guideline." He had previously trimmed *Paths of Glory* between preview and release and, of course, *Dr. Strangelove* had its intended pie-throwing ending taken out by Kubrick for reasons referred to in the text.

A Clockwork Orange (Great Britain, 1971)

Production Company	Warner Brothers/Hawk Films
Producer-Director	Stanley Kubrick
Associate Producer	Bernard Williams
Assistant to Producer	Jan Harlan
Script	Stanley Kubrick, based on the novel by Anthony Burgess
Photography	John Alcott
Editor	Bill Butler
Production Designer	John Barry
Production Assistant	Andros Epaminondas
Art Directors	Russell Hagg, Peter Sheilds
Special Paintings and Sculpture	Herman Makkink, Cornelius Makkink, Liz Moore, Christiane Kubrick
Costumes	Milena Canonero
Electronic Music	Walter Carlos
Music	Henry Purcell
	Gioacchino Rossini
	Ludwig van Beethoven
	James Yorkston
	Arthur Freed, Nacio Herb Brown
	Sir Edward Elgar
	Rimsky Korsakoff
	Erika Eigen
Songs	Gene Kelly, Erika Eigen
Sound	Brian Blamey
Executive Producers	Max Raab, Si Litvinoff

Malcolm McDowell (Alex), Patrick Magee (Mr. Alexander), Michael Bates (Chief Guard), Warren Clarke (Dim), John Clive (Stage Actor), Adrienne Corri (Mrs. Alexander), Carl Duering (Dr. Brodsky), Paul Farrell (Tramp), Clive Francis (Lodger), Michael Gover (Prison Governor), Miriam Karlin (Cat Lady), James Marcus (Georgie), Aubrey Morris (P. R. Deltoid), Godfrey Quigley (Prison Chaplain), Sheila Raynor (Mum), Madge Ryan (Dr. Branom), John Savident (Conspirator), Anthony Sharp (Minister of the Interior), Philip Stone (Dad), Pauline Taylor (Psychiatrist), Margaret Tyzack (Conspirator), Steven Berkoff (Constable), Lindsay Campbell (Inspector), Michael Tarn (Pete), David Prowse (Julian), Jan Adair, Vivienne Chandler, Prudence Drage (Handmaidens), John J. Carney (CID Man), Richard Connaught (Billyboy), Carol Drinkwater (Nurse Feeley), Cheryl Grunwald (Rape Girl), Gillian Hills (Sonietta), Barbara Scott (Marty), Virginia Wetherell (Stage Actress), Katya Wyeth (Girl), Barrie Cookson, Gaye Brown, Peter Burton, Lee Fox, Craig Hunter, Shirley Jaffe, Neil Wilson

Running time: 137 minutes

Distributor: Columbia Pictures/Warner Brothers (U.K.), Warner Brothers (U.S.A.)